LIVE

SEX

ACTS

LIVE SEX ACTS
Women Performing Erotic Labor

Wendy Chapkis

Routledge
New York

Published in the United States of America in 1997 by

Routledge
29 West 35th Street
New York, NY 10001

Printed in the United States of America on acid-free paper

Excerpt from "Golden Showers" by Pat Califia on p. 68
reprinted with permission of the author.

Library of Congress Cataloging-in-Publication Data

Chapkis, W. (Wendy)
    Live sex acts : women performing erotic labor / Wendy Chapkis.
        p.   cm.
    Includes bibliographical references and index.
    ISBN 0-415-91287-3 (hb). — ISBN 0-415-91288-1 (pb)
    1. Prostitution. 2. Prostitutes—Interviews. 3. Feminist ethics.
4. Sexual ethics. I. Title.
HQ115.C43 1996   96-34633
306.74—dc20   CIP

CONTENTS

Section III: Strategic Responses

Acknowledgments

This book has been a labor of love, desire, and desperation. Without the support—intellectual, financial, and personal—of many individuals and organizations, it never would have been completed. I am most indebted to the women and men who agreed to be interviewed for this project; may the result prove useful to them.

I also would like to express special thanks to four of my colleagues at the University of California at Santa Cruz: Wendy Brown, John Brown Childs, Robert Connell, and Sherri Paris. Each of them exhibited a tremendous generosity of time and spirit. Other UCSC colleagues who assisted me in this work include, James Clifford, Susan Curtis, Nicolette Czarrunchick, Gillian Greensite, Donna Hagler, Donna Haraway, Earl Jackson Jr., Kat Lawrence, Marcia Millman, Helene Moglen, Lynne Sheehan, Nancy Stoller, Carter Wilson, and Besty Wooten. The Sociology Department, Women's Studies Board, and the Feminist Studies Research Cluster at the University of California at Santa Cruz all provided invaluable intellectual and financial support.

I am also grateful to the Netherlands/America Fulbright Foundation for fellowship support which made possible comparative research in Amsterdam. This work further reflects the careful attention and expert editorial and production assistance I received from Anne Sanow, Jayne Fargnoli, Karen Deaver, and Alex Mummery of Routledge, and Roz Hopkins of Cassell.

During my final year of writing, I relocated to the University of Southern Maine. I am very appreciative of the willingness of my new colleagues in Women's Studies and Sociology to carry more than their share of departmental responsibilities while I immersed myself in the completion of this book; special thanks to Nancy Gish, Susan Feiner, Cathlynn DiFrancesco, Doug Anderson, Donald Anspach, David Fullam, Jill Kendall, Cheryl Laz, Peter Lehman and, in particular, to my assistant, Lisa Marie Rippy.

This book owes a tremendous debt to the work and wisdom of many other writers, artists, and activists who have inspired and challenged my own thinking on the subject of sex, especially

Priscilla Alexander, Dorothy Allison, Margot Alvarez, Ariane Amsberg, Kathleen Barry, Kat Beaulieu, Kate Bornstein, Licia Brussa, Gon Buurman, Pat Califia, Karen Davis, Jo Doezema, Liv Finstad, Dolores French, Jane Gelfand, Evelina Giobbe, Terry Goodson, Cecilie Hoigard, Nina Hartley, Sheila Jeffreys, Valerie Jenness, Aimee Jolson, Theodora Kerry, Bobby Lilly, Gloria Lockett, Anne McClintock, Samantha Miller, Kathy Miriam, Sandy O'Neill, Laddawan Passar, Carole Pateman, Gail Pheterson, Jill Posener, Carol Queen, Laurie Shrage, Alena Smith, Margo St. James, and Annie Sprinkle.

Finally, I would like to thank my family and my family of friends for their kindness, passion, and commitment: Kiki Amsberg, Peter Brown, Andy Chapkis, Karen Chapkis, Marjorie Chapkis, Martina Leutgeb Chapkis, Robert Chapkis, Stephen Chapkis, Valerie Corral, Michael Corral, Ans van Dale, Leah Warn Fortin, Esther Hagler, Bruce Lee, Liliane Maesen, Nathalie Magnan, Martha McDevitt, Sal Mendolia, Sig Moglen, Linda Niemann, John O'Brien, Karen Peifer, Maryann Peterson, Lin Pugh, Tuija Pulkkinen, Del Rey, Piet Rodenburg, Cynthia Saffir, Merrie Schaller, Abbie Sommer, David Talamo, Terez, Dana Williams, and, most especially, to Gabriel, who fed the flame.

This book is dedicated to
the differences among us
and the solidarity
between us.

Introduction

My older, urban cousins, Nancy and Cheryl, always knew everything before I did. They introduced me to dirty words, cigarettes, and the latest fashions. I worshipped and feared them. During one exciting visit when I was eight, Cheryl told us what she had learned about how babies were made. After my cousins left, I climbed into the back of a closet and huddled among the winter coats. I was unwilling to believe but unable to seriously doubt my worldly-wise cousins. I stayed there until my mother climbed in with me and retold the story with a more romantic gloss.

I greeted their next visit with excitement and trepidation; who knew what valuable and terrifying information I might receive this time? But as we sat out on the back porch, I realized they were angry with me, the "tattletale." "You are such a good girl. You never get into any trouble." "I am not!" "You are too, goody-goody." My reputation on the line, I jumped up, opened the back door, and slammed it hard. Then I reopened it and yelled out, "Sorry, Mom." My cousins' hoots and laughter wiped the triumphant smile off my face before I even turned around.

Now, thirty years later, our positions are less clear. Nancy and Cheryl have "settled down" as respectable married homeowners while—in some circles at least—I've become known as a "celebrity apologist" for prostitution.[1] But I suspect that, in many ways, I'm still a good girl fascinated by those more bold.

When I began working on this book, my ambitious intent was not only to pose a challenge to the enduring divisions between "good girls" and "bad girls," but also to help heal the schism within feminism that had developed around the subject of commercial sex. I was horrified by the bloodletting within the feminist community occasioned by differences of perspective on prostitution and pornography. On the one side, there were feminists who saw commodified sex as a form of—and incitement to—sexual violence. On the other, there were those who embraced recreational (including commercial) sex as a potentially liberatory terrain for women. The one side viewed prostitutes as victims of sexual slavery, while the other side understood them to be sexual renegades and exploited workers. These conflicting perspectives produced radically opposing feminist politics and competing proposals for change.

I watched most of the pitched battles of the "feminist sex wars" from a comfortable distance. Through much of the 1970s and 1980s, I lived in Amsterdam. There, differences among feminists at least appeared to be less fraught than in the United States, and the tone of debate seemed more civil. I read with alarm the reports of the U.S. conflict, but I remained optimistic. After all, I was living in a country with both a vibrant women's movement and a largely decriminalized and openly practiced sex trade. Conflicts between feminists—and between feminism and commercial sex—seemed manageable. I assumed such reasonableness eventually would prevail.

As I began spending more time in the United States in the late 1980s, however, I discovered that reconciliation among feminists appeared as distant as ever. The camps remained firmly in place, and even before I knew exactly where I stood relative to the key issues in the sex debates, other American feminists knew just where to position me. My first encounter with the feminist litmus test on sex occurred in 1986 shortly after my book, *Beauty Secrets: Women and the Politics of Appearance*,[2] was published. In that moment of celebrity, I was invited to speak at a number of American universities, including one in New Orleans. There, I was asked to share the podium with another prominent American feminist best known for her militant activism against pornography. I was honored (and a little daunted) at the prospect of sharing the stage with her. Then I received a phone call from the campus organizer. She explained, with some embarrassment, that the other speaker's assistant had called to ask some questions about me. Since she wasn't quite sure how to answer, would I mind telling her what my position was on prostitution, pornography, and s/m? I stumbled through my answers, but I must have failed the test: the other feminist chose not to participate.

A few months later, while residing in the small California coastal town of Santa Cruz, I had another opportunity to consider my own position on prostitution. While reading the local paper, I came across an article reporting on the forced closure of all the county's "massage" parlors. Law enforcement had tolerated the existence of the parlors for more than a decade as a cover for the community's sex trade; suddenly, however, in a more conservative political climate, the sheriff and district attorney decided to clean up the town. I glanced at the story and turned the page, comfortable that, for once, the law seemed to be on the side of women.

Then I turned back to the story, wondering about the women workers suddenly without a place of employment. Shutting the parlors meant that they would be forced into potentially more unsafe environments, such as the streets. Or perhaps they were expected to turn to more "legitimate" minimum-wage jobs? Or to the poverty of welfare? This concern was brought home to me in an article on the next page regarding a labor dispute at a local cannery employing mostly Latina workers. Those women were portrayed as heroes, fighting to save jobs paying $5.40 an hour, despite the fact that conditions in the cannery—just as in the parlors—were undoubtedly exploitive. Still, one labor struggle was applauded, and the other not even recognized as such.

This disturbing realization inspired me to action. In collaboration with two women working in the Santa Cruz sex trade, I helped mobilize a broad feminist coalition against the crackdown on the parlors. Over thirty prominent women's rights activists eventually signed a letter of protest. Members of the "Don't Turn Pros Into Cons" coalition varied widely in their overall assessment of prostitution, ranging from those who advocated abolition to those committed to normalization and destigmatization. But all felt comfortable expressing concern about the safety and well-being of women in the sex trades. This promising model of collaboration across difference within feminism was short-lived, however.

Soon, some members of the coalition were actively demanding that local law enforcement "prosecute the johns who purchase women and children instead of the prostitutes."[3] The sex workers in the coalition denounced the proposal and I found myself sharing their concern. Perhaps it was my identity as a lesbian that made me wary of a strategy calling for the arrest and punishment of any party to consensual adult sexual activity. This point was underscored when the same sheriff responsible for the massage parlor crackdown also organized a campaign to entrap and arrest gay men at a local outdoor cruising area.

Also about the same time as the massage parlor sweep, I attended a lesbian "leather and lace" formal dance at an old hotel in the center of San Francisco. The other hotel guests, mostly out-of-town tourists, were puzzled by what they were seeing: hundreds of women dressed for sex with no men around. Finally, one man turned to his wife and exclaimed: "I get it—it's a hookers' convention!" His confusion was understandable. Sex workers, I was discovering, often wear their outlaw status in a way that reminds me of my own defiant attitude toward having a moustache or being a lesbian. The "queerer" I became, the more I found myself admiring and identifying with politicized whores. Clearly, a "position" was being born, and I started to admit that I probably wasn't good bridge material between opposing camps in the sex debates. Still, it seemed improbable to me that in the United States in the 1990s, feminists could possibly continue to see one another as the biggest problem around. This was a time of extreme right-wing retrenchment featuring deep cuts in welfare, federal rules prohibiting state-funded health clinics from even discussing abortion with clients, restrictions on the sexual content of federal arts grants, and war with Panama and Iraq. In this political context, disagreements over pornography, prostitution, and perversion seemed much less urgent if no less interesting.

Once again though, I had underestimated the single-minded determination some feminists bring to the sex wars. I soon found myself having to defend both my reputation and my right to call myself a feminist because of my "perverse" sexual politics. The temptation here is to catalogue injuries I sustained in skirmishes with *radical feminists* over sexual culture, politics, and practices. Someday, reconciliation within American feminism might allow for just such an airing of "war crimes." At this point, though, it would only serve to add fuel to a fire that needs to be doused. I will say that, in my experience, feminists opposed to prostitution, pornography, and s/m fight with a passion reserved for the truly self-righteous. It is not only that they know they are right, but that they know that the safety of women

4

everywhere depends on the triumph of their position. Women who would disagree are not only enemies but traitors. Given such conviction, it should come as no surprise that they find it appropriate to use almost any means necessary to secure victory. My own experience as a designated enemy has not only intensified my hatred of war in any context, it has also raised the stakes for me in wishing to see this conflict resolved.

That resolution, however, remains maddeningly elusive—and not only in the United States. In 1994 in Amsterdam, I watched with dismay while a prominent Dutch journalist vented her rage at a TV talk-show host who had the temerity to ask her, a serious, professional woman (read: fashion columnist), to share air time with a couple of working whores. I was similarly shocked when, just weeks later, residents of one of Amsterdam's more politicized squatted buildings, the "Vrangrijk," refused to allow a working prostitute, Jo Doezema, to live in their housing collective. The woman's political credentials were impeccable as a labor organizer, except that the labor involved was sex. For some of the anarcho-feminist anticapitalists at the Vrangrijk, the prospect of having such a person in the house was the equivalent of living with the enemy.[4]

In short, events on both sides of the Atlantic indicate that prostitution, pornography, and other forms of commercial sex still function as land mines within feminism. It is with no small amount of fear, then, that I venture into this explosive territory. The various "sides" in this dispute have faces and names and histories that are well-known to me. I am concerned about exposing myself to the righteous wrath of one, further injuring another, or misrepresenting a third. The certainty and conviction of those who disagree with me make my own enthusiasm for partial and contradictory truths feel inadequate. But I remain convinced that the key to the resolution of this conflict is the recognition that the truth about sex, including commercial sex, is necessarily more complex than any one position can express. Some positions in these debates make more sense to me than others (as will become apparent in the pages to follow), but clearly no one voice has a monopoly on Truth. From where I stand, it is easy to see some of the dead ends in analyses with which I disagree.

No doubt I am less able to detect the blind spots in perspectives closest to my own. I trust, though, that these will be made known to me by those better able to see them.

Just the "Facts"

The material in this book is derived primarily from comparative research conducted from 1986 through 1995 in the United States (in the Northern California communities of Santa Cruz and San Francisco) and the Netherlands (particularly in Amsterdam). Several interviews were also conducted with women working in the sex trades in a limited number of other locations such as Britain, Finland, and the East Coast of the United States.

To immerse myself in the sex debates, I carefully examined the question of state intervention and regulation of (commercial) sexual practice[5] and re-read contemporary feminist accounts of the meaning and experience of prostitution and other stigmatized forms of sex.[6] Secondary research, however, felt inadequate to fully understanding this subject. As a result, I committed myself to "participant observation" in the field—with a primary emphasis on "observation"—but including some very minimal participation. Prostitution, after all, is not only about contested meaning and competing policy; it is also about buying and selling sex. For this reason, I attempted to reproduce for myself some of the embodied reality of commodified touch, but very much under conditions of optimal control and choice.

For instance, several years into this research, I became a certified massage practitioner and began seeing clients in California and Amsterdam. On one occasion, I arranged to pay for sexual services in the form of hands-on sexual instruction from two professional sex workers. And, finally, I also arranged to work one afternoon selling sex to women clients in Amsterdam. None of these experiences duplicates prostitution conventionally understood. I make no claims of "insider's" status or knowledge based on them. But putting my own body on the line served to reveal something more about my own resistances to and fascination with the sale of "intimate services."

More important in helping me understand the complexity of commercial sex than my own minimal firsthand experiences were the more than fifty interviews I conducted with individuals actively involved in prostitution politics. These interviews included workers in a wide range of occupational locations, such as call girls, escort workers, pornography actresses and models, brothel workers, exotic dancers, peep show workers, phone sex workers, street workers, and window prostitutes. One restriction I imposed on myself early in the research was the decision to narrow the already dauntingly broad subject by limiting my study to *women* performing erotic labor. While many of the concerns raised in this work are applicable to male prostitution, that subject deserves and requires separate consideration. Each of my interviews lasted at least one hour, and many exceeded that time. I strived to conduct those conversations in an environment in which the subjects felt secure, often their homes or mine. In order to enhance the sense of safety and minimize the awkwardness of discussing intimate and stigmatized subjects, most of the interviews conducted in the Netherlands were done in Dutch (which I later translated into English).[7]

Each taped interview was open-ended and reciprocal (that is, they were conversational sessions in which I guided discussion through my questions, but also responded to comments directed at me). There is perhaps no other aspect of so-called "qualitative research" that so clearly reveals (or, by slight of hand, conceals) the power of the writer as that of editing interview material. I alone was in the position to decide what to include and what to discard from among the dozens of conversations that inform this book. One of the ways I attempted to diminish the effect of my own bias was to seek out voices with perspectives different from my own, and to attempt to always include rather than edit out material that made me uncomfortable. In fact, it was in such moments of unease that I most directly confronted my own "agenda" in conducting this research. By consciously including material with which I disagree or which challenges my preferred presentation of the subject, I have attempted to minimize the danger of simply using sex workers' stories as authenticating evidence for my own position. Anne McClintock refers to this as the problem of the "ventriloquist's dummy":

> In the arguments of the anti–sex work lobby, the prostitute becomes the other's other. A mute, cut-out paper doll onto which relatively empowered professional

women often project their feelings of sexual frustration,
political impotence, and rage. The slave doll image serves
as a ventriloquist's dummy through which (generally
white, middle-class) women voice their interests, at the
expense of the sex workers' needs.[8]

Similarly, American call girl and writer Carol Queen warns of the
power of the researcher to shape a particular version of the truth:

If a researcher or therapist only encourages someone to
look at the down and difficult side of sex work, without
asking any questions about what feels healthy and
vibrant and alive about it to you, they're going to get a
very partial story. And by the end of the interview, the sex
worker is going to be saying "you know, I never put into
words before how terrible this is." I could give that interview, too, except I would have to interrupt myself after
every answer to say "but I've also had an experience that
contradicts the one you asked me about."[9]

These warnings are well taken, and should be heeded no less by
those researchers, such as myself, often designated as members of the
"pro-prostitution lobby." But in conducting this research, it has been
my observation that sex workers are nobody's dummy. Prostitutes are
no more passive objects in their encounters with researchers than
they are in their interactions with clients. By choosing to reveal or to
withhold information, sex workers help shape the "ethnographic
encounter." Amsterdam sex worker Jo Doezema admits:

I think for almost everybody, I make it [the experience of
prostitution] more positive than it is, because everybody
has such a negative idea about it already. So you tend to
talk about only the good things or the funny things.[10]

The following accounts, then, are not unmediated Truth. Like all
narratives, they are stories to be interpreted. It is both unnerving and
exhilarating to know that the subjects of my research, as well as other
readers examining it, will be answering back to this text by challenging errors in it and by reinterpreting the findings, each according to
their own strategic needs.

SECTION I
SEX WARS

Chapter 1
The Meaning of Sex

The sexualization of the female body historically has been a concern for women's rights activists. According to feminist historian Sheila Jeffreys, many prominent suffragists at the turn of the century believed that the "sexualization of women led to her being considered fit for no other career than that of sexual object and affected the opportunities of all women for education, work, and general self-development."[1] As a result, they often endorsed purity campaigns which aimed "to free women from the 'degradation of her temple to solely animal uses,' so that she might take a full part in all the areas of life previously arrogated to man."[2] Women's identification with sex was understood, then, to be an important obstacle in the recognition of women as civil subjects rather than simply sexual objects.

Other early women's rights activists challenged this understanding of sex as primarily an expression of women's oppression, arguing instead that sex could and should be an arena of expanded freedom for women. *Freewoman* magazine, for example, founded in 1911 by a former suffragist activist, Dora Marsden, did not shy away from discussions of marriage reform, extramarital and nonmonogamous sex, and (male) homosexuality. From the perspective of the "freewoman," "spinsters" advocating male sexual restraint and purified sexual practices were not only politically misguided but personally repressed. As one correspondent to the *Freewoman* declared:

> it will be an unspeakable catastrophe if our richly complex Feminist movement with its possibilities of power and joy, falls under the domination of sexually deficient and disappointed women ...[3]

Similarly acrimonious disputes over the role of sexuality in women's liberation and oppression have dominated debate among women in "second-wave" feminism of the late twentieth century. By the 1980s, these disputes had escalated into feminist "sex wars." One effect of organizing conversations around sex as a "war" of positions was the need to define neatly dichotomous and hostile camps. Typically positioned on the one side are "Radical Feminists," portrayed as unrelentingly hostile to sex, which is seen as the source of women's oppression. On the other side, are "Sex Radical" feminists, who are portrayed in equally oversimplified terms as unvaryingly positive toward sex, which is understood as no more than a source of pleasure and power in women's lives.

The reality is far more complex. Feminist thinking on the subject of sex defies simple division into two coherent positions. Not only have many feminists argued in favor of a third camp[4] beyond the two polarized ones, but important differences of perspective exist within the two identified camps. Within so-called Radical Feminism, for instance, there exist at least two distinctive visions of sex. One of these perspectives selectively embraces some limited number of sexual practices as long as they are mutual and loving in their expression, while the other opposes all practices of sexuality because they are understood to be, invariably, expressions of male dominance over women. Similarly, within so-called Sex Radical feminism, distinctions can be made between those who understand sex to be inherently benign; those who see sex as potentially oppressive but only for those women who "choose" to embrace an identity as "victim"; those who view sex as neither inherently empowering nor oppressive but a contested terrain in which women must organize and demand their rights; and those who understand sex to be a cultural practice open to subversive performance and resignification. Within these debates over the meaning and function of sex, practices of prostitution serve as a central trope. The prostitute thus comes to function as both the most literal of sexual slaves and as the most subversive of sexual agents within a sexist social order.

Radical Feminism

Sociologist Steven Seidman argues that within American culture there exist two opposing perspectives on sexuality: "sexual romanticism" and "libertarianism." While libertarians, according to Seidman, believe sex to be benign whether as an expression of love or of pleasure, romanticists firmly tie sex to affection, intimacy, and love:

> Sex, say romanticists, is a way to express intimate feel-
> ings; it always implicates the core inner aspects of the
> self. It should never be approached casually or with an
> eye to mere erotic pleasure.... It should be gentle, caring,
> nurturing, respectful and entail reciprocal obligations.[5]

Within Seidman's system of classification, all feminists who oppose prostitution and pornography are relegated to the category of sexual romanticist. But, as Radical Feminist Karen Davis argues, "there are lots of good reasons to dislike objectified sex that do not reduce to a morality of love."[6] While some Radical Feminists do attack prostitution and pornography as corrupting practices under-mining a natural foundation of "positive" sex, or eros, based on love, other anti-prostitution feminists see commercial sex as only the most demystified form of sex, which is, by definition, oppressive to women. While the former position might be called a kind of pro-"positive" sex feminism, the latter is outspokenly anti-sex.

PRO-"POSITIVE" SEX FEMINISM

For those feminists engaged in the recuperative project of attempt-ing to uncover an eros free of the distortions of patriarchy, prostitu-tion and pornography represent a useful foil. They serve as the antithesis of "positive" sexuality. Gloria Steinem, for example, defines the erotic as a "mutually pleasurable sexual expression ... rooted in eros or passionate love, and thus in the idea of positive choice, free will, the yearning for a particular person." This she distinguishes from the "pornographic" which

> begins with a root meaning "prostitution" ... thus let-
> ting us know that the subject is not mutual love, or love
> at all, but domination and violence against women.... It
> ends with a root meaning "writing about" ... which puts
> still more distance between subject and object, and
> replaces a spontaneous yearning for closeness with objec-
> tification and a voyeur.[7]

From this perspective, then, sex can be divided between its "posi-tive" expression in passionate love and its violent articulation in pornographic objectification.

In the hyperbolic terms of feminist writer Jean Bethke Elshtain,

> does not anonymous lovemaking, free from constraints, mimic rather than challenge the anonymous killing of war? ... [We must] rethink whether the sexual liberation standard was from its inception the generalization of a norm of adolescent male sexuality writ large onto the wider social fabric.[8]

As Elshtain's comments suggest, for feminist sexual romanticists, certain sexual practices are not only understood to be inherently bad, but also, and not coincidentally, gendered male. Robin Morgan, for instance, argues against a "male sexual style" which emphasizes "genital sexuality, objectification, promiscuity, emotional noninvolvement" in favor of a female-centered sexuality, which would place a "greater trust in love, sensuality, humor, tenderness, commitment."[9] Similarly, Dutch feminist Ariane Amsberg argues:

> It seems to me that prostitution is something that only men could have invented. Women need more of an emotional connection when they are sexually active.... For most people, or at least for most women, sex is absolutely about intimacy and a safe, loving relationship.[10]

When love, relationship, and mutual pleasure are the only appropriate context for sex, cash and contract cannot substitute as evidence of reciprocity. Kathleen Barry thus argues that positive sex "must be earned through trust and sharing. It follows then that sex cannot be purchased.... "[11] From this perspective, the practice of prostitution is not really sex at all, but an abuse of sex. This misrepresentation sold as sex through prostitution and pornography endangers the possibility of real, positive sexual experience. Commercial sexual culture is seen to be as contaminating as a virus. Kathleen Barry states:

> Pornography no longer describes only the sexual activities between prostitutes and their customers. Sexual liberation has brought into the home many of the bizarre sexual activities that men have demanded with prostitutes. Pornography depicts not just what one can do with a whore but with one's lover, one's wife, and even one's daughter. Through pornography, time-honored distinctions of society are now blurring and the gap is quickly closing between love and violence, madonnas and whores.[12]

Prostitution, then, is seen to be increasingly the model for private sexuality even when there is no formal exchange of money for sex:

> Public sexuality is institutionalized through the massive production and distribution of pornography and through the industrialization of prostitution which has the effect of reducing sex to an object and reducing women to sex [which] objectifies sex into a thing to be gotten, had or taken, disengages sex from its human experience, its dimensionality and places it in a marketing condition *whether in fact it is marketed or not....* Public sexual exploitation increasingly is becoming the model for private sexual behavior.[13]

Commercial sex, therefore, can be held responsible for both literal and symbolic violence against women. In order to protect women and to preserve the possibility of positive sexual experience, prostitution and pornography must not only be abolished, but their contaminating effect on sexual fantasy and practice must be actively challenged.

This has led some pro-"positive" sex feminists to advocate a politics of cultural cleansing. At "The Sexual Liberals and the Attack on Feminism Conference,"[14] organized in 1987 by Radical Feminists,

Photo © Annie Sprinkle

participants discussed whether it was possible to reclaim any aspect of sex for use by women:

> Ultimately, [British author Sheila]Jeffreys believes that it is possible for lesbians to come up with a vision of egalitarian sexuality, one that doesn't have *all the residue* of heteropatriarchal society. She is doubtful, however, whether heterosexual relations can ever be *cleansed* to the point of equality.[15]

> ... Jeffreys was asked to elaborate on her earlier admission that she has had disturbing fantasies or has been aroused by pornographic material. In response, she commented on her efforts to *purge herself* of undesirable fantasies. She said she has given up fantasizing altogether; she took some time off from sex in order to try something *completely different*.... She suggested that giving up fantasies was a strategy to *cleanse the movement of* S/M.[16]

> ... The answer, according to [feminist sex therapist] Stock is to develop our own model.... We should continue to question sexuality in order to *detoxify* ourselves from this culture.[17]

For pro-"positive" sex feminists, then, sexuality may be able to be reclaimed from the patriarchy, but not in forms easily recognizable to us as sex. Because prostitution and pornography have already infiltrated our imaginations, women's fantasies and sexual activities must be cleansed of their residue. Pro-"positive" sex feminists advocate the abolition of practices of prostitution both in order to prevent further contamination of the erotic by the pornographic, and to free women from the burdens of sexual objectification by men. The objectification of women through the commodification of sex is understood to reinforce what Carole Pateman calls "male sex-right":

> when women's bodies are on sale as commodities in the capitalist market, the terms of the original [sexual] contract cannot be forgotten; the law of male sex-right is publicly affirmed, and men gain public acknowledgment as women's sexual masters—that is what is wrong with prostitution.[18]

Nancy Fraser, in a sympathetic critique of Pateman's argument, notes, however, that it is marriage and not prostitution that "establishes a long-term, hierarchical status relation whose terms are predetermined and unalterable, and whose roles are assigned according to sex." While a notion of male sex-right may well underlie the patriarchal meaning of sexual difference defining femininity as "subjection," the commodified version of that relationship through prostitution may offer a (limited) challenge to notions of boundless male dominance. The client or employer does not acquire unlimited command over the worker (except significantly, in cases of outright slavery). Thus, Fraser suggests, it is misleading to assimilate "commodification to command" because "even as the wage contract establishes workers as subject to the boss's command in the employment sphere, it simultaneously constitutes that sphere as a limited sphere."[19]

ANTI-SEX FEMINISM

If, from the vantage point of romanticist feminism, a form of positive sexuality can be recovered through purification and selective abolition (of prostitution and pornography), from the perspective of other Radical Feminists, sex itself must be abolished. From the perspective of anti-sex feminists, there is nothing sexual to recover or reclaim because the very meaning of sex is male domination. Prostitution and pornography only reveal this message most clearly. Catharine MacKinnon, for example, argues that

> sexuality itself is a social construct, gendered to the ground. Male dominance here is not an artificial overlay upon an underlying inalterable substratum of uncorrupted essential sexual being.[20]

For this reason, MacKinnon dismisses romanticist feminism as liberal:

> The critical yet formally liberal view of Susan Griffin [*Pornography and Silence: Culture's Revenge Against Nature.* 1981] conceptualizes eroticism as natural and healthy but corrupted and confused by the "pornographic mind." Pornography distorts Eros, which preexists and persists, despite male culture's pornographic "revenge" upon it. Eros is, unaccountably, still there.[21]

Because sex is understood not to be "contaminated" but rather constituted by male domination, these feminists argue that the practice itself must be abandoned. Karen Davis argues that

> being "anti-sex" is not being against sexuality per se, merely against everything that has been organized as sex,

everything one has been able to experience as sex within the constraints of our culture.[22]

One of the most explicit statements of this position has been articulated by the Southern Women's Writing Collective, who organized under the title "Women Against Sex." WAS advocates a strategy of "sex resistance":

> All sex acts subordinate women ... all actions that are part of the practice of sexuality partake of the practice's political function or goal.... Thus all sex acts (and their depictions) mean the same thing, though some mean it more than others.[23]

Apparently, while sex always means male dominance, some forms of sexual practice—such as prostitution, s/m, or heterosexual penetration—are more clearly expressive of that dynamic than others (lesbian "vanilla" sex within the bonds of loving relationship, for example). Still, even the most apparently benign kinds of sex are still sex, and hence still an enactment of male supremacy.

From this perspective, it is not enough to reject some of the more apparently abusive sexual practices, it is also necessary to recognize that the language and symbolism of those acts are the building blocks for even that which women perceive to be their most authentic sexual selves. According to WAS, feminist sex resistance must involve resisting "patriarchy's attempt to make its work of subordinating women easier by 'consensually' constructing her desire in its own oppressive image."[24] Female desire must be recreated entirely outside the practices and symbols of contemporary culture. What desire would look like divorced from sex cannot be known:

> Any act which did not subordinate women would literally not be a sex act, but would be "something else."... The practice that could make this happen does not exist. In our feminist future, an act outwardly identical to a sex act might be informed by an entirely different practice. It might stand in a different relationship to conceptual and empirical male force. But the feminist future is where we want to go/be after the defeat of male supremacy—and that is to say, after dismantling the practice of sexuality.[25]

Sex, therefore, cannot be a tool for dismantling male supremacy because it is created by and for it, and is thus inextricably implicated in it. Sex, from this perspective, is "in" us but not "of" us. It is not ours to do with as we would, it does us. The only possible strategic response is opposition to sex:

> There is no way out on the inside of the practice of sexuality except out.... The function of this practice permits no true metamorphoses.[26]

Similarly, Andrea Dworkin insists that sex resists resignification:

> Experience is chosen for us, then imposed on us, especially in intercourse, *and so is its meaning*.... We have no freedom and no extravagance in the questions we can ask or the interpretations we can make.... Our bodies speak their language. Our minds think in it. The men are inside us through and through.[27]

Within the anti-sex framework, woman is constituted as and through sex. Thus, not only is sex synonymous with male supremacy and female objectification, but woman is synonymous with whore. Andrea Dworkin states:

> The metaphysics of male sexual domination is that all women are whores. This basic truth transcends all lesser truths in the male system ...[28]

In the anti-sex invocation of "whore" (much like that of the romanticists), the prostitute is divorced from the notion of sex *worker* who negotiates a literal exchange of sex for money and is reduced to the position of sex *object* (that is, woman-as-sex, not women-does-sex). "Whore," like "woman," becomes a passive condition rather than a place of active engagement within the social and cultural order. Thus, Catharine MacKinnon insists "... men say all women are whores. We say men have the power to make this our fundamental condition."[29] Similarly, Kathleen Barry warns that "women exist as objects and as such will be taken if they don't give themselves."[30]

Women exist only as passive bodies because men have the power to make it so. Within anti-sex and romanticist feminist rhetoric, the prostitute becomes the symbol of women's abject powerlessness under conditions of male objectification and domination; they are simply objects in a marketplace.

> That is what prostitution is about: it is about bodies being exchanged on a market.... So what you have is a

lot of bodies in Manila, a lot of bodies in Thailand, a lot
of bodies in Saigon that have been used for prostitution.
Now what do you do with them [after the U.S. troops
withdraw from the region and no longer support the sex
trade]? You don't send them home to mother.
Prostitution doesn't work that way.[31]

Kathleen Barry thus explains the development of sex tourism in
areas that once served as "rest and recreation" centers for American
soldiers as strictly the result of traffickers' ingenuity. Women's need
for continued employment plays no part; they are only "bodies that
have been used for prostitution," soiled and thus no longer suitable
to be sent home to mother.[32] Such language joins forces with the
power it seeks to challenge. The dialectics of struggle disappear
entirely into an apparently seamless system of male supremacy.[33]
Male power is constantly reaffirmed even as it is denounced. In this
way, anti-sex and romanticist feminist rhetoric tends to reproduce the
very ideology it intends to destablize.

By constantly reiterating that women are whores, and that whores
are no more than objects, such feminists blind themselves to the fact
that prostitutes, no less than any other worker, and no less than any
other woman, engage in acts of negotiation, resistance, and subversion that belie their designation as passive objects. Anti-sex feminism,
like pro-"positive" sex feminism, cannot accommodate this reality.
Indeed, reality is understood to be identical to the image of it men
would wish to impose. MacKinnon states:

> Gender is sexual. Pornography constitutes the meaning
> of that sexuality. Men treat women as who they see
> women as being. Pornography constructs who that is.
> *Men's power over women means that the way men see women
> defines who women can be.*[34]

Because the positions "inside" culture are defined as fixed, to act
defiantly from within the sexual order by making subversive use of
that culture is understood to be impossible. The only "radical" feminist act is one of opposition and resistance. The cultural order must
be refused.

Sex Radical Feminism and the Meaning of Sex

Contemporary feminist sexual politics encompass positions beyond those of purification and resistance. Some feminists reject the distinction between "positive" and "perverted" sexuality and simultaneously insist on active engagement within the sexual order rather than the abolition of it. Steven Seidman categorizes these alternative positions as sexual "libertarianism." According to Seidman, while sexual romanticists assume that "certain sexual acts carry an intrinsic moral meaning," libertarians "frame sex as having multiple meanings … and [see it as] legitimate in multiple social settings."[35] Because libertarians resist the idea that sexual meaning is fixed, individuals (rather than the community) must determine whether an act is right or wrong for him or her. A libertarian notion of "consent" thus replaces a romanticist notion of "responsibility" as the ultimate measure of the ethics of any sexual activity. Seidman insists that this has the effect of individualizing the meaning of sex to the point where social structures such as gender inequality necessarily disappear from the account.[36]

Just as Seidman's category of sexual romanticism is too narrow to account for the divergent perspectives within Radical Feminism, so too is his designation libertarian inadequate to describe the diversity of positions within feminist Sex Radicalism. Among feminists broadly defined as Sex Radicals, a distinction can be drawn between those most closely aligned with the extreme individualism of libertarian ethics and politics, and those who explicitly situate sex (and the individuals enacting it) within structures of power and privilege.

SEXUAL LIBERTARIANISM

Sexual libertarianism offers a reversal of the image of sex presented in anti-sex feminism. Both insist that sex, as represented in prostitution and pornography, must be read as reality, and both conclude that the encoded message is one of power. Where these groups diverge is on the question of who holds that power. One of the most prominent voices of the libertarian perspective is Camille Paglia, whose uncompromising pronouncements on sex make her a fair match for such anti-sex feminists as Andrea Dworkin and Catharine MacKinnon. According to Paglia,

> What you see in pornography and prostitution is the reality of sex. It is not a patriarchal distortion. It is the ultimate physical reality. So a feminist who claims to understand sexuality but cannot deal with pornography or topless clubs is no expert. She is a censor. She is a prude.[37]

While Dworkin and MacKinnon read messages of male power and female subjection in commercial sexual culture, Paglia sees the reverse:

> Men are run ragged by female sexuality all their lives. From the beginning of his life to the end, no man ever fully commands any woman. It's an illusion…. That's what the strip clubs are about: not woman as victim, not woman as slave, but woman as goddess.[38]

Paglia insists that women's association with sex should be seen as her source of greatest power, not as the root of her oppression and abuse. Paglia thus intends not only to complicate the notion of women's sexual victimization by men, but to reverse it. It is men who are "run ragged" and feel powerless in the presence of women's sexuality:

> The feminist line is, strippers and topless dancers are degraded, subordinated, and enslaved; they are victims, turned into objects by the display of their anatomy. But women are far from being victims—women *rule*; they are in total control…. The feminist analysis of prostitution says that men are using money as power over women. I'd say, yes, that's all that men *have*. The money is a confession of weakness. They have to buy women's attention. It's not a sign of power; it's a sign of weakness.[39]

If women rule sexually and enjoy total control in their encounters with men, then those who claim to be victims of male sexual violence have only themselves to blame. In this way, sexual power is removed from any social or political context and instead becomes an attribute available to any individual alert enough to claim it.[40] Author bell hooks criticizes this libertarian feminist position for "embracing outmoded sexist visions of female sexual agency and pleasure." Such a politics, she argues, lacks imagination as it conceives of "sexual agency only by inverting the patriarchal standpoint and claiming it as their [women's] own." [41]

Hooks is not alone among contemporary feminists in rejecting both the radical individualism of libertarianism as well as the ubiquitous female sexual victimization of Radical Feminism. Many Sex Radical feminists explicitly situate sex within a culture of male domination; sex is understood to be constructed by this culture without being fully determined by it. Carole Vance, for example, suggests that

> to focus only on pleasure and gratification ignores the patriarchal structure in which women act, yet to speak only of sexual violence and oppression ignores women's experience with sexual agency and choice and unwittingly increases the sexual terror and despair in which women live. [42]

Unlike libertarians, feminist Sex Radicals do not fully substitute an ethic of consent for one of responsibility. Social and political context beyond the individual continue to figure prominently in their interpretation and assessment of sex. For example, during her tenure as editor of the lesbian sex magazine, *On Our Backs,* Marcy Sheiner objected to photos in another erotic publication, *Future Sex,* on the grounds that they were both racist and sexist. Sheiner challenged these images of sex tourism for glossing over a context of unequal power and privilege:

> I'm the first to admit that these images and ideas generate sexual excitement in many people, even those who are ethically opposed to them. But is arousal potential the sole criteria for what goes into a sex magazine? ... [this question] has plagued me since I penned and sold my first pornographic story several years ago. So while I champion freedom of expression, and continue to create sexual materials, I can't kid myself into believing there are black and white answers to the ethical questions raised during the course of my work. [43]

A similar tension was revealed in 1991 when Bobby Lilly, a leader of a mixed gender anti-censorship organization in California, CAL-ACT, reported on the struggles of sex workers and Sex Radical feminists to gain a voice within the largest American feminist organization, the

National Organization for Women. A male reader returned the issue with the words "what irrelevant garbage" scrawled across the top. He also circled the words "Equal Rights Amendment" and "patriarchal" in the article, commenting that "this has nothing to do with the fight against censorship." Lilly, who "didn't know whether to laugh, cry, or spit," replied that as a feminist and a Sex Radical, her anti-censorship politics could never be gender-blind.[44] Sex Radical feminists and libertarians may both embrace a politics of sexual "free speech," but they diverge on the issue of whether an erotic ethic needs to extend beyond the formal question of consent.

———

In the early 1990s, a workshop on pornography was organized at the National Organization for Women's annual conference in New York. One presenter, a male academic, reported on the causal relationship he believed to exist between pornography and violence against women. After the presentation, an audience member approached him. "Isn't there some way," she asked, "to educate people about the difference between violence and consensual fantasies, something besides resorting to censorship? Maybe s/m photos could be captioned: 'This is a negotiated fantasy between two consenting adults.'" The man slowly shook his head. "I understand your concern. But while that might be enough for you or me, what about a group of Black teenagers at a newsstand on 42nd Street? They won't read or understand a message like that." Overhearing this exchange, I found myself wondering about the problematic alliances some women have made with "good" (White, professional) men out to protect the sisterhood from the "bad" (Black, poor) ones. But I was soon reminded that my own alliances can be no less embarrassing.

The group I was associated with at the conference, "Union Labia: Sex Workers and Sex Radical Feminists," had a number of male "supporters" attached to it. Some of them were fans of the various high profile porn stars in the delegation. The presence of these men made me acutely uncomfortable, but the pros simply treated them with the cursory courtesy reserved for johns. One man, however, received a more respectful sort of attention. He was a short, chubby, middle-aged fellow in a business suit. This man, I learned, was no average john; he was a journalist on assignment from Playboy magazine hoping to cover a catfight between sex workers and other NOW feminists.

Playboy had access to our group because the Playboy Foundation had contributed a small sum toward the airfare necessary to bring an international prostitution expert from the World Health Organization in Geneva to the meeting. In return, he was to see if there was a story to be had. I was profoundly ambivalent about his presence. While pornography may no longer be the declared enemy for feminists such as myself, Playboy's fondness for airbrushed "perfection" has never endeared them to me.

Throughout the conference, the Playboy reporter secreted himself away with one or another of the "Union Labia" members attempting, I assumed, to dig up dirt that wasn't being thrown. I managed to avoid him until the final afternoon. He opened our conversation with the offer of a marijuana cookie. Our alliance as outlaws thus cemented, I proceeded to give him my standard feminist critique of both the anti-pornography/anti-prostitution movement and of the male violence that inspires it. This is a familiar role for me in sex worker/sex radical settings where there are already many articulate voices asserting women's right to fuck convention by being sluts and whores.

Because I was talking to a Playboy, it felt especially satisfying to remind him that anti-porn feminists were responding to a very real state of emergency over women's sexual integrity and safety. "Still," I confided, "their insistence that people like me are the enemy is distressing, especially in this political moment when we so desperately need each other. We have to form a united front against the real and declared enemies." "Like who?" he asked. "Well, you know, like the President, the Supreme Court, the whole Reagan/Bush Right Wing." "Now, wait a minute," he interrupted, "what makes you think they're the enemy? I'm a contributor to the National Review myself. William Buckley is a personal friend. They've been very receptive to my articles defending free speech and pornography." I felt the room shift slightly, and it wasn't just the marijuana kicking in. The whole encounter reminded me that anti-pornography feminists have no monopoly on courting or tolerating the support of dubious allies to "advance the cause."

———

SEXUAL SUBVERSION

Unlike sexual libertarians, feminist Sex Radicals generally accept romanticist and anti-sex feminists analyses of sex as deeply implicated in structures of inequality. But what distinguishes the Sex Radical perspective is the notion that sex is a terrain of struggle, not a fixed field of gender and power positions. Jana Sawicki explains:

> Neither wholly a source of domination nor of resistance, sexuality is also neither outside power nor wholly circumscribed by it. Instead, it is itself an arena of struggle. There are no inherently liberatory or repressive sexual practices, for any practice is co-optable and any is capable of becoming a source of resistance.[45]

Sex Radical feminists thus share with romanticist and anti-sex feminists a sense of outrage at the existing sexual order, but reject a politics of purification or abolition in favor of one of subversion from within sexual practice. This offers a vision of political struggle not predicated on a cleansing of culture or on a move outside of culture.

From this perspective, acts of apparent complicity may also be acts of subversive resistance. Just as a colonized people may make use of the language of the colonizer in transgressive ways,[46] women are understood to be able to subversively resignify sexual language and practices through using them in unintended ways. Pat Califia, for example, argues that lesbians can liberate a sexual vocabulary for their own use by seizing words previously used against them:

> Words that have been used in anti-sex, anti-lesbian ways can be coopted. By using these terms with pride, lesbians can liberate them and change their meaning. The word "dyke" has already been transformed this way.[47]

Daphne Marlatt has described this subversive relationship to the symbolic order in terms of being "an inhabitant of language, not master, nor even mistress ... inside language she leaps for joy, shoving out the walls of taboo and propriety ..."[48] Such attempts to redefine and reinhabit the sexual order are in part a response to the impossibility of moving to a place outside of culture to create entirely anew. Teresa de Lauretis argues that

> paradoxically, the only way to position oneself outside of that discourse is to displace oneself within it—to refuse

the question as formulated, or to answer deviously (though in its words), even to quote (but against the grain).[49]

In addition to the impossibility of moving to a place outside of culture, some feminists argue that a politics predicated on an abolition of the sexual order rather than engagement with it leaves women further impoverished. Betsy Warland, for example, acknowledges the shortcomings of sexual speech in describing women's experiences and desires, but urges women nonetheless to refuse to abandon it:

> the language itself does not reflect women's sensual experience. For most of us, however, it is our native tongue. The only language we have … so when we abandon words, it isn't a simple matter of leaving them behind but rather a turning over of our power to those who keep them: speechlessness the consequence.[50]

Ntozake Shange wrestles with a similar concern in her decision to make use of sexual speech in her writing:

> One part of the exploitation of people of color—especially women—has been to rob us of any inner life, to rob us of our own sexuality and sensuality…. I hesitate to strip

Photo © Annie Sprinkle

us of a concrete and vital language for sexual activities and
desires and fantasies, because I don't think we can afford
to lose too much more.[51]

But feminists like Shange who regard sexual language as a crucial
resource for women are far from reverent in their uses of it:

> I'm taking words that men have used to make us dirty.
> I'm taking them to make us able to use them any way we
> choose ... I can get myself in a big bind and never be able
> to write anything that is honest if I can't somehow uproot
> words or images that have been malignant and make
> them constructive for me.[52]

Pat Califia further argues that the meaning of sexual practice no
less than sexual language is dependent on the context in which it
is employed:

> No erotic act has an intrinsic meaning. A particular sex-
> ual activity may symbolize one thing in the majority cul-
> ture, another thing to members of a sexual subculture ....
> The context within which an erotic act occurs can also
> alter its meaning.[53]

It is precisely this commitment to locating sex within a cultural and
political context that distinguishes feminist Sex Radicals such as
Califia from libertarians such as Paglia. While Paglia would general-
ize the apparent control a performer has over a client in a strip club
to assert that all women "are in total control" of sexual interactions
with men, Califia would read the interaction and its meaning as context dependent.

Even in sub-cultural enactments of sex, dominant culture always
remains important. Anne McClintock notes that within the "control
frame of cash and fantasy" of commercial s/m, for example, men can
"surrender" power to women while still maintaining control outside
of that limited frame:

> In the private security of fantasy, men can indulge secret-
> ly and guiltily their knowledge of women's power, while
> enclosing female power in a fantasy land that lies far
> beyond the cities and towns of genuine feminist change.[54]

McClintock concludes that within the "magic circle" of subcultural
sex, "social and personal contradictions can be deployed or negotiated,

but need not be finally resolved, for the sources and ends of these paradoxes lie beyond the individual...."[55] As sociologist Robert Connell concludes, a true "democracy of pleasure" requires an equalization of resources among and between men and women.[56]

While sexual libertarianism can ignore what lies beyond the individual, feminism cannot. Women are still disproportionately poor, overworked, and underpaid; women are still the deliberate targets of male sexual violence; women's bodies are still heavily regulated by state policies criminalizing subcultural sexual practices and restricting access to birth control and abortion; and women are still stigmatized and punished for sexual activity beyond the confines of monogamous heterosexual marriage. These realities co-determine women's experience of sex.

The key difference, then, between Sex Radical feminists and Radical Feminists does not rest on whether attention should be paid to the structures of gender inequality in which sex is constructed, enacted, and represented. Rather, the two perspectives differ in their assessments of whether the meaning and function of sex is fully determined by that sexist social order. While Radical Feminists insist that the sexual (mis)representations of patriarchy create "reality" because of the absolute power of men to make them function as such, feminist Sex Radicals understand sex to be a cultural tactic which can be used both to destablize male power as well as to reinforce it. In much the same way, Michel de Certeau argues that culture

> articulates conflicts and alternately legitimizes, displaces, or controls the superior force. It develops in an atmosphere of tensions, and often of violence [and] the tactics of consumption, the ingenious ways in which the weak make use of the strong, thus lend a political dimension to everyday practices.[57]

Practices of prostitution, like other forms of commodification and consumption, can be read in more complex ways than simply as a confirmation of male domination. They may also be seen as sites of ingenious resistance and cultural subversion. For this reason, Sex Radical feminists insist that the position of the prostitute cannot be reduced to one of a passive object used in a male sexual practice, but instead can be understood as a place of agency where the sex worker makes active use of the existing sexual order. Indeed, the Whore is often invoked by feminist Sex Radicals as a symbol of women's sexual autonomy and, as such, as a potential threat to patriarchal control over women's sexuality. Rebecca Kaplan suggests:

> Women are usually called whores for being openly or highly sexual. Men who yell at women will often call them a "whore" and a "dyke" in the same breath. How is it that a woman can be simultaneously accused of having too much sex with men (whore) and too little sex with men (dyke)? This should make us realize that both of these terms condemn women's sexual autonomy. Whores and dykes are a threat to heteropatriarchy because both set their own rules for sex—rules which deny men the right to unlimited access to women's sexuality. Of course, prostitution can be critiqued like any other capitalist venture, but in a world in which a woman's body is so devalued, telling a man that he has to pay for access to it can be a radical act of self-determination.[58]

Pat Califia concurs:

> The slut is, in Dworkin's parlance, male property—a victim of male violence—a woman who accepts male definition of her sexuality. Instead, I believe that she is someone men hate because she is potentially beyond their control.... A whore does not sell her body. She sells her time. So she has time that is not for sale, that belongs to no one but herself. Domesticated women don't dare put a price on their time.[59]

The slut, the dyke, and the whore are thus embraced by Sex Radicals as a potent symbolic challenge to confining notions of proper womanhood and conventional sexuality. Because Sex Radicals, like libertarians, embrace a vision of sex freed of the constraints of love, commitment, and convention, prostitution and pornography are understood to be useful to enhance sexual exploration and diversity. While Kathleen Barry and other pro-"positive" sex feminists condemn prostitution for introducing "bizarre" pornographic practices into private sexual behavior, Pat Califia celebrates commercial sex for very similar reasons:

> If you don't know that there's a whole group of people who engage in a particular sexual behavior, it makes it

much more difficult to imagine yourself ever being able to do it. And porn is one of the commonest ways that people discover there are other folks out there who like to do cunnilingus, anal sex, gay sex, get tied up, have threesomes …[60]

Similarly, Lisa Duggan, Nan Hunter, and Carole Vance argue that

pornography carries many messages other than woman-hating: it advocates sexual adventure, sex outside of marriage, anonymous sex, group sex, voyeuristic sex, illegal sex, public sex…. Women's experience of pornography is not as universally victimizing as the [MacKinnon/ Dworkin anti-pornography] ordinance would have it.[61]

Of course, Sex Radicals' invocation of prostitution and pornography as tools of liberation forged by undomesticated outlaw whores is as much of a rhetorical trope as the Radical Feminists depiction of commercial sex as realm of oppression populated by sexual slaves and exploited objects. Ira Levine, who has long worked in the adult film industry, reports, for example, that "outlaw" is not an identity all sex workers embrace:

It's amazing how in so many ways, many people in the porn industry have the same rather conventional values as people in any other industry. Do not assume that this is a bunch of wild bohemian personalities. We have our share of them, but we have an awful lot of people who struggle to lead conventional lives in spite of what they're doing. I think a lot of those people are missing out on the one real advantage of this job: the freedom of being a leper. After you've already done something loathsome to the majority of the population, you have a certain amount of latitude. I think it's a shame that these people feel an obligation to prove to everyone that they're really just perfectly normal people.[62]

Similarly, Carol Queen, a California sex worker and writer, notes that, far from being sexually enlightened, many prostitutes share the sexual prejudices of dominant culture:

Unlike many women working in the sex trades, I actually have a background in sex education. I want to think well of the erotic desires of the people who come to me. I don't think of clients as kinky or perverted. I like it that they can come to me and say "I would like you to put your hand in my butt" or "I would like you to piss on me." One of the things that I know I am providing is a sexual safe space for people who haven't had that before. And I'm probably more safe for them than most prostitutes because I honor their desire. One piece of the puzzle of how to improve sex work is that sex workers could be trained in human sexuality, and other people could be assisted in developing both their own sex awareness and their communication skills.[63]

The reality of commercial sex (and the experiences of those performing erotic labor) is far more varied than either Radical or Sex Radical feminist rhetoric can express. Prostitution functions as an effective trope in these competing discourses of female sexuality, but the use of the sex worker as a symbol has also served to obscure the real complexity of her life.

▼ ▼ ▼

Nina Hartley, *adult film actress*
Berkeley, CA, 1991

I came across explicit adult sexual material for the first time when I was about fourteen. I was immediately fascinated by it, especially by the portrayal of women as sexual free agents. Now I realize that that's just a fantasy of men, but it was a pretty powerful concept for me at that age. It wasn't an entirely new message because my mother had always had feminist books like *Our Bodies, Ourselves* and *Liberating Masturbation* around the house, but the explicitness of porn appealed to me.

It wasn't until I was about twenty-three, though, that I did any sex work myself—first stripping and then adult films. It all happened under very favorable circumstances: the first film I did, *Educating Nina*, was written, directed, and produced by a woman, Juliette Anderson. Since then, I've done almost three hundred more videos and, while the energy is the same, my performances are way more polished.

It's a skill learning how to open up to the camera, how to give head in a photogenic fashion. You know, there's real sex and there's camera sex; my skill is in fusing the reality of camera sex with the intensity of real sex. I have to pull together a lot of different dynamics: who my partner is, what kind of mood we're in, and whether it's the beginning of a shoot so the producers are still a little more generous with time, or at the end of the day and we're running late and have to rush. All those things have to be brought together in a way that appears effortless. And usually it's a challenge I enjoy.

The frustrating part is that, with budget limitations, there's not a lot of time to do much character development, rehearse, do several takes, and really try to hone things down. In the 1970s, adult films were shot with a lot more care, over a period of several days and with real budgets and serious actors. A lot of the best movies still date from that time like *Autobiography of a Flea*, *The Opening of Misty Beethoven*, and *The Private Afternoons of Pamela Mann*. Those are movies that will stand the test of time. And I think some of my best work will, too. *Debbie Does Dishes* from 1985, for instance, was hugely popular and it still sells well. I received a best actress and best comedy scene award for it. It also spawned five sequels featuring the Debbie character who is a kind of a utopian Nina Hartley/Judy Holiday combo.

Generally, though, most of the films these days are rushed through production. You come in and have to do five sex scenes. It would really improve the job to have fewer sex scenes per day so you could spend a little more time on each one. But these are relatively minor complaints. I'd still say that my bad days at work don't have that much to do with the fact that I'm making a sex film. Some days I do have a sore back or my feet hurt or I'm just in a bad mood. It's no big deal. I've had experiences from the sublime to the ridiculous, but very few really unpleasant ones. Work is work: you have good days and bad days, but my worst day at work is still better than the best day selling shoes at Kinney's.

What I do often long for is more creativity and variety in the work. Pornography as we know it has only been around for twenty or twenty-five years. A lot of the guys making it have been in the business forever; they're real dinosaurs. As they retire or die, new blood is starting to appear. I think in the next ten or fifteen years there could be some exciting developments with younger people, amateurs, and especially more women making movies. Most of the product you see now is made by businessmen for a profit. They're not committed artists; they're just in it for the money.

I've worked with a number of alternative production companies run by women like Tigress, Blush, and Femme Productions. The key difference is the boss/worker relationship. To start with, all three of those companies are run by women who used to be adult actresses or strippers. Because they've been sexual entertainers themselves, they understand the process differently. These alternative companies are not only female-oriented but feminist. I love that because it can get a little old sometimes to be the person with the highest consciousness on the set. I take my work very seriously and I see part of my job to be feminist consciousness-raising around issues of health and self-determination.

If another woman on the set is new to the business, especially if she's young, I make a particular point of checking in with her to make sure she understands her rights and privileges. It's not so much that I'm worried that someone has hit her over the head and dragged her in front of the camera, but I am always concerned that she may not have fully considered the impact the work can have on her life twenty years down the road. The societal reaction to the woman who has not only crossed the line from "good girl" to "bad girl" but has left a photographic record of her sexual activity can be intense. The movies provide undeniable evidence that you have done something society doesn't want women to do. You are a whore, an outcast, a bad woman, and they can punish you unmercifully for it. I try to make sure that actresses understand what it means to have a permanent record of you with a man's penis in your mouth. When this comes up later, will you be prepared to deal with it? It's not good enough to just do it for the money because, while it's not a bad living, you ain't gonna get rich doing it.

I've had a wonderful time making movies for seven years in large part because of how I have done it: I don't do anything I don't like already, and if I like it I'll really go for it. I think a big part of feeling used and abused in this profession is having taken money for something you didn't really like and that won't sit well with you after a while. I really wish there was a pamphlet to hand out to every actress on the set. Something with phone numbers of community counseling centers, substance abuse clinics, rape crisis lines, job training programs, and career planning advisors. Women need to be able to approach things with clarity. You need to save money and pay taxes. It's not just a big party, it's work.

I have to be careful though. When I first got into this business, I had a lot of value judgements about some of the women: they smoked, they drank, they didn't wear their seat belts, they didn't eat their vegetables, and they didn't finish school. These were really street smart women, and I had to admit that I was having a tremendous classist reaction to them. I've done a lot of growing up myself over the past few years. As much as I don't like the fact that some women in this business are only 19 or 20, or don't seem to be together enough to do the work, I also know that a woman has got to do what a woman has got to do. I may not like her path, I may want to shout "Don't take that road, take a left, take a left, the right is a real bummer ...", but I've finally gotten to the point where I just say, "If you ever need to talk, I'm here. Here's my number."

And who's to say that my limits should be their limits anyway? I've never done any outright prostitution, for example, because, as a middle-class girl, I'm terrified of arrest. If I can't say "This much money will get you exactly this; there's my bodyguard; here's my bedroom; shall we?" then I'm not into it. You know, despite my work, I don't really feel much like a "bad girl." I don't even think I do porn out of a need to rebel. Sure, I'm militantly sexual but only in places where that's expected and appropriate behavior. At heart, I'm a "good girl" who wants to make the world a better place for everybody. I want an end to hunger, no more war, no more rape. I pay my taxes, I help old ladies across the street, I'm kind to animals, I visit my grandma.

The funny thing is, given the objections some feminists have to porn, I really see my work as important for women. I think sex is a very valid area to explore on an artistic level and women need to reclaim that. We need to be less afraid of our sexuality, of becoming frenzied, our eyes glazing over, getting sweaty, and feeling out of control. This is a good state; it's called approaching orgasm. But because we so rarely see it, it can really seem scary. Part of the problem is that in Hollywood films, when a women is in that state she's either in danger or dangerous. I hate slasher films and movies like *Fatal Attraction* where the sexually aggressive woman is a victim or insane. In 99% of commercially available pornography, a woman is depicted desiring sex, pursuing sex, having sex, having orgasms and at the end of the movie she's still alive, happy, healthy, and well. Women really need to look at that message in light of what Hollywood has to offer and get off the kick that it's pornography that's violent.

▼

Ariane Amsberg, *writer and sexologist*
Amsterdam, *1994*

I'm a feminist; I think prostitution is bad for women. I don't want to see women treated as though we were just a hole men can use whenever and however they want. We'll never be equal, if men think "Ha! For money I can have you!" Men despise women profoundly and the possibility of buying sex only increases that contempt.

Look in the paper, there are two full pages of sex advertisements every day. The phone sex lines advertise things like "young school girls, 18 years old" but the stories they tell are all about being twelve or thirteen and saying "No, no, no, don't do that" to the doorman who almost rapes them. By the end, of course, it always turns into "Oh yes, oh yes, how wonderful." Men listen to this and it stimulates their appetite for younger and younger girls. I'm concerned about rape and battery; such violence is only possible where there is a complete lack of respect for women. Surely that must partly be the responsibility of the sex industry.

One of the sex ads I saw in the paper today read something like "help students: call to negotiate what they will give you in bed in exchange for your financial support." This is terrible for the women's movement; any man, whether he's highly educated or a worker, living in the gutter or even a criminal, any man now thinks that he can get an intelligent woman, a student in need of money, to lie on her back and put his prick in her. Is that what the women's movement is about? To get women educated, to obtain equal rights, just so that any man can still fuck her for a little money? That's very reassuring to men. The message is "Don't worry about women who go to the university, you have nothing to fear from intelligent women. You can still pay to fuck them at Yab Yum [an 'exclusive' sex club in Amsterdam]." I used to write a column in the *Algemene Dagblad* [national Dutch daily paper] until they ran an interview with the guy who runs Yab Yum. He described his business as a respectable one employing very intelligent and highly educated women. After that, I refused to write for the paper anymore. The article was nothing more than a big advertisement for the place.

These men who are involved with prostitution are not nice men. I'll say it just like that: every man who goes to a prostitute is not a nice man. His actions must come from total disrespect. Maybe he has feelings of inferiority so that he has to go to someone who he thinks is even more inferior to do things that nobody else would do with him or that he would be too ashamed to tell anyone about. I know that some prostitutes think that they have power over the men, and I believe them. It's a kind of professionalism knowing exactly what a man wants the minute he walks in the door. But no matter what kind of power the woman seems to have in that setting, the man will always have more.

In the bedroom, power is almost always in the hands of the man. That's because men have been socialized to feel much more confident about their sexual performance than women. Women are so badly informed and so insecure about their bodies that, in the bedroom, the man just takes over and determines what's going to happen. On top of that, he can also say, "if you don't have enough sex with me, there are thousands of prostitutes who will." That gives him all the power in sex. Imagine how different it would be without that possibility of escape, without him being able to say "if you don't do what I like, then I'm going to a prostitute or I'll take a girlfriend."

Besides, if a woman doesn't want to have sex with her husband, it's probably because he's such a bad lover. And who makes men bad lovers? The prostitutes! I want this to be noted: prostitutes teach men to be bad lovers because, in prostitution, the faster the men come the better. So they learn to ejaculate fast but they never learn to touch a shoulder or caress a face. And, after they've performed so badly, it's the prostitute's job to build up their ego. No matter how ugly and filthy he is, no matter how bad a lover he may be, she always builds him up: "No one has ever made me feel like this …" It's so fake, I don't know how they can do it. How can they play that little piece of theater for men and their pricks? What happened to those girls? Where's their self-respect?

I've always had the idea that they must have been damaged to want to do this. Unless, of course, they're just curious. One woman I know tried prostituting herself one night in Paris just out of curiosity. That's fine if someone wants to do that; I would never look down on anyone for that. But if I try to visualize myself as a prostitute, I immediately see the client. I don't know how he smells, but he probably doesn't smell very good. And then I see myself going around his prick and caressing it, and pretending to lick it or kiss it, and put it inside me. I would totally lose respect for myself if I did that because it would be something I wouldn't enjoy. Maybe I'd only enjoy the money. Of course, if I worked in a factory all day, I might not enjoy that either. Or if I worked in a hospital; I know that nurses have to touch people's bodies and clean up the urine and shit, which obviously isn't so pleasant either. But prostitution is worse. It cannot be compared to a normal job because it's bad for all women.

[handwritten margin note: Why? need elaboration]

One of the things that I regret is that our feminist movement doesn't think enough about the long-term effects of prostitution on society as a whole. They only seem to be concerned about the women who want to prostitute themselves and how they can best be protected. But they don't think about what prostitution means, how it changes society and affects the possibility of equality between men and women. In the Dutch feminist movement, women are really afraid of being critical of prostitution. *Opzij* [the national Dutch feminist magazine] doesn't even take a stand; they're too afraid. Very few women will say what they really think.

But it just goes too far when the Women's Movement is promoting prostitution by saying that it's a job like any other. I've even heard it compared to marriage where a housewife goes to bed with her husband in order to improve the atmosphere at home, or to convince him to buy her a new dress. Of course it's true that men have money, women have what men want, and the rest is negotiation. But to compare prostitution with a good relationship is bullshit. You choose to be in a relationship and you share very nice moments. That's totally different than pure commercial sex. The women have no choice, absolutely no choice. Anyone who comes in, they have to please. Sure the women from the Red Thread will say "I only take this one, or I only take that one." Of course they would say that. What no one will say is that it's outrageous for the Red Thread to get state subsidies to hold their Whores' Congresses. Community tax money is paying for their get-togethers! Well, personally, I don't want to pay for prostitutes to get together and promote their "jobs." Prostitution is extremely bad for all women, including non-prostitutes. Why, then, are we agreeing to support it?

[handwritten margin note: Is that a good relationship?]

[handwritten margin note: again... why?]

39

Apparently, though, anybody who uses the label "feminist" is invited into the movement without first finding out who these women really are. Just because you are a woman and say you are a feminist doesn't mean that you are. What could it possibly have to do with feminism that someone likes s/m, for example, or works as a prostitute? They're just using feminism to give themselves some sort of status. They feel safer in the feminist fortress, but they have nothing to contribute to feminism except in a negative sense.

I'm not saying that prostitution and pornography are *bad* in themselves, I'm saying that they are bad for *women*. I know that there are some extremely interesting lesbian porn movies and I've certainly found some of them are very exciting. There's something in the rhythm or the story that's completely different than hetero pornography. As far as I'm concerned, free and consenting adults can do whatever they want to do with each other. It's fine with me if people want to experiment with sex parties, or want to be tied up, or want to be pierced. But once money enters into it, that changes things. It makes it unfree. If you are paid, you have to give the service that you were paid to render no matter how disgusting or painful it is.

Besides, it's not a safe job for women. Prostitutes have to surrender all their money to whoever demands it because they have absolutely no rights. Especially the foreign women. It's terrible to promote prostitution so that all these foreign women come to the Netherlands to prostitute themselves. How can anybody imagine that's a good thing? When they go back to their countries, they'll have to keep their past totally secret or be despised. If it's known what they did, they'll have no chance of marrying or ever being respected. Prostitution works against whatever is good for them. Sure you could argue that it would help them if people stopped despising prostitutes. But isn't it better to say that women shouldn't be used in prostitution in the first place?

▼

Chapter 2
Sexual Slavery

White Slavery is not just a figment of the imagination of pornographic writers; it has gained considerable impetus in recent years.... The girls are recruited from all over Europe and their destinations are the ports and capitals of the world, some going to private clients of one race or another before being passed on to brothels.[1]

For over a hundred years, such images have had a tenacious grip on the public psyche for reasons which have not always been conscious or articulate. This depiction of commercial sex as a form of slavery, and prostitutes as women "trafficked" into the trade against their will, has endured in part because it resonates well with long-standing assumptions about women's sexual vulnerability and the proper relationship of women to sex, commerce, and travel.

"Beautiful White Girls Sold Into Ruin"

Organized movements against what was once known as "White Slavery" formed in the late nineteenth century in both Western Europe and the United States. One of the first widely read exposes of sexual trafficking appeared in 1885 when a British journalist, W. T. Stead, described his purchase of a young London girl from her mother,ß purportedly for use in Parisian prostitution. Public response was overwhelming, and included a demonstration of more than 200,000 people in London demanding, among other things, legislation to raise the age of sexual consent for girls.[2] Stead's story, and others like it, created the impression that prostitution was little more than the sexual enslavement of young girls. Historical records, however, suggest that most British prostitutes were not children sold into the trade but rather young women who consciously engaged in prostitution for economic reasons.[3]

Still, it was the image of the sexual slave that captured both the headlines and the public imagination, a phenomenon which might partially be explained by the effective mix of moral outrage and sexual sensationalism in the reporting. One tract, for example, promised readers: "Beautiful White Girls Sold Into Ruin.... Illustrated with a Large Number of Startling Pictures."[4]

Despite meager evidence of a widespread phenomenon of involuntary prostitution, anti-trafficking campaigns quickly spread beyond Britain. In the United States, federal investigators attempting to uncover evidence of white slavery reported with frustration that few of the women they interviewed pointed to slave trafficking as their means of entry into the trade. A more typical explanation, they found, was economic need. One former domestic explained to U.S. investigators: "[I was] tired of drudgery as a servant ... I'd rather do this than be kicked around like a dog in a kitchen by some woman who calls herself a lady."[5] Nonetheless, in the U.S. as in Britain, it was easier for both investigators and the public to believe in "a vast underground traffic in women than to accept that working-class women might choose sex either for money or the excitement it brought."[6]

The belief in a pervasive sexual slave trade in the absence of widespread evidence suggests that the notion of white slavery was not dependent on large numbers of documented cases. Instead, it was fueled by more general anxieties about changing gender, sex, class, and race relations at the turn of the century. The idea of a "white slave" unconsciously spoke not only to the experience of the white working class laboring under harsh conditions of early industrial capitalism, but also to the racial fears of an increasingly ethnically diverse population.

In the first sixty years of U.S. history, from Independence through 1840, total immigration was only three-quarters of a million people. But in the next forty, between 1840 and 1880, over eight million Europeans, mostly from northwestern Europe, emigrated to the U.S. And from 1880 to 1930, during the height of the White Slavery campaigns, more than twenty-three million immigrants came to the United States, this time primarily from eastern and southern Europe, including Italians, Poles, Russian Jews, and Slavs. This represented the largest population movement recorded in history.[7] Such massive trafficking across borders produced fears of cultural contamination and moral pollution. Not surprisingly, these foreigners became the target of nativist rhetoric and provided a focus for early anti-trafficking legislation. A 1901 U.S. Senate report, for example, asserted that "the vilest practices are brought here from continental Europe ... the most bestial refinements of depravity."[8] Investigators especially warned against Jews "engaged in importation ... prey[ing] upon young girls whom they find on the streets, in dance halls and similar places."[9]

Adding to racial anxieties in the U.S. was the recent emancipation of African American slaves, which was perceived as a threat to both sexual and racial purity. As Lynne Segal notes:

> the emancipation of Black slaves in the southern states of America had been followed by the immediate violent upsurge of lynchings of Black men, at least one every three days between 1885 and 1890 ... the justification given referred to the protection of white womanhood from bestial Black men.[10]

Even without the effective scapegoating of Blacks, Jews, and immigrants, fears of white slavery resonated with the prevailing gendered belief that travel, commerce, and sex were all properly the province of men. A woman found operating in such foreign territory—especially a White woman—was not only out of place, but highly suspect. Cynthia Enloe notes:

> feminist geographers and ethnographers have been amassing evidence revealing that a principal difference between women and men in countless societies has been the license to travel away from a place thought of as "home." A woman who travels ... without the protection of an acceptable male escort is likely to be tarred with the brush of "unrespectability." She risks losing her honor ...[11]

In the late nineteenth century, only a handful of women had assumed the public identity of "lady traveler." Their class status as "ladies" offered some protection from public condemnation as did their willingness to package themselves as handmaids to colonization. Nonetheless, as Enloe reports, they were still "viewed with suspicion because they dared to travel such long distances with so little proper male protection."[12] It was assumed that few women above reproach would willingly travel far from home; it was easier to conclude

43

that she had been trafficked there against her will and better judgment. While far more women were "trafficked" out of the home by the forces of industrial capitalism than sexual slave traders, prostitution served as a convenient symbol for anxiety over women's entry into industry.[13] Prostitutes, who traveled not only across physical distance but also through symbolic space, served as an effective trope for traffic across identity: sexual innocent to world-weary woman, sheltered daughter to working girl, madonna to whore. Anti-trafficking campaigns thus gave expression to popular concern for—as well as about—a new generation of working girls laboring and socializing outside the home. Public life was understood to be dangerously seductive. Places of urban commerce and recreation were described as dangerous recruiting grounds for traffickers and, more generally, as "the breeding ground of vice."[14] The danger, then, was not only forced prostitution but also the lure of casual or recreational sex engaged in by so-called "charity girls." Women who engaged in sex outside of marriage—whether for pay, trade, or pleasure—challenged notions of proper womanhood, especially White womanhood.

Despite the use of the generic term "women" in anti-trafficking rhetoric, not all women were seen as equally positioned to fall from grace. The presence of White women in a world of carnality and commerce demanded an explanation which "trafficking" provided. Black women's involvement in the sex trade was considered less remarkable, merely confirming their exclusion from the status of "true womanhood." Patricia Hill Collins notes that "according to the cult of true womanhood, 'true' women possessed four cardinal virtues: piety, purity, submissiveness, and domesticity.... African American women encountered a different set of controlling images."[15] According to Collins, the stereotypical image of the Black woman included the sexualized Jezebel: "Jezebel's function was to relegate all Black women to the category of sexually aggressive women, thus providing a powerful rationale for the widespread sexual assaults by White men typically reported by Black slave women."[16]

Until the abolition of trade in and possession of African slaves in the British territories in 1833 and in the United States in 1863, the sexual abuse of enslaved African women was not only commonplace but considered to be a right of ownership. As Sander Gillman points out, both Black women and those prostitutes unable or unwilling to claim the identity of trafficked innocents were believed to possess inherent biological "abnormalities" that set them apart.[17] The idea that Black women were congenitally inclined to whorish behavior was matched by a comparable belief that Black men were highly sexed and dangerously out of control. The stereotypes produced and justified racist violence. As Patricia Hill Collins concludes, "lynching and rape, two race/gender specific forms of sexual violence, merged with their ideological justifications of the rapist and prostitute in order to provide an effective system of social control over African Americans."[18]

The unfortunate term "white slavery" was also a mystifying misnomer for the sexual exploitation of Asian women in the United States during the late nineteenth century. In the 1870s, several hundred women were purchased in China to be resold into either domestic labor or prostitution in California.[19] Popular reports of Chinese "sex slaves" trafficked to California melded sexual titillation and racism. Sucheta Mazumdar argues that the publicity about these "'debauched' Chinese prostitutes fueled fears and hostility among many Americans toward the 'inassimilable Chinese.'"[20] Despite the fact that the numbers of women imported from China to California for prostitution were never large, the presence of even limited numbers of Chinese prostitutes was seen as a serious threat to the moral order.[21] In 1876, one observer argued that there were enough Chinese prostitutes "to disgrace the city and greatly facilitate the spreading of … immorality and vice among the youth of all classes."[22]

The issue of forced prostitution became a justification for racist immigration legislation, culminating in the Chinese Exclusion Act of 1882. The Exclusion Act, the first such law directed against a specific nationality, entirely suspended Chinese immigration into the United States including, rather incidentally, that by Chinese prostitutes. Even the far more compassionate "rescue work" undertaken by White missionary women in San Francisco shared some of the racism fueling the exclusionary laws. For the missionaries, Chinese prostitutes were victims not only of sexual slave trading but also of a heathen culture. Rehabilitation centrally required both religious conversion and commitment to Christian marriage. "Success" was measured by the adoption of White, middle-class, American standards of feminine behavior. Those Chinese prostitutes unwilling to conform to this model were offered little assistance. Mission Home files suggest that many young prostitutes found the terms of their "liberation" unattractive enough to reject the offer of rescue "with scorn and derision."[23]

Anti-Trafficking in the Contemporary Period

Echoes of racism and ethnocentricism have remained in the rhetoric of some abolitionist organizations well into the late twentieth century.[24] In general, however, contemporary anti-trafficking campaigns have distanced themselves from the defense of White womanhood by explicitly reframing the problem as one that confronts women of all races. One of the most important texts that helped to transform and update the concept of sexual slavery in the late twentieth century was written by American feminist Kathleen Barry. Barry's 1979 work, *Female Sexual Slavery*, redefined the problem of trafficking in the broadest possible terms:

> All kinds of women are vulnerable to slave procurers.
> The assumption that only women of a particular class,
> race, or age group are potential victims [is wrong] ... sexual slavery lurks at the corners of every woman's life.[25]

Barry argued not only that sexual slavery was a general threat to all women, but also greatly expanded its meaning beyond forced prostitution. Sexual slavery, according to Barry, is

> the business that merchandises women's bodies to brothels and harems around the world ... [as well as that which is] practiced individually without an organizational network, it is supported by pimps ... [and] by husbands and fathers who use battery and sexual abuse as a personal measure of their power over their wives and daughters.[26]

By defining sexual slavery so broadly, Barry generally avoided the racist reduction of sexual violence to that which is enacted on the White female body by the ethnic Other.[27] Barry also challenged the belief that abuses in the commercial sex trade are of an entirely different order than that which might occur within more respectable institutions such as marriage or the family. But Barry's goal was more ambitious than simply to draw complex connections between related phenomena across race and class lines. Barry wished to argue that there was in fact *no* significant difference between such practices as sex work, sexual slavery, incest, and rape: "Female sexual slavery is present in *all* situations where women and girls ... are subject to sexual violence and exploitation."[28] Thus, victims of sexual slavery might equally be "a prostitute, battered wife, incestuously assaulted child, veiled woman, purchased bride."[29] This collapse of all forms of sexual violence into a broadly defined category of "sexual slavery" effectively sidestepped debates about how widespread coercion might be within the specific practice of prostitution. Arguing against the need for a careful accounting of the actual numbers of those forced into prostitution, Barry claimed only that sexual slavery was "pervasive throughout patriarchal society."[30] Indeed, the author argued that an attempt to be more precise would be both irrelevant and impossible:

> Amassing one hundred, one thousand, or many thousands of sex slavery cases will not prove the existence of the practice to those who have a vested interest in keeping it invisible.... There is no way to estimate what proportion of prostitution results from cases like the ones presented [in *Female Sexual Slavery*].[31]

Barry's claim, however, is a reflection of an ideological and not a methodological problem. Scholars and activists less committed to the abolitionist equation of prostitution with slavery have found far fewer difficulties in estimating the prevalence of deception and coercion as "recruiting" devices in the commercial sex trades. In one study of prostitution in South East Asia, for example, author Wendy Lee reports that "about ten percent of prostitutes in Thailand are deceived or forced into the profession. But more commonly families act as agents of recruitment."[32] Lee, who is highly critical of prostitution and presumably has no "vested interest" in discounting the role of trafficking in the trade, suggests that for the vast majority of Thai prostitutes working in Europe, entry is facilitated not by "traffickers" but by family members, "aunts, sisters, or cousins already in the trade."[33] Licia Brussa, director of the migrant prostitutes' AIDS prevention project in the Netherlands, concurs:

> If you look at the way women really get into the trade here, it's mostly in the hands of other women through chain migration. They bring their sisters and cousins over to work, partly out of a desire to help, partly because it provides a feeling of solidarity to have family and friends here. But sometimes it's also simple exploitation: you can earn a lot of money by taking care of the travel arrangements and getting someone else settled into the business. Besides it's safer than bringing over strangers; you aren't as likely to turn in your aunt.[34]

A similar conclusion is reached by the Dutch Foundation Against Trafficking in Women (STV) who estimate that no more than twenty percent of foreign prostitutes in the Netherlands have entered the trade through coercion or deception.[35]

Kathleen Barry refuses to quantify the problem of sexual slavery. Instead she insists that, for anyone really concerned about violence against women, one case is evidence enough. A file cabinet full of documentation won't make the problem any more compelling to those who just don't care. I bristle at the suggestion that to ask "how many? what percentage? how widespread?" suggests I have a stake in denying that such abuse might actually exist. But I also appreciate her reluctance to play the numbers game. Numbers are not simply neutral "data"; their meaning is always political. As a lesbian, I have watched the "Christian" Right celebrate studies purporting to show that gays comprise less than the proverbial ten percent of the population. No mention is made of how difficult it might be to accurately count the members of a despised minority. No questions are asked about why human rights should be dependent on numerical status. During the 1993 March on Washington for Gay, Lesbian, Bisexual, and Transgender Civil Rights, about a dozen anti-gay protesters held signs declaring "Only 1%" and "Two Gay Rights: AIDS and Death." It was comforting to me that there were only twelve of them and close to a million of us.

While numbers can never tell the whole story, they are not unimportant. It is useful to know that more than half of the women working behind the windows in Amsterdam's Red Light district are foreigners. It is also useful to know that the great majority of them are not there against their will. I honor the efforts of feminists committed to rescuing those coerced into the trade, and I tolerate the attempts by the Christian Right to rehabilitate homosexuals "recruited" into a life they wish to leave. But in both instances it is disingenuous at best to portray a stigmatized sexual practice as inevitably coercive, and insist that all counterclaims are irrelevant. That's just another twist in the numbers game.

———

The seriousness of forced prostitution is in no way diminished by evidence that trafficking is not the most common form of "recruitment" into the sex trade. Even using low estimates, the reality remains that many thousands of women and children are involved in commercial sex against their will. Many more have "chosen" prostitution from a desperately limited range of options, and most prostitutes work under exploitative labor conditions. This, however, is a different set of claims than the argument that commercial sex is inevitably a form of slavery.

It is not only those, as Barry suggests, with a stake in denying the existence of abuse who have an interest in knowing the extent of trafficking within the trade. Activists committed to effectively combating sexual violence, too, are well served by the knowledge that deception and coercion do not account for all, or even most, prostitution. If prostitutes have not been simply trafficked into the trade as slaves, rescue work may be a less productive strategy than labor organizing. But many anti-prostitution activists' commitment to abolition causes them to view strategies of reform as not only inappropriate but dangerously counterproductive. Reforms are seen only to "normalize" a practice they insist is invariably abusive. As Cecilie Hoigard and Liv Finstad suggest, without a commitment to abolition, it becomes easy to

> to oppose some types of prostitution without having to take a stand on the fundamental and threatening question of 'voluntary' adult prostitution. 'Fight prostitution

controlled by pushers and pimps, fight prostitution which exploits incest-victims or children. But leave 'voluntary' prostitution alone.'[36]

This is a suggestion they vehemently reject; the practice in all of its forms must be abolished.

Abolitionist ideology actually stands in the way of attempts such as those made by Kathleen Barry to reposition prostitution within a broader range of practices including marriage ("battered wife" or "purchased bride"), family life ("incested child" and mandatory motherhood), and gendered appearance ("veiled woman" and, by extension, other less exotic forms of compulsory female self-presentation). Despite clear evidence that state-sanctioned heterosexual marriage and family life is often violent, coercive, and abusive, there is no comparable argument that these institutions must be prohibited in all of their varied forms including those which participants claim to be consensual.[37] Campaigns against wife abuse and child abuse typically challenge the idea of women and children as property of husbands, propose reforms intended to increase structural equality between participants, promote legal changes to increase protection for victims and facilitate prosecution of those who commit abuses. Rarely is abolition suggested as the most appropriate tactic, nor are claims made that research into the prevalence of sexualized violence within marriage or the family is a methodological impossibility, that those who choose marriage (or defend another's right to do so) are "pseudo-feminists," or that an adequate understanding of these institutions can be attained by studying only those who have "escaped" them. All these are claims freely made about prostitution, however.[38] In short, despite attempts in the 1970s by anti-trafficking activists to expand the meaning of "sexual slavery" beyond the institution of commercial sex, prostitution remains a "special case," uniquely suited to abolition.

The contradictory impulse to consider prostitution as only one among many sites of sexual abuse and to simultaneously position it as a case apart was reinforced in the early 1990s when the Coalition Against Trafficking in Women issued a statement redefining sexual slavery as "sexual exploitation." "Sexual exploitation" was defined as "sexual harassment, rape, incest abuse, wife abuse, pornography and prostitution."[39] In other words, the *abuse* of a wife or a child, the *harassment* of a worker, and the practice of sexual *assault* (rape), were all to be considered instances of "sexual exploitation," whereas consensual participation in marriage, family life, and heterosexuality were not. "Consent" and "choice" were meaningful in all areas except commercial sex. From the perspective of abolitionists, prostitution and pornography alone required no modifiers to signal abuse because, there, no meaningful distinction could be made between "forced" and "free." Indeed, for abolitionists, prostitution can no more be a "chosen" or consensual activity than rape. Thus, Hoigard and Finstad conclude that "it is not mere rhetoric to counter the absurdity of the demand for legalization of prostitution with 'Legalize rape and incest. Recognize these as normal activities.'"[40]

But defining prostitution as exactly the same, whether consensually enacted or forced, poses a serious problem for sex workers. If prostitution is a form of sexual violence exactly like rape and incest, then the rape of a prostitute becomes predictable, indeed redundant.[41] If a prostitute always already has been violated, rape is unremarkable, no more than a sign of excess. And if a prostitute can never consent, then she can never be said to refuse consent, an assertion challenged by a Melbourne street prostitute raped in 1991: "Sure I'm a working girl, but that doesn't mean I have to put up with such violent behavior. The fact that I sell sex for a living in no way invalidates my right to say no. I don't consent to violent attacks on my body."[42]

One of the justifications for insisting that prostitution, unlike marriage, is necessarily abusive is the belief that no one could ever really choose to participate in such an activity. Coercion, therefore, must be responsible. Hoigard and Finstad insist that "No one 'wants' to rent out her vagina as a garbage can for hordes of anonymous men's ejaculations."[43] Sex worker Carol Queen calls this a "politics of 'ick'":

> The assumption is that because I find something icky no one else could ever consent to doing it. The question I always ask is whether "oh ick!" is really the basis for a politics. For a lot of years, heterosexual people said "oh, I could never have sex with people of the same sex, so

therefore it must be sick, it must be immoral, it must be criminalized." Well, some of us really can do this.[44]

To argue that there is an important difference to be made between consensual and forced prostitution, is not, however, the same as arguing that all consensual prostitution is necessarily "free." As Hoigard and Finstad point out:

> voluntary choice assumes that there exists good, realistic alternatives to choose among.... Both material and cultural processes leave some women feeling pushed into a corner where prostitution emerges as the best alternative.[45]

Prostitutes' rights activist Jo Doezema agrees that the concept of "free choice" is less than useful in discussing prostitution:

> There is no way to combat the anti-prostitution position that all prostitution is forced by using their language and insisting that what I do is "freely chosen." If I say "I choose to do it because I need the money," well, that's economic coercion. For every "free choice" you can think up, they just point out how it wasn't entirely free. The idea that there are two distinct poles of "forced" and "free" is a false dichotomy. I mean who really freely chooses to work at any kind of job? I want to get the whole choice argument off the prostitutes' political agenda. We'll never win it and it's useless as a political strategy. And ultimately it's not important if you're fighting for things like workers' rights, or fighting to challenge the stigma around being a prostitute. It doesn't matter if you were forced to be a prostitute or so-called chose to be one; you're dealing with the same stigma and you'd be benefitted by better working conditions.[46]

Very few women's lives are models of "free choice." Most women's "choices" are severely limited by their disadvantaged position within hierarchical structures of sex, race, and class. Gender inequality, coupled with extreme differences of wealth within and among nations, creates tremendous pressure on women to engage in any available form of employment, including sex work. Indeed, there is good evidence that participation in prostitution increases in times of economic crisis and diminished options. At the Second European Meeting on

Migratory Prostitution held in 1994, for instance, a huge increase in the number of East European women working illegally in Istanbul's sex trade was reported. Women, primarily from Rumania, were flee-ing "extreme economic hardship. The majority had had either no personal income or had earned less than $13 a month" prior to emi-gration.[47] In this study of about three hundred women, only six per-cent reported having been trafficked to Turkey against their will. Yet it clearly would be a misrepresentation to suggest that the other nine-ty-four percent had "freely chosen" migratory prostitution from among a range of occupational opportunities. In a similar study of two hundred prostitutes in contemporary Bulgaria, investigators found that economic hardship motivated most to enter the trade. Women were "often unemployed before becoming a prostitute ... [Once working in the sex trade] their income per day was often high-er than that of their parents' monthly salary." The study further notes that "many had plans to go abroad as migratory prostitutes."[48] These women are neither classic "victims of trafficking" nor are they fully empowered free agents. The complexity of their situation has led to a deep rift within the contemporary anti-trafficking movement dividing those who insist on abolitionist strategies from those who defend migrant prostitutes' right to "self-determination."

A Movement Divided: Abolitionism and Self-Determination

While the Coalition Against Trafficking in Women has been strik-ingly successful over the past two decades in promoting the prostitu-tion-as-slavery perspective within influential international bodies such as the United Nations, anti-trafficking activism is no longer synonymous with abolitionism. Increasingly, voices supporting reform over prohibition are surfacing from within the anti-trafficking movement itself. The Dutch Foundation Against Trafficking in Women (STV) is one of those organizations challenging the aboli-tionist imperative. Almost since its inception in 1985, the STV has explicitly targeted coercion and abuse, rather than the practice of prostitution as such. This perspective may be a reflection of the largely decriminalized status of the sex trade in that country. Unlike in the United States, where policies of prohibition have produced clandestine prostitution and created problems of access for those attempting to assist women trafficked into the trade, decriminalization in the Netherlands has created a highly visible, partially organized, and relatively accessible population of sex workers.

Prostitutes in the Netherlands have long resisted easy definition as victims of sexual commerce, and instead have demanded rights and respect as workers. This has produced an unusually collaborative effort between the Dutch prostitutes' rights movement and anti-trafficking activists, with both advocating the importance of increased worker control and "self-determination." Lisa Hofman, director of the Dutch Foundation Against Trafficking in Women explains that her organization quickly concluded that

> the best place to start is to improve the circumstances under which [prostitution] takes place.... Of course we are here to help those trying to leave, but we also recognize the importance of working with those who decide to stay to improve conditions in the trade.[49]

This pragmatic perspective is increasingly characteristic of anti-trafficking activity in Western Europe. In 1991, European anti-trafficking groups held an international conference attended by ninety participants from women's, migrant's, and prostitute's rights organizations from fourteen different countries. The meeting produced a series of recommendations submitted to the United Nations Working Group on Contemporary Forms of Slavery, part of the UN Commission on Human Rights, to "initiate steps to formulate a new international convention for the suppression of the traffic in persons."[50] The existing UN Convention dates from 1949 and is explicitly abolitionist in objective. Under its current wording, signatories commit to "punish any person who, to gratify the passions of another ... exploits the prostitution of another person, *even with the consent of that person.*"[51] The European conference proposed a revision of this agreement "based on the principle of the right of self-determination of women which would differentiate between prostitution as work and forced prostitution."[52] Furthermore, the group advised that an updated convention on trafficking "avoid the moral rejection of prostitution."[53]

Two years after the first European anti-trafficking meetings, a second international gathering was held to further discuss proposed revisions to the UN Convention. The resulting recommendations were submitted to the UN World Conference on Human Rights in Vienna by the Dutch National Council of Churches, the STV, the Asian Women's Human Rights Council of the Philippines, and the Thai Foundation for Women. These recommendations were endorsed by fifty-three organizations from Europe, Africa, and Asia, including the Women's International League for Peace and Freedom, Physicians for Human Rights, and Sisters in Islam. The proposed revisions strongly emphasize the role of violence and coercion in determining instances of trafficking, and encourage an expanded definition of trafficking to include "modern manifestations like malafide marriage bureaus or employment agencies."[54] The groups argued that the existing convention does not "cover contemporary practices … in which people are traded and end up in slavery or slavery-like conditions."[55]

These efforts to revise anti-trafficking agreements on the basis of a distinction between consensual labor and slavery (whether sexual or otherwise) were almost immediately denounced by the Coalition Against Trafficking in Women. Positioning itself in direct opposition to such efforts, the Coalition declared: "Trade in sex *is* a moral transgression … Prostitution exploits women. The erroneous distinction between 'free' and 'forced' ignores that reality."[56] While the Coalition agrees that the existing convention requires revision, the direction of their proposed changes is diametrically opposed to proposals made by those emphasizing prostitutes' rights to self-determination. From the Coalition's perspective, the existing agreement is not severe enough in its rejection of the significance of consent. The Convention as written, the Coalition notes, is "directed specifically at prohibiting pimping, procuring, and brothels because they constitute coercion. Therefore, the 1949 Convention implies a distinction between coerced and 'voluntary' prostitution."[57] Because the Convention admits the possibility of consent even while dismissing its relevance in determining instances of trafficking, neo-abolitionists believe the agreement to have "only limited value in protecting women's human rights because ... it reduces the victimization of women to only the most extreme examples of torture and slavery, thus obscuring how prostitution violates human rights...."[58]

The Coalition Against Trafficking in Women thus reiterates the abolitionist view that *all* instances of prostitution are abusive, not only those that are most obviously nonconsensual. Indeed, it is not the issue of coercion that interests the Coalition, but rather the problem of *sex*. Thus, while the European Working Group proposes expanding the definition of "trafficking" to emphasize the common features of "deception, coercion, violence and financial exploitation," the Coalition argues instead that the pertinent commonality is "the abuse of a person's sexuality." It is sexual *commerce*, not sexual *coercion*, that is identified as a threat to human rights. For this reason, the Coalition proposes rewriting the agreement to replace the notion of "trafficking" with that of "sexual exploitation" including:

> casual, brothel, military, pornographic prostitution, and sex tourism, mail order bride markets, and trafficking in women ... [which] violates the rights of anyone, female or male, adult or child, Western or Third World.... Therefore this definition rejects the use of any of these distinctions to determine exploitation as artificial and serving to legitimize prostitution.[59]

The Coalition's proposals have met with serious criticism from European anti-trafficking activists. One member of the Dutch National Council of Churches has argued that the Coalition's proposal to revise existing UN conventions on trafficking "denies the right of self-determination of adult women.... The whole draft convention breathes a patronizing air.... "[60] Similarly, in a document signed by "women's, children's and development groups in Thailand" (including EMPOWER, Friends of Women Migrant Workers in Asia, Terre des Hommes, and the YMCA), the Coalition's proposed changes are criticized for

> not allowing the differences between forced prostitution and prostitution chosen by women in both industrialized

> and developing nations ... [in the Coalition's document]
> prostitution is prohibited without exception, absolutely.
> This is not in accordance with the present reality, and
> more regressive than the basic principle stated in the
> 1949 Convention.[61]

For activists who resist the abolitionist imperative—including those involved in anti-trafficking work—the context and conditions of sexual labor become a paramount concern. Those who are enslaved must be made free either to leave the trade or to join those who are "merely" exploited in demanding better wages, safer working conditions, and greater control over the labor process. Such a perspective allows prostitution to be examined critically as a form of service work, with attention focused on factors enhancing or limiting a worker's power relative to clients, employers, and colleagues. When erotic labor is viewed as work, it is transformed from a simple act of affirmation of man's command over woman, and instead is revealed to be an arena of struggle, where the meaning and terms of the sexual exchange are vulnerable to cultural and political contestation.

▼ ▼ ▼

Grazyna, *victim of forced prostitution and trafficking*
Amsterdam, 1993

My name is Grazyna, I'm thirty years old, and I come from Poland. I used to work in the shipbuilding industry, but since the so-called "revolution" there is no more work for me. I'm divorced and have two children to support. The economic crisis turned my life upside down. In September of 1991, I was working in a restaurant in Yugoslavia and had just come to the end of my contract. Through some acquaintances, I met a man who asked me whether I was interested in going to work in a restaurant in Germany where I would earn three times as much for the same kind of work. I was interested because the situation in Yugoslavia was becoming more and more unstable. It was agreed that I would work as kitchen help and would be paid a salary between DM 1,500 and DM 1,800 a month. A few days later, Robert came with two other men to fetch me. There was also another woman with them who was going to work in Germany, too.

At the German border I had to give him my passport because he somehow convinced me that it was better if he was the one to hand it to the immigration officers. He never gave it back to me. We stopped at a hotel somewhere in Germany and Robert and one of the other men stayed with me while the other man went somewhere with the other woman. I never did see her again. That's when I was told that I was going to work as a prostitute. I protested, but it didn't help. When I kept refusing, one of the men raped me while Robert took photographs which he threatened to send to my mother if I continued to resist. I was taken to the Netherlands, where I was forced to work as a prostitute behind a window in a street full of "prostitution windows." They said they would be watching me all the time so I shouldn't even think about escaping. They also said it was no use going to the police because they were paying off the police, too. I was supposed to earn at least 600 guilders a day, and if I didn't I was beaten and kicked. It was terrifying.

Sometimes I was allowed to keep some money, which I sent to my mother and children in Poland, but I didn't dare tell them about my real situation. After I had been working a few weeks under close guard, I saw a chance to escape. A client seemed to like me so I asked him for help. After some hesitation, he took me to his apartment. Two weeks later, a man appeared at the door; the client was afraid and let me go. From then on I was guarded even more closely and not allowed to go anywhere unaccompanied. I pretended to submit. I worked, I laughed, and I hoped that my captors would relax their guard. I was still determined to escape.

It finally worked. In an unguarded moment, I fled, not knowing where to go. On the street I spoke to a woman passerby who couldn't understand me. But at least she figured out that I was Polish. It turned out that she had a Polish neighbor and this neighbor understood my story. The woman let me sleep in her house that night, and the next day she brought me to a center for asylum-seekers. But the Ministry of Justice eventually decided I didn't fulfill the criteria for recognition as a political refugee and rejected my request for asylum. Luckily my lawyer understood that I was a victim of trafficking and contacted the Foundation Against Trafficking in Women, the STV. They explained about the laws against trafficking in the Netherlands and told me what my rights were. Since I had nothing more to lose, I decided to press criminal charges.

The STV contacted the Vice Police, but they didn't believe me. They thought I made up the charge of trafficking after my asylum request had been denied so that I could stay in the Netherlands. They wanted to know why I hadn't filed the trafficking charges in the first place. Fortunately, the woman I had been brought to Germany with had ended up in another city in the Netherlands and had also filed charges against Josef and Robert. The police in that town had contacted the STV for assistance for her. So finally my case was taken seriously. That meant I would be allowed to stay in the Netherlands until all legal procedures were completed. But my relief was short-lived. Josef was arrested but, through a procedural mistake, he was released. Robert was never found.

After some time, my case was dismissed for lack of evidence and I knew I would have to leave the country. Meanwhile my mother informed me that "some strange people" had visited her and were asking where I was. I can't imagine going back. The STV and my lawyer are trying to get me a residence permit for the Netherlands on humanitarian grounds, but it will take months, maybe years for a decision. In the meantime, I miss my children and my family.

[This testimony was presented by a staff worker at the Dutch Foundation Against Trafficking in Women at the U.N. World Conference on Human Rights, Vienna, June 15, 1993.]

▼

Luisa, *indentured brothel worker*
Amsterdam, *1993*

I'm 23 years old and I was born in a small village in Colombia where I lived most of my life. My parents earned very little money so, to help support my family, I began working as a prostitute in a bar in Panama, and later in Aruba. There I met a man who told me he had two sex clubs in the Netherlands and asked if I was interested in coming to Holland to work. The promise of more money was something I just couldn't pass up. I told him I could buy my own plane ticket, but he said he would arrange everything and I could pay him back later. He said that if I tried to arrange things myself, the police might make trouble and send me back to Colombia after taking all my money. He arranged for me to fly into Germany. A man named Ronny and his friend picked me up at the airport and drove me to the Netherlands. At first they were very friendly and we chatted about the weather and my flight. Then Ronny and the other man began to talk in Papamiento; I understood enough to know that they wanted me to pay them a lot of money and I started to get really frightened.

I was tired and wanted something to eat, but Ronny took me to one of his clubs and had me work until 4:00 a.m. Then he took me back to his house which became my prison when I wasn't working. I asked Ronny when I would get paid but he said that I had to first pay him 15,000 guilders. I'd have to work in his clubs and I wouldn't get any money until I had earned everything I "owed" him. He wanted my passport and became furious when I tried to keep it from him. I felt like I had no choice but to give it to him.

When I started working, I had no idea how much I was earning because the clients paid the two men behind the bar. Finally I heard that the clients paid 150 guilders a session and that I was going to earn about 55 or 60 of that. But I never saw any of it. Ronny kept it all because he said I had to pay him back the money I owed him first. From the time I arrived in the Netherlands, I worked six days a week, and saw eight or nine clients each night. My earnings were recorded by the bar keepers but, even if they forgot to do it, I kept my own records. After about eight weeks, I went to Ronny and told him that I thought I had paid off my debt and I wanted my passport back. I figured that I had seen at least 250 clients by then and showed him the records I had been keeping. He got really angry and told me I owed him another 15,000 guilders for rent and all sorts of expenses. Then he tore up my records, grabbed my head and tried to stuff my mouth with them. He picked up a chair and started beating me with it.

I decided I had to run away; I wasn't going to earn another 15,000 guilders for him. So I took a chance, called an acquaintance and asked for help. I had really thought that in the Netherlands I would be able to find legitimate work as a prostitute. If I had known beforehand that I would be so abused and have no control over my life, then I never would have come here.

[This material is from a 1993 interview conducted by the Dutch Foundation Against Trafficking in Women.]

▼

Lisa Hofman,
Director of Dutch Foundation Against Trafficking in Women
Utrecht, Netherlands, 1994

At the Dutch Foundation Against Trafficking in Women we're terribly pragmatic. We start from the basic reality that prostitution exists; it probably always has and probably always will. There are millions of women in the world who see prostitution as the best means of survival for themselves and their families. It seems to us, then, that the best place to start is to improve the circumstances under which it takes place, thereby strengthening the ability these women have to negotiate better conditions for themselves. We've adopted this approach because we've seen what a dangerous illusion it is to look to the state to abolish prostitution. Just like with drugs, when you criminalize prostitution you only drive it underground and make it more dangerous.

I think that this kind of pragmatism is very common among anti-trafficking organizations with real contacts in the field. When you start working with these women and really develop respect for them, it becomes clear how important it is to change the very practical circumstances of their life. The point is, given existing conditions, some women do make a rational choice to do this work. We would never call it a "free choice," but "free choice" in the contemporary labor market is something that very few people really have. I think it's a good long-term goal, but it's not a very practical guide to immediate action. What is urgent is to help these women increase their options and gain more control over their lives. So for those of us in anti-trafficking groups in places like Belgium, Switzerland, Germany, and the Netherlands, we've all concluded that decriminalization has to be the priority. Prostitution itself should never be an offense. What has to be punished is coercion, violence, and deception. That is a crucial distinction; without it, you can't work effectively with the women in the field.

We were shocked when we went to an anti-trafficking conference in New York in 1988 and discovered how out of touch with working women the U.S. Coalition [Coalition Against Trafficking in Women] seemed to be. I think it's very significant that that particular group only works with women who have already left prostitution. The whole thing felt kind of religious: "I am a survivor who was saved from this evil. I escaped and can now distance myself from my terrible past thanks to these good people who helped rescue me." That's a really different approach. Here we're primarily working with women who are still involved in prostitution. Of course we are here to help those who are trying to leave, but we also recognize the importance of working with those who decide to stay to improve conditions in the trade.

The problem is that these two approaches aren't able to comfortably coexist; the U.S. Coalition was one of the very first organizations concerned with trafficking and that means that they set the tone. They have a high profile and excellent contacts with the UN. The Coalition tends to present itself as if they are *the* international representative of all anti-trafficking groups. If you've ever had anything to do with them, shared information with them, whatever, then suddenly you are part of their network. But in my opinion, it's not a network. A network means real cooperation and an acknowledgment of our differences.

Two years ago we held a European-wide conference with representatives from eighteen countries from around the continent. A really different perspective came out of that meeting but it's been hard to get our voices heard. It seems that the Americans have convinced everyone that they speak for all of us. I suppose we need to be more diligent in attending international conferences, but we really aren't big-time professional conference goers. Our work is in the field. Other people seem to specialize in attending conferences. It's almost a career, going from meeting to meeting like that. The result is that you develop lots of contacts, but you also start to operate in a kind of closed circuit and run the risk that you lose contact with your base. I keep thinking it shouldn't be a choice between the two, but practically speaking, we experience a certain amount of tension knowing that we can't do it all. In general, it seems to me that the movement here is different in style from the Americans. We always try to work together despite our differences whereas it seems like nobody there will talk to you if you don't already agree with them. Well, I'm sorry, but we really aren't used to that style of working. It's all so unproductive when we share such important goals like strengthening women's right to self-determination. More and better choices has been such an important goal for feminists whether you're talking about abortion, reproduction, or prostitution.

If you depend only on the state, you end up with repressive strategies which often interfere with the rights of women to make decisions about their own lives. For instance, the Dutch state recently imposed new regulations designed to fight "paper marriages," partly using the argument that it would help curtail trafficking in women. Actually, among our clients the use of paper marriages is pretty unusual. But because the government is so intent on denying residency to foreigners, this paper marriage law was very popular and passed without any problem. The result is that foreign residents now have fewer rights. A Dutch person can decide to marry for any reason at all: for financial gain, tax purposes, convenience, whatever. But migrants who marry are strictly controlled; now all migrant women interested in getting married have an additional hurdle to jump. That doesn't increase their independence or their ability to determine what's going to happen in their lives.

The problem with repressive strategies is maybe the clearest if you look at the new visa requirements for women from some Third World countries. By requiring visas for these women to travel to the Netherlands, they just become more dependent on "go-betweens" who can get them into the country. Again, the new requirements are part of a much broader campaign against foreigners, and absolutely not effective in addressing the problem of trafficking. Visas are just a tried and true method of discouraging immigration; so the authorities don't get much more creative than that. The Justice Department doesn't think: "Okay, how can we best get rid of the pimps, the go-betweens and the traffickers?" They just immediately think "visas." We keep trying to point out to them that that kind of strategy only strengthens the hand of the traffickers and weakens the position of the women themselves. But they have a "Fort Europa" mentality and are trying to close the gates. If you really want to stem the flow of foreign prostitutes into Europe, the only real solution is to do something about the inequality between the rich and poor parts of the world. But that again is a very long-term strategy. For the moment, the state seems to have decided that the most politically popular thing to do is simply to try and close the borders. There are very few people willing to say that we have to come to terms with the fact that Europe is an immigration magnet. Instead foreigners are targeted as the source of all of our problems and excluding them becomes some kind of solution.

This year the Dutch government came close to abolishing the prohibition on brothels, but in exchange they almost instituted a ban against women from outside the European Community working in prostitution. The STV immediately responded that this would be a violation of migrants' rights. If you are going to regulate prostitution for foreigners it should never be done through the criminal code but through regular immigration law and labor law—just like for all other professions. The assumption that foreign women shouldn't have the right to decide whether they will work in prostitution is patronizing. Under the proposed regulations they would have been put in the same category as children who, by definition, cannot choose prostitution. That's a complete denial of their right to self-determination. We were also opposed to the prohibition on foreign prostitutes because we knew that it would put them at greater risk. They are still going to come, of course; you aren't going to stop them. But under the proposed changes they would have ended up in the illegal circuit, where they would be much less visible and much less accessible to those of us doing outreach work.

It was difficult for us to decide to publicly oppose the proposed revisions. Our position wasn't always appreciated by the other groups involved [The Red Thread and the prostitution policy group, the de Graaf Foundation]. We certainly agree that brothels should be removed from the criminal code; that's something we've supported for a long time. But then replace it with legislation advantageous to more than just the brothel *owners*. The new law should be an improvement for the *women* in the trade.

Some people initially thought it was better to accept what they saw as partial success, than to leave the old law on the books. So it was especially crucial that we were there defending the interests of migrant women. It isn't clear to me that the other organizations take those concerns seriously enough even though a very significant proportion of prostitutes in this country are foreigners. There are probably thirteen to fifteen thousand migrant women working in the Netherlands in prostitution; that means 40 to 60 percent of the prostitutes in the big cities are foreign. Among those women, there are several hundred cases each year of trafficking. And no matter how they got here, all of those women would have been made more vulnerable under the new law. That's just bad policy.

▼

SECTION II
WORKING IT

I keep trying to accept the fact
That all my days wear a "for sale" sign.
I'm too poor to save much time for myself,
And I'll do almost anything for money.
I keep trying to accept the fact
That people expect to pay for what they need.
If they try to make you feel bad about your wares,
It's just because they have nothing to barter.

I would rather be a whore
Than be ignorant about that.
Don't let it go too cheap,
My dears.
Money's dirty but your hands stay clean.
You can never hang onto it long enough
To be stained.
You always have to hurry to
Put bread on your table.

It doesn't mean you are a thing,
An object, a doll, a dummy.
It means
You are like Midas,
Because anything you sit on, wear, or step on
Turns to gold.
There is no base metal in you.

Pat Califia
from "Golden Showers"

Chapter 3
The Emotional Labor
of Sex

Magda Sade   © *Annie Sprinkle*

In the 1970s, a new understanding of prostitution began to emerge which repositioned the prostitute not as a "social deviant" or a "sexual slave" but as a "sex worker" engaged in legitimate service work. This project of "making it work," to use Valerie Jenness' fortuitous phrase, involved the efforts of both those directly performing sexual labor as well as advocates outside of the trade.[1] In 1975, legal scholars Jennifer James, Jan Withers, Marilyn Haft, and Sara Theiss advanced the position that feminists should offer critical support to workers in the sex trade:

> Whether a woman chooses prostitution at a dollar a minute or a clerk-typist at two dollars an hour, feminists eventually recognize that our response to a woman's choice must be essentially the same. We can legitimately explain to a woman how we believe her situation is discriminatory. We can write, lobby for and pass laws which open better options for women and which make their current situation more tolerable. But when a woman decides, "If you've ever been a clerk-typist, you'd rather be a prostitute," we cannot annul her choice.[2]

Similarly, in 1977, the U.S. prostitutes' rights group COYOTE asserted, "To make a great distinction between being paid for an hour's sexual services, or an hour's typing, or an hour's acting on a stage is to make a distinction that is not there."[3]

Immediately on the heels of efforts to redefine prostitution as work came challenges to that project. These challenges have taken three forms. The first rests on the notion that consent in the context of prostitution is impossible, or at least meaningless. Prostitution, therefore, should be defined as slavery, not as work. The second argument relies on the belief that prostitutes are "only doing what comes naturally" and thus cannot be said really to be "working." Santa Cruz Sheriff Al Noren remarks:

> Calling it a "profession," that's just a bunch of crap, you know. I think most people define as professional where study and effort are put forth. Having sex is no great accomplishment. It's like saying when you have breakfast that you are a professional breakfast eater.[4]

A similar objection is raised by some Radical Feminists who dismiss the comparison of sex work to other forms of physical labor such as massage, arguing that in massage "the commodity being offered and paid for is technical expertise" whereas "the mechanics of sexual stimulation are so basic and uncomplex, particularly in the male, that no enormous lore or expertise is required."[5]

The third objection to conferring the status of work on commercial sexual practices is the insistence that, because sexuality cannot be separated from the person of the prostitute, the sale of sexuality involves a fundamental sale of *self*. "Sexual services" related to prostitution, it is argued, can no more be considered work than "gestational services" related to pregnancy.[6] Anti-prostitution activists thus argue that payment for prostitution services is not merely inadequate but mystifying, serving to disguise abuse as work.[7] Prostitution, then, is understood to involve a fundamentally "self-estranging process" as a woman develops an instrumental relationship to her sex and hence to herself. Norwegian researchers Cecilie Hoigard and Liv Finstad assert:

> [In order to] trade her sexuality in the marketplace …
> she must treat it as an object that can be relinquished
> and made use of as the possession of a stranger.… She
> must have learned to split herself into an object and a
> subject. Her own sexuality must be an object that she
> can manipulate and transfer.[8]

Of course, the process of alienation described by Hoigard and Finstad is not unique to sexual labor. Karl Marx has argued that alienation is a fundamental dynamic in all productive labor under conditions of capitalism. As the worker loses control over the work, the product of that labor becomes an object with a power of its own, hostile and alien.[9] Such labor is

> not voluntary, but coerced; it is *forced* labor. It is therefore
> not the satisfaction of a need, it is merely a *means* to sat-
> isfy needs external to it. Its alien character emerges clear-
> ly in the fact that as soon as no physical or other com-
> pulsion exists, labour is shunned like the plague.

External labor, labor in which man alienates himself, is a labor of self-sacrifice, of mortification.[10]

Anti-prostitution feminists such as Carole Pateman insist, however, that prostitution can and must be distinguished from other forms of labor because the trade in sex involves a more profound sale of the self:

Prostitution differs from wage slavery. No form of labor power can be separated from the body, but only through the prostitution contract does the buyer obtain unilateral right of direct sexual use of a woman's body.[11]

From Pateman's perspective, what is "unique" (and thus uniquely abusive) in the commercial sexual exchange is not the use of the human body, but the very particular *sexual* use of a *woman's* body. According to Pateman:

In modern patriarchy, sale of women's bodies in the capitalist market involves *sale of self* in a different manner, and *in a more profound sense* than sale of the body of a male baseball player or sale of command over the use of the labor (body) of a wage slave.[12]

Thus, for Pateman, prostitution must be distinguished from work because only in prostitution does a woman sell her essential *self*:

When a prostitute contracts out use of her body, she is thus selling herself in a very real sense. Women's selves are involved in prostitution in a very different manner from the involvement of the self in other occupations. Workers of all kinds may be more or less "bound up in their work," but the integral connection between sexuality and sense of self means that, for self-protection, a prostitute must distance herself from her sexual use.[13]

As Pateman suggests, in physically and emotionally intimate work such as prostitution, boundary maintenance is essential. Whether this is necessarily problematic or even uniquely true of prostitution is much less clear.

Since the mid 1970s, a body of work has developed exploring the "sociology of emotion."[14] By applying a sociological perspective to emotion and emotional expression, researchers have uncovered how "exogenous macro factors, such as organizations, occupational structures, and broad cultural ideologies" help to shape emotion both as inwardly felt and as expressed.[15] One important advantage of this perspective is the possibility of "denaturalizing" emotion by depriving it of its special status as innate and thus pre-social.[16] Emotion, then, is not viewed as an unmediated communication from the soul to the socialized self but rather as itself a product of socialization. The insight that emotion is always already social—and thus can be performed, created, objectified, and exchanged—challenges its characterization as uniquely unalienable.

This radical insight can be usefully applied to the specific set of emotions comprising "sexual desire" and expression. As we have seen, sex is often understood to be the "most intimate" of emotional connections and, therefore, a marker for the authentic self.[17] In her influential piece "The Uses of the Erotic; the Erotic as Power," Audre Lorde distinguishes between "the erotic" which is noninstrumental and "true," and "the pornographic" which is its conceptual opposite: "pornography is a direct denial of the power of the erotic, for it represents the suppression of true feeling." The erotic, on the other hand, is that which is "deepest, strongest and richest within each of us …"[18] For Lorde, the erotic is "our deepest feelings," that which is most our own, that which is "within" rather than an "external directive." To tap into the erotic, then, is to access "internal knowledge and needs." Non-intimate sex (pornography specifically, but clearly also prostitution) is not only condemned as objectified— "using another's feelings as we would use a kleenex"—but is also described as "an abuse of feeling."[19] From this perspective, selling sex—which, in a telling elision, becomes "selling one*self*— alienates the unalienable. Some critics, such as Hoigard and Finstad, assume that sexual feeling is not merely transformed but *destroyed* in the process: "… it's not just feelings connected with sexuality that are destroyed. One's entire emotional life is attacked."[20]

The idea that feeling is a true and vulnerable part of the self in danger of destruction through commodification is directly examined in one of the early, and still exemplary, studies of emotional labor, *The Managed Heart*, by Arlie Russell Hochschild. Hochschild's exploration of the effects of the "commercialization of human feeling" among flight attendants can be usefully applied to the sale of sexual services. In investigating the possible costs and benefits of emotional labor (both to the worker and to society as a whole), Hochschild first must establish what "emotion" is, and what its relationship to the "self" might be. To this end, she begins by examining the notion that emotion is something pre-social, perhaps even biological. For those who subscribe to this view, emotion acts as a messenger from the pre-social to the conscious self-in-the-world. Hochschild finds something compelling in this designation of emotion as serving a signal function: "Many emotions signal the secret hopes, fears, and expectations with which we actively greet any news, any occupance."[21] The hopes, fears, and expectations are, in other words, secret even to the conscious self. "It is this signal function that is impaired when the private management of feeling is socially engineered and transformed into emotional labor for a wage."[22]

If emotion is a messenger from the self to the conscious mind, overriding that "authentic" feeling in favor of a commercially appropriate one could be assumed to impair that critical function: "... the worker can become estranged or alienated from an aspect of self—either the body or *the margins of the soul*—that is used to do the work."[23] While Hochschild acknowledges "the poetic accuracy"[24] of describing emotion as the authentic voice of the inner self, she concludes that this actually impedes our understanding of how emotion works and how we work with emotion. Hochschild thus rejects attempts to create a protected status for emotion as a natural and endangered resource. Instead she notes that, by using techniques of "deep acting," we actually can create or summon emotions that are experienced as real both to the audience and to the self. "In surface acting we deceive others about what we really feel, but we do not deceive ourselves.... In deep acting, we make feigning easy by making it unnecessary."[25] Sex worker Annie Sprinkle confirms that in managing her emotions through the commercial sexual exchange, she is able to create real compassion for a client for whom she otherwise would have no interest:

> [S]omehow when the money is there, we can have a fabulous time with these people, really give and be loving and totally be of service. And if the money isn't there,

forget it, don't want you in the same room with me. It's so weird. What is that? What is it that the money provides? Maybe it's just a clear exchange, especially when you are with someone that you don't like that much, somehow if they give to you, you can give to them. You've been compensated in a clear, clean way. I mean I can actually *like* a person if they pay me that I wouldn't if they didn't.[26]

From this perspective, then, emotion is not something that exists independent of its social expression and management. Hochschild concludes that feelings "are not stored 'inside' us, and they are not independent of acts of management ... In managing feeling, we contribute to the creation of it."[27] Hochschild thus abandons the rigid distinction between emotion in its "natural" state and "objectified" or commodified emotion. Indeed, she suggests that the awareness and expression of feeling is necessarily a form of objectification: "Feeling—whether at the time, or as it is recalled, or as it is later evoked in action—is an object. It may be a valuable object in a worthy pursuit, but it is an object nonetheless."[28] Hochschild does not romanticize the transformation of the relationship between emotion and the self which occurs in the performance of emotional labor, but neither does she reduce it to an inevitably destructive process. Significantly, while the majority of the flight attendants in Hochschild's study believed that they had been changed by the demands of performing emotional labor, they most often described that transformation as a positive one, of gaining greater control. Emotion was no longer something that simply happened to them, they felt practiced in also creating and controlling it.

For sex workers, too, the ability to summon and contain emotion within the commercial transaction may be experienced as a useful tool in boundary maintenance rather than as a loss of self. Amsterdam sex worker Jo Doezema reports:

Now it is true that there are parts of myself that I don't want to share with my clients. But drawing boundaries in my work doesn't mean that I am in danger of being destroyed by it. The way you deal with clients is different than the way you deal with friends or sweethearts.[29]

For these workers, at least, the performance of emotional labor cannot be reduced to an "abuse of feeling"; it is experienced in more complex terms contributing to a sense of a multiply-positioned self. Hochschild notes that among the population that she studied:

> Some workers conclude that only one self (usually the nonwork self) is the "real" self. Others, and they are in the majority, will decide that each self is meaningful and real in its own different way and time.... [for such workers] the idea of a separation between the two selves [commodified and private] is not only acceptable but welcome to them.... They talk of their feelings not as spontaneous, natural occurrences but as objects they have learned to govern and control.[30]

Ans, who worked behind the windows in the Amsterdam Red Light district, describes the ways in which she consciously utilized an aspect of herself in her work:

> Normally, I wouldn't have had anything to do with those guys, and I didn't really care about the stuff they wanted to talk about. But while I was there, in my blonde wig and lingerie, it was okay. I was really able to give them my attention. I felt like they weren't really talking to me, they were talking to the woman they saw in front of them. No, that's not quite right; it was part of me, of course. The wig didn't create it. But it was useful that I looked totally different when I was working, otherwise I would have felt much more naked. I don't think that any whore totally reveals herself in her work. You just show a part of yourself, the part they can have sex with, but you keep the rest for yourself.[31]

Once sex and emotion have been stripped of their presumed unique relationship to nature and the self, it no longer automatically follows that their alienation or commodification is simply and necessarily destructive. As Hochschild points out "... many experienced workers develop a healthy estrangement, a clear separation of self from role. They clearly define for themselves when they are acting and when they are not...."[32] One San Francisco call girl, Lupe, describes the creation of a work persona that provides her with a sense of control and professionalism:

> I have this persona that I really like; the word that comes to mind is "professional." She's a pro. I tend to be rather sloppy, you know my house isn't particularly clean and I

don't care. But when this woman kicks in, things get
done. When she answers the phone, her voice is business-
like and her house is in order ... there are condoms by
the bed, the lube bottle is open and I'm in control. I feel
one of the things that prostitution really gave me was this
tight sense of professionalism.[33]

Anti-prostitution activists dispute this notion of control, arguing
instead that the commodification of sex destroys the ability of sex
workers to experience real sexual intimacy even outside of the marketplace. Again Hoigard and Finstad strongly articulate this position:
sex workers are "forced to protect themselves against a massive inva-
sion of strange men. They will be left with an impoverished sexual
and emotional life."[34] In selling the illusion of sexual desire, they
argue, the prostitute loses her ability to experience sex in a noninstrumental way:

When sexuality becomes a commodity for exchange, it
assumes the character of an object. You have to be ready
to hand it over and let a stranger use it as his own property. When this occurs, sexuality as a part of the
woman's own unfolding is destroyed.... When sexuality
becomes the means to an end, when sexuality is calculated,
then its potential for personal unfolding is undermined.[35]

But many sex workers insist that techniques of boundary maintenance are often successful in protecting both worker and client. San
Francisco sex worker Carol Queen argues:

We create sexual situations with very clear boundaries,
for ourselves and for our clients. In fact, one of the things
that people are paying us for is clear boundaries. It's like
the person going to the massage therapist; you're paying
to be touched without having to worry about intimacy,
reciprocity, and long-term consequences. We can argue
about whether that is a good model for human relationships, but the fact of the matter is that there are plenty of
people happy to have access to a massage therapist. Same
thing with seeing a psychotherapist; there you are paying
someone to tell your secrets to, someone you can trust
will not judge you and who at least won't interrupt you
in the middle and start telling you their secrets. Instead
you are getting focused attention.[36]

Lupe conceives of her boundaries in architectural terms:

> I think of my sexuality like a house. My clients come in
> the front door and they can rumpus around that room all
> they want. And then they walk out that front door and I
> lock the door behind them. They don't get to go in the
> rest of my house. I have this feeling that I'll give the image
> of sex, I'll give the body of sex, but I'm not going to give
> you my sex.[37]

One Dutch researcher, Ine Vanwessenbeek, suggests that this ability to create boundaries within the work through emotional distancing is considered a positive sign of professionalism by many sex workers: "It appears that a certain ability to separate feelings is required to continue to do the work well. In that sense, disassociative ability means professionalism for the prostitute."[38] Hochschild agrees that boundary maintenance through emotional control does not need to be seen as a pathology. Rather, it simply may be evidence of the plasticity of emotion:

> If we conceive of feeling not as a periodic abdication to
> biology but as something we do by attending to inner
> sensation in a given way, by defining situations in a given
> way, by managing in given ways, then it becomes plainer
> just how plastic ... feeling can be.[39]

Using the tools provided by Hochschild, it is possible to rethink the assumption that sex work inevitably destroys the emotional life of the worker. Sex work is no more a pact with the devil (in which the "soul" is exchanged for worldly fortune) than any other form of emotional labor. Sex workers may be assumed to run the same risks as others involved in emotional labor. Clearly, performing emotional labor, including sex work, can negatively effect the emotional life of the worker.[40] But there is no more reason to expect that the effect is necessarily and simply destructive. Hochschild outlines three possible stances for emotion laborers to take toward their work. The first is complete identification with the demands of the job which, she warns, leads to burn-out. The second is a conscious but guilty separation of aspects of the self from the emotional demands of the work, producing guilt arising from the belief that such a division represents insincerity. And lastly, there can be a positive separation of aspects of the self from role: "the worker distinguishes herself from her act, does not blame herself for this, and sees the job as positively requiring the capacity to act."[41] In other words, Hochschild suggests that the danger lies not in the separation from role but in too close an identification with it.

The conceptualization of sex as inalienable pathologizes sex workers who have successfully distanced themselves from their work, and thereby deprives them of professional pride in what Hochschild describes as the most effective strategy they can adopt on the job. California sex worker Cheyenne expresses her frustration over this lack of acknowledgment of her hard-learned skills:

> Sex work hasn't all been a bed of roses and I've learned some painful things. But I also feel strong in what I do. I'm good at it and I know how to maintain my emotional distance. Just like if you are a fire fighter or a brain surgeon or a psychiatrist, you have to deal with some heavy stuff and that means divorcing yourself from your feelings on a certain level. You just have to be able to do that to do your job. But if you're a prostitute who can separate herself from her emotions while you're working everybody condemns you for it. I don't get it.[42]

As Cheyenne suggests, the assumption that a separation of feeling and face is necessarily destructive is challenged when we look at less stigmatized areas of emotional labor. Hochschild presents several examples where such labor is socially rewarded and personally gratifying: "We do not think twice about the use of feeling in the theater, or in psychotherapy, or in forms of group life that we admire."[43] Here it is understood to be "an honorable act to make maximum use of the resources of memory and feeling …"[44] But in other less exalted forms of labor, we begin to "look at these otherwise helpful separations of 'me' from my face and my feeling as potentially estranging."[45] The respect given to emotional labor in the theater, a psychotherapist's office, or a day care center rarely extends to the brothel.[46] Just as day care workers or psychotherapists who sell nurturing and empathy may still be able to summon similar feelings for a loved one outside of the workplace, Hochschild suggests that flight attendants who put on a smile along with the uniform are still be able to express genuine delight off the job. In the same way, sex workers who sell sexual services may be fully capable of accessing those feelings for non-instrumental ends. The common assumption that this is otherwise is partly due to the special status assigned sexual feeling, especially in women's lives.

Nonetheless, some emotion workers, including those performing erotic labor, do report feeling damaged as a result of their work. If the commodification of emotion itself does not necessarily lead to these negative effects, what does? Hochschild suggests it may have to do with such mundane concerns as intensity of labor, level of maturity in entering the profession, customer attitudes and cultural biases toward the work and the workers, and control over the conditions and terms of the exploitation of one's emotional resources. In the performance of emotional labor, Hochschild argues that potential harm could be reduced "if workers could feel a greater sense of control over the conditions of their work lives."[47]

A number of factors can serve to reduce workers' control over their labor. For instance, when emotions have not been merely commodified, but sold to an employer for a wage, control over when, how, and to what ends those emotional resources will be used passes, in large part, from the worker to a boss. Hochschild notes that among flight attendants, their sense of exploitation was intensified by the fact as they were "not making an independent profit from their emotional labor, they are working for a fixed wage. They are not selling themselves, they are selling the company."[48]

Wage labor transforms the work experience regardless of the commodity sold. However, when the commodity is emotional labor—especially erotic labor—its exploitation by a third party is often considered uniquely egregious. Santa Cruz District Attorney, Art Danner, who generally upholds the right of employers to the profits produced by their workers, condemns the same dynamic between massage parlor owners and prostitutes:

> My view of the business is that the women are exploited
> for financial gain. It is organized such that money is
> syphoned off by operators. It's an exploitation kind of
> activity and the community doesn't need this.[49]

When control over the conditions of labor pass from worker to employer, workers in all trades are subject to speed ups, increased duties (with no necessary increase in pay), and supervision intended to reinforce their position as ever-compliant servants. Hochschild notes that, for airline flight attendants for instance, in the 1950s and 60s, they were "asked to take pride in making an instrument of feeling," and generally did. However with cost-cutting and speed-ups resulting from deregulation in the 1970s, "... workers came to see that instrument as overused, underappreciated, and susceptible to damage."[50] A similar dynamic can be found in the sex trades, when control moves from the worker to a brothel owner, a pimp, or the state.

Other factors, too, may diminish the power of a worker relative to the client. For instance, structural inequalities often exist between those likely to perform and those likely to receive emotional labor. Not surprisingly, women are found in far greater numbers than men in jobs requiring emotional work. Hochschild estimates that only a quarter of all jobs performed by men—but over half of all jobs held by women—involve emotional labor.[51] Women are expected to do emotional labor and to do it willingly:

> The deferential behavior of servants and women ... come to seem normal, even built into personality rather than inherent in the kinds of exchanges that low-status people commonly enter into.[52]

Male customers thus come equipped with an ideological justification for believing that female workers "owe" them respectful service independent of their own behavior. It can seem only "natural" that women are servicing their emotional needs.

In sex work, where the vast majority of prostitutes are women and the vast majority of clients are men, men's negative attitudes toward women (and toward whores) contribute to negative experiences in the work. Maryann, who worked as a call girl in California, reports:

> I often got the feeling that the men felt they had a right to whatever they were getting, and I did resent that. The most difficult moments were when I had to deal with a guy who had the attitude of "I'm a man. I have the power. You do this for me."[53]

Terez, who worked as a "hostess" in a club, describes the fundamental power difference between male clients and women workers:

> Some of the men like to wear women's clothing under
> their suits. This one time, I had a customer who kept say-
> ing "make me feel like a woman." So after a couple of
> drinks, I finally said to him "Oh, baby, you just give me
> all your money; that's the first step to feeling like a
> woman."[54]

In other words, mundane concerns like status differences between
worker and client, employee/employer relations, and negative cultural attitudes toward the work performed, may be at the root of the dis-
tress and damage experienced by some workers. This is less grand,
less poetic, than the image of a soul in necessary and mortal danger
through the commodification of its most intimate aspects. Such a for-
mulation, however, has the advantage of pointing critics in the direction of practical interventions such as workplace organizing and
broader political campaigns to increase the status and respect accord-
ed to those performing the labor.

▼ ▼ ▼

Maryann, *nurse and former prostitute*
Santa Cruz, CA, 1995

When I worked as a prostitute, I saw it the way I've seen many of the jobs I've held in my life: as a means of getting to someplace else. At the time, what I wanted was to go to nursing school and I needed to find a way to make some money. A friend who was doing it made it sound like something I could do.

The thing is, it's really hard work. In fact, it turned out to be some of the most emotionally draining work I've ever done. I found that I didn't have the emotional stamina to do it more than a day or two a week during the two years of outcall and parlor work. And I couldn't do it again because it's just so much work. So much.

I took it all a little bit too much to heart probably, but I sometimes found it kind of sad. There is so much shit around sex that we can't just go out there and get what we need or want. And that's really all that people were trying to do. Sometimes they needed way more than anybody could give them in a one-hour session.

I'm sure part of the problem is who I am as a worker. It's typical of me that in any job I want to do the best I possibly can. I'm always trying to figure out what people need or want and then it's my desire to fulfill that. Look at me: I'm a nurse now. It's that caretaking kind of stuff that I tend to take on with people.

With prostitution, not unlike other jobs I guess, you have to be who they want you to be. At least in most jobs, your roles are defined. You get a job description that says "this is what we expect out of you." In sex work, you have to use a bunch of intuition because most people are so bad at saying what they want when it comes to sex. I mean the men have an image of what they want when you arrive at their door, and maybe they'll be able to communicate that to you. But more likely, they'll expect you will be able to just figure it out. That was really difficult. There you are doing your job and you want to do a good job, but you have to figure out what it is that that means for this particular client. Sometimes they wanted the typical trashy, sexy kind of woman, and other times they wanted a much more innocent young girl. Sometimes they wanted you to be more dominating; sometimes they wanted you to be really passive. I'd think "Shit, just tell me what you want. I can do this. But I can't fucking always figure it out."

That was the hard part of the job; the sex itself wasn't a big deal. Maybe that's because I've never valued sex the way that society suggests that a woman should. I don't know if that's a result of "free love" or what, but I never felt that sex was something I should "save" for somebody. From about the time I was sixteen, I remember thinking that virginity was this thing used to keep men and women unequal. The last thing I wanted to be was a virgin. I felt like it put me in a role I didn't want. I decided that sex was something I should do if I wanted to and not do if I didn't. I could never figure out the big price put on sex for girls. In fact, when I got older and got into sex work I was actually kind of amazed that you really could make money off of it. What an incredible thing.

I suppose I should also say that I have a history of sexual abuse as a child. I'm kind of reluctant to mention the abuse because it seems like people assume that's all they need to know about me: I was abused as a child and I worked as a prostitute. Then they can dismiss anything else I might say about sex. That really brings the dragons out in me; the experience of abuse no more defines my sexuality or who I am than does the experience in prostitution or the kind of sex I have with someone I care about. It seems to me that the attempt to see it otherwise is all part of cubbyholing women into those who have a "good" view of sex and those who don't, those who are sexual victims and those who aren't. It's like sex can only mean one thing for women.

I think that the assumption that being a prostitute ruins a woman's experience of sex is part of that. Men need to think that women can't have sex without intimacy, and that if they do that it's bad for them. Like a woman only has sex with a man because he and he alone has something she can't live without. In fact, an important part of prostitution for me was realizing that sex didn't have to be about intimacy. There is great power in the realization that you are, in fact, in control.

In sex work, there's this real issue around having orgasms on the job. One of the things that I realized was that those orgasms were mine. They didn't belong to anybody else. It was up to me to let them be known or not. But they were really mine in that I was the one creating them. It had nothing to do with who I was with; it wasn't about being so turned on by this guy instead of that one. It was about me. It really challenged the idea that orgasms are something a man "gives" you. That's part of the traditional belief that women aren't supposed to be in control of sex. Instead, you're supposed to be passive and accept whatever happens. But, as a prostitute, you really do determine what goes on, you guide the entire experience. There was a tremendous power in that for me; not only was I able to say "I can make this go whatever direction I want it to" but I also got to experiment in all these different roles and see where I fit in, which ones I liked. I didn't have to be just one thing. I could be this straight-A student going to nursing school and at the same time be a prostitute. Go figure: Florence Nightingale or the Whore? Which one are we? I was both of them, all of that.

The problem is, there is still this real virgin/whore thing for most people. I was very aware when I got into prostitution that I couldn't tell certain people about it. If they saw me as a sex worker, that would be all they would see. It wasn't that I minded if people found out; if they knew, they knew. But I didn't want to be defined by it.

On the other hand, I used my real name at work. It was really funny because sex workers generally use professional names so the guys would always go: "Well, what's your real name?" And I'd tell them "It's Maryann." "No, really, what's your real name?" "No, really, it's Maryann." Even if you are being real with them, that's not what they see. They're always going to make you into whoever they need you to be.

And, you know, while it was exhausting to have to reinvent myself for each new client, the work I do now requires similar skills in a lot of ways. Part of my job as a nurse is to walk into a room and assess the situation and figure out what is needed. Since I work with women who are in labor, those aren't just physical needs but emotional needs, too. The big difference for me is that I'm working with women so it's much more of a two-way street.

When I worked as a prostitute, I often got the feeling that the men felt they had a right to whatever they were getting, and I did resent that. The most difficult moments were when I had to deal with a guy who had the attitude of "I'm a man. I have the power. You do this for me." Sometimes that was an attitude they walked in with, sometimes it was what they left with. I used to wonder if it wasn't because I was too clearly in control. It was the attitude, not the sex, that was abusive because I can tell you I see a lot of the same thing from doctors: you're there to serve them and whatever they need they should have. Nurses are there to carry out doctors' orders and to intuit their needs. It's something we're always battling.

The truth is, your best skill can be your worst enemy. I *am* intuitive; I'm good at figuring out people's needs. It can really work against me, but it can also work for me. Nursing is a good place to put those skills to use; you certainly get more respect doing this than sex work. My point is, don't battle prostitution; go deeper than that. Abuse is about power and the intentions behind it. It's that attitude we have to battle wherever it appears.

▼

Vision and Annie Sprinkle, *Sluts and Goddesses*
Amsterdam, 1993

Vision: I have a degree in sociology and spent a few years working for a major corporation doing that whole game. But at the same time, I was involved in a lot of personal growth work. I got tired of my job not really reflecting my heart and then it happened that I got laid off. So instead of looking for another nine-to-fiver, I decided to go to bodywork school and get into deep tissue massage. I loved it; I was doing this great thing for people but still keeping a lot of flexibility in my life. I'd work for six months and then take off and travel. And when I came back my clients were thrilled to see me. They loved my work. Doing massage allowed me to stay in the alternative community, it was legitimate and I made decent money for someone who didn't have a straight job.

Because I was working out of a chiropractic office, it was very clear that what I was doing was therapeutic massage; the issue of sex never came up. But I did have some girlfriends who were doing sensuous massage and, at first, I had a lot of judgments about it. It was this kind of taboo thing that I thought was basically bad. In any case, I was pretty sure I wasn't comfortable dealing with that kind of sexual energy. Then I got into doing a lot of tantra in my private life, and as I did, I became more comfortable being sensual. At the same time, I realized I had gotten to the point with massage where the amount of energy I was putting out to earn enough to just keep my survival needs handled was starting to drain my battery. At $25 an hour in a chiropractor's office, I needed to do five or six massages a day and it was clear that I didn't have that kind of juice anymore. And there were my friends, girls who had *no* training, making $120 an hour with "sensuous massage." A couple of the girls said, "The guys would love you because you work deep and most of them need that. And you're totally sensuous." I saw that I could basically quadruple my income for the energy output: I could do one massage and make the same kind of money that had taken five.

It also gave me time and space to meditate and exercise and skin brush and do all those things that are part of keeping the temple in good shape, so to speak. And I was just not having that kind of space in my life. In the beginning I worked for a girlfriend who had done this kind of work for a long time. She really holds the work as sacred and has created the kind of context around sensuous massage that made it safe for me to step into. It was important to me that it was-n't just sex for money. It wasn't really even about sex: it was about healing and giving men the opportunity to be in the presence of god-dess energy. My friend really initiated me; she held my hand through the whole thing. I remember the first client I did, I was totally scared. My biggest fear was "what if I can't make him come?" She just laughed, "That's the last thing you need to worry about."

She was very clear that the men were to be in a receptive mode. It was not about them touching us, getting us off. It was an hour for them to receive and to be given to. And it was very clearly a hand release only, no blow jobs or fucking. I've found that most of the men are willing to be in that receptive posture. They know the routine: they come in, they take their clothes off, they lay down on the table, they receive and sometimes at the end, there'll be some touching. I don't mind some exchange if its respectful and sensitive and honoring, but I still don't let them get into my genitals. Skin-to-skin contact is nice, though. I really think that if everyone had skin-to-skin and breath-to-breath contact with another human being once a day, the planet would be a very different place. And I am very happy to provide that space in the world. For me its mostly about affection and nurturing and love, not so much a heavy sex vibe. It really helps that they come to my environment, so the energetic is set up by me. They are walking into my game. I'm the priestess and its my temple.

I've never had a bad session in the year and a half I've been working. A lot of it is screening clients. Energy is real clear on the phone. If they call up and say, "How big are your nipples and are your legs apart right now?" then I know I don't want to deal with their energy. I just say, "Listen, this isn't what is available here" and I hang up. Although one of the things that I have experienced shifting in myself since having had this Annie Sprinkle encounter over the past few months, is a lot less judgment about the work, about what is good and bad, spiritual and not spiritual in sex. I've noticed, for instance, if somebody calls up now and says "Will you wear high heels and lingerie for me?" I may not choose to do that but I'm more inclined to say "No. But who do I know who you could call? I'm very happy to do the referral." I try to be clear that whatever he wants is okay. My immediate response has shifted from "It's wrong for you to want that" to just "I can't provide what you want, but who do I know that could?"

And I must admit that I've gotten more playful in exploring my own boundaries. I'm starting to feel more comfortable with not necessarily staying within the rigid format of a great massage and a quick hand release at the end. I'm not so afraid that if I let the sexual energy come up a little bit more, they are going to want to fuck me and then I'm going to have to play gestapo. One of the things I've always liked about bodywork is that I know I'm giving something valuable to my clients. There have been periods in my life when I've taken a few months off and sometimes I'll get into that place of the Big Doubt: Who am I, and what am I doing in the world, and what is my value? And, man, I do one massage and I totally come back into that place of knowing that I am a valuable human being with things to contribute. My work is valuable. But I have to say it is great to not be in the factory massage clinic, cranking out six of them a day. Now I only do five to ten sensuous massages in a week; five being an okay week, ten being a great week. If I do one a day I feel happy.

Living in Marin [California] makes it easier for me to do this kind of work. There's probably more tantra being taught here than anywhere on the planet right now. So within that context, within this community, what I do isn't even called "prostitution." You can call it "private tantra session." So you recontextualize it and within that context what I do is legitimate. That's important to me.

Annie: Hearing her story, it strikes me that we started off on such different roads but ended up on the same path. What's really interesting is that in my community of prostitutes, people in pornography, sexual radicals, the really hard thing has been for me to come out as spiritual. That was the Big Taboo. A lot of my friends just do not want to know about tantra, they still think it's a passing phase. These are people who are really out there sexually, totally out there. And yet they think tantra and meditation and yoga are just ridiculous.

Vision: One of the things I realized when we first got together and did this "Sluts and Goddess Workshop" was that some people have "slut shame" and some people have "goddess shame." And Annie had goddess shame.

Annie: Yeah, I still do.

Vision: If the energy would get too spiritual, too powerful in that way, she would flip into little girl mode and blow it off. Whereas for me, if the energy would get too sexual, I tried to blow it off. We've been a great mirror for each other that way, embracing those really different aspects.

Annie: The "Sluts and Goddesses Workshop" that we just did in San Francisco was amazing. It was really sluts meet goddesses. The people who attended because they've been following my work came from this new generation of young sex workers. Jwala, who I co-led the workshop with, lives in Mill Valley and she brought all these tantra goddesses who have never really explored their slutty side. It was amazing, that kind of integration, tearing down our prejudices toward each other. When I made up the name "Sluts and Goddesses" I thought it was kind of funny, but now I am becoming more and more convinced of the power of that symbology, those archetypes. It allows you to give a persona to those different parts of yourself and it's about embracing both.

I was a full-time prostitute for ten or twelve years, four or five days a week. I did three tricks a day, sometimes five or six, in the biggest massage parlor in New York. They used to call them "leisure spas" because they had showers and a sauna in addition to twelve women working there. You wore a uniform and the rooms all had massage tables in them and red flocked wall paper. Nevertheless, it was "massage work." And I did give a lot of massages, actually. In fact, I used to give a great massage when I was 18, 19, 20. Then I lost it. I also used to give the best blow job; every guy I gave a blow job to said "that was the best blow job I ever had." And then at a certain point I never heard another guy say that again. I lost it. It has to do with where my interest lies. I just burned out on it, I guess.

Vision: For me, the burn out comes from being out of integrity with yourself. Even in doing straight massage, the burn out came when I was doing six massages a day when the truth for me was that I only wanted to do three. To continue past that point creates that burn-out factor. I haven't experienced that yet in sensuous massage work. Admittedly, I've only been doing it a year and a half; I don't have that experience of doing it for ten years full time. So I am still very turned on to the work; I don't find it jading me to my own personal sexual expression. I think if anything it juices that place for me. But I am also really staying within my own personal boundaries in the work.

Annie: But a lot of times, to find out where boundaries are, where your integrity lies, you have to make some mistakes and go over your limits. Maybe even on a regular basis. Working in prostitution was that kind of challenge for me. I still like to keep my finger in the pie; it's like I have to remember my roots or something. So I still turn an occasional trick with my friend, Karen, who lives downstairs. She's a male-to-female transsexual and a born whore. She loves being a whore. The tricks I turn with her are the most basic, average Joe-Shmo tricks in the world. There is nothing spiritual or tantric about these guys. And I can't tell you what a kick and thrill I get out of it. Just putting on my gear, getting dressed up as your average whore, going down, getting the money and doing the most dumb, stupid, adolescent sexuality. It's all totally safe sex, of course, so there is all this saran wrap and gloves. It almost feels like arts and crafts. But turning a trick every so often with Karen is totally different than working full time. I could never do now what I did then. Never. Even with Karen, I tell her, if the guy is a creep, I'm just leaving. I can't handle it. She does. She deals with six creeps a day. I mean, some of them are nice guys, but she sees a lot of clients. She is saving up for a sex change, so she's working her cock off.

Ninety percent of what I do with Karen is just fuck her clients in the ass. They come to Karen because she's a transsexual, and most guys that go to transsexuals want to get fucked in the ass. So I fuck them, and I spank them and I call them a few names. And I feel great afterwards. I'll feel totally rebalanced, like I can find myself again. Because most of the time I'm upstairs doing all this mental and creative work, being an artist who explores the outer edges of sexuality. That's a lot harder than turning those totally predictable tricks. I mean, creating new visions of sexuality for the future can be pretty heavy stuff and it's scary sometimes.

What's happening right now is that, at some level, I really feel like I've acquired some power. In my performances, I talk about how sexuality empowers you, and I have these young girls come up to me after my show and tell me how much it means to them. It's great but it's also kind of strange. The thing is, it's real for me. I talk about reaching states of total bliss and ecstasy. And that's real. I talk about getting enlightened through sexual ecstasy, and that's real. But then I think, "You're getting such a fucking big ego, what is this? Get off it, you're full of shit." Because I have met people who are on ego trips and I don't want to be like that. I don't want to be one of those spiritual types that walks around really believing they are enlightened but you look at them and know they're not.

So I like my fantasy of being both this down-and-dirty whore who is also an enlightened being who can heal people with her touch.

Because being that down-and-dirty whore sometimes is very ground-ing, it's who I am, too. On the other hand, I really feel that what Vision is doing, is paving the way for the future. I so much honor that. I wonder, though, how does it feel if I call you a "prostitute"?

Vision: It's hard. If you even say "sacred prostitute," it helps me hold it in a different way than if you just say "prostitute." I had this one client who I had seen kind of personally, and then he came back in a professional sense. It got to the point of the money, and it was like should I ask him for it, is he going to pay me? There was this awkwardness which forced me to confront the fact that I was a pros-titute. I was doing it for the money. If the money wasn't there, I wouldn't be doing it. I really came up against some judgment in myself, some bad girl stuff. There are certain words that trigger that for me, and the word "prostitute" is absolutely one of them.

Annie: We had an interesting conversation about all this the other night. The money is important. And it's not because we are desper-ate for it, like we're on drugs and need the money, 'cause we aren't, or that we are money hungry, because neither of us is. But somehow when the money is there we can have a fabulous time with these peo-ple, really give and be loving and totally be of service. And if the money isn't there, forget it, don't want you in the same room with me. It's so weird. What is that? What is it that the money provides? Maybe it's just a clear exchange, especially when you are with some-one that you don't like that much, somehow if they give to you, you can give to them. You've been compensated in a clear, clean way. I mean I can actually like a person if they pay me that I wouldn't if they didn't. It's amazing.

Vision: Or for me, it's that I can be with them in a different way than if they didn't pay me. If I related to this man on a personal level, I felt a need to guard my own emotional space, to be concerned and have attention to his emotional well-being. Is he going to fall in love with me? Is he going to want something I don't want to give? In the con-text of a professional relationship, I have none of that. I can totally be there, completely be his lover for the one hour and provide that ener-getic space that I wouldn't on a personal level.

Annie: I think prostitutes are so compassionate and giving. And that's harder and harder for me. I feel like I paid my dues, I gave so much to a lot of guys. I'm a very generous person. I gave and gave. And then I couldn't give anymore. And it does make me sad that I can't do that anymore. [crying]

I don't want to start thinking that I'm better than someone else. Women who are still giving. Clients. Bad tricks. A porn star who's still playing some empty-headed role. It's an emotional thing for me, obviously. But there are things I just can't do anymore. And some of them are things that I wish I could.

I don't want to be hurt physically anymore. I mean, I used to really put my body through some heavy shit. And not just because I "had to." Because I *liked* it. I really liked it. I like really intense hard sex and I wish I could still do that. I miss it. The masochist in me is disappearing and I miss it. Isn't that weird? I'm a weird girl.

Vision: When I'm with you, I can feel that edge. It feels like a place that you have been abused in the past, and one of the things that I want to bring to loving you is just that space of honoring the sacredness that it is, too, the sweetness, and a place of never hurting you or never treating you in a way that is dishonoring ...

Annie: But I like that part of me.

▼

Susanne, *"high class" call girl*
Helsinki, 1995

I used to just work evenings and weekends as a part-time prostitute. During the day, I had a completely different life as a respectable secretary in a company doing foreign trade. Prostitution was only a secret hobby. But the company moved, so now I'm doing this full time and I have to lie to everybody. My family is already suspicious. My mother knows something is going on. I suppose someday they'll find out about it. Maybe we'll get arrested. Now that I work together with my friend, Anna, I worry more about that. We're making lots of money and we have big plans for a studio here in Helsinki with a special room for sadomasochism. We're doing everything very professionally. If the police find out that we're running a business, they might decide to arrest us. It's a frightening thought that my family, my friends, even my ex-colleagues, everyone, could find out about all this. The magazines would love a story like this: two high-class hookers with all these powerful clients get arrested.

I've been covering my identity for years now. I don't even carry my ID with me, just in case I have to go to the bathroom and my client opens my purse to check out who I am. I have a secret phone number, and I always watch behind me when I'm coming home to make sure no one is following me. But working with Anna, I have to give up some of that security. She's getting us clients every day. I have no idea who they are; they could even be people who know me. But that risk is just part of the price you have to pay. At least I'm getting paid very well for it.

I do have a lot of professional pride. I set standards for myself and I protect myself in many ways. First of all, I choose my company. I don't want to date anyone who uses drugs, for example. And I charge a lot, so I only see middle-class men, businessmen, husbands, fathers, people who are afraid of getting caught and are concerned about their health. I'm careful about even ordinary germs. I don't like the guys to touch themselves before they touch me. I don't mind kissing but I don't do it much because of the germs. If we do fellatio, it's always with a condom. Besides, the thought of doing it without is so disgusting. It's important to maintain boundaries.

I put a lot of my real self into some parts of my work, for instance, when I'm creating the atmosphere by talking to them about themselves. Most of the men like to talk a little and have a cup of coffee. They don't want to go straight to bed. And I use a lot of the real me for that part of the work. I don't want to have to do that too often every day. It would be easier to work in a window or a brothel, because you don't have to socialize. You just have to say your rates, take the money, and fuck. Of course there's no such thing as "easy money" in this business. I hate it when people say, "Oh it's so easy, you don't have to do anything." They know nothing about this business.

I do a lot of disgusting things every day. Not all days are bad days, but there are those bad days, too. The act itself, intercourse, is very

94

easy. At least it is as long as the client is okay. But sometimes, fortunately not every day, I meet a man I don't like. And then I have to force myself to smile, show a positive attitude and act like a high-class hooker. We have to look eager to please and appear sexually excited because that's what they expect. With some men, I have to close my eyes and think of the money, otherwise I would get up and run out of the room yelling, "Keep your money and get out of here. I don't want to see you, don't touch my face." Those are the bad times.

Some parts of the work are harder than others. A lot of what Anna and I are going to be doing together, is this sadism business. I already know it's something I'm not going to like. It's not going to be easy. There will be nights when I'll hate myself, hate what I see in the mirror. I remember after one spanking session, I caught a look at my face. It was a familiar face, it was my face, but the eyes weren't mine.

But a trick only lasts an hour or two and then the only thing that's left is the money. Last night I had a client and already I can't remember his face. I make myself forget. Ideally, I'd like to see only a couple of clients a day. But since I don't plan on doing this for long, I want to grab everything I can get. We want our club to specialize in services you can't get any place else in Helsinki. Anyone can tie a man to the bed and fuck him, but we plan to offer services men have to go to Amsterdam for right now, like really working with pain. That part of our business scares me. But Anna's an expert and she's going to teach me.

I protect myself: it's "Susanne" who's doing those tricks. After a trick, I'm always very excited, full of adrenaline, talking like a gangster in the streets. I'm finding something very tough in me: "Shut up, I'm the Queen." But I worry it's starting to be the only part of me that I show, I'm just working so much . Maybe it would be good for me to get away for a few days and try to forget the world I'm stepping into, because this is nothing yet. The future will be much worse. Then there will be hardly any time for a normal life. We plan on spending all our time at the club. We are tough businesswomen. We have a plan and whatever it takes, we'll do it.

I don't go out much because I don't want my face to be known, but I've heard that in the nightclubs and places like that there's so much competition between the girls now that the rates have gone down a lot. On the streets, it's as cheap as 100 marks for ten minutes in a car. For me, I charge a minimum of 2,000 marks for a two-hour session. That gives us time to have coffee or drinks, and then do it. The client feels he has all the time he needs. Actually they don't need much time. But I don't want to do fifteen-minute tricks. When new clients call about my rates and I tell them its 2,000 for two hours, they sometimes ask, "What about if I just pop in for ten minutes?" They've gotten used to doing business with those street girls. Some of them can't understand the difference between a quick fuck in a car and going somewhere where you get a smile and good service and all the time you need. That's the fault of those cheap girls. They're something quite new here in Finland. There have always been street prostitutes, but they have been alcoholics and drug addicts and lower-class people. But now, suddenly, there are all those foreign girls, too.

A hundred marks is a huge amount for them, while for me it's nothing. I'm not going to lower my rates though. We can't compete in price but we can compete with service. There are men who want that service and are willing to pay more for a girl who is healthy, decent, and sober. A nice girl who can shut up and keep their secrets. The fact is that I charge a lot. I don't sell myself, my services cheap. That's not any excuse for being in this profession, but I pretend it is. I try to convince myself that I'm not so bad because I charge so much. I have to find something positive in this. I'm afraid of getting caught, but if I do, at least I can say, "Look at how much money I made. Don't you think this is a very high-class activity?"

Anna and I are businesswomen. We both have a little bit of education and we're not going to stop here. Maybe we'll get married and quit this business or something. But there is no limit to what we can do. We're businesswomen and we have a plan. I'm not a sad story. I've succeeded.

▼

Chapter 4
Locating Difference

© Laddawan Passar

Sex workers all perform erotic labor, but their accounts of that experience vary dramatically from the "happy hooker" to the "sex work survivor." The source of those differences may lie less in the "nature" of erotic labor than in the social location of the worker performing it and the conditions under which the work takes place.

Sex work can be radically transformed, for example, when control passes from a worker to a third party (brothel owner, escort agency manager, or pimp). In such a situation, restrictions are often placed on a worker's right to select among clients and to determine which services will be offered. The most classic case of such third-party control is pimp-run prostitution. Here a combination of psychological dependence, drug use, and violence may be used to exercise control over a worker. Evelina Giobbe, founder of the American abolitionist anti-prostitution groupß WHISPER (Women Hurt in Systems of Prostitution Engaged in Revolt), describes her experiences in prostitution as an exercise in domination. Giobbe entered prostitution as a runaway at age thirteen after fleeing a rape by a friend's uncle. She came under the control of a pimp who determined every aspect of her life: "He made the dates, he sent me, he bought my clothes ... I never had more than cab fare."[1] Her seven-year ordeal was further intensified by heroin addiction. Not surprisingly, Giobbe's experiences have led her to define prostitution as "system of exploitation and abuse" and to devote her energies to "rescuing women and girls attempting to escape the sex industry."[2]

Control by pimps is only the most dramatic form of third-party power exercised over sex workers. For indoor workers, management-imposed "house rules" may limit a brothel, club, or escort worker's ability to select among clients and services. Jo Doezema, who worked in the Amsterdam brothels, explains:

> It's very difficult to refuse a client. Most clubs won't come right out and say, "You have to go with everybody that wants you," but they put a lot of pressure on you. If somebody wants you and you say to the management, "No, I don't think so," they go, "What's the matter with him? You're not here for your fun, you're here to make

money." It's really difficult to stand up under that kind of pressure. And if you do hold your ground, they can just say, "Well, get out then, we don't need that."[3]

Similarly, Terez, an erotic dancer and "hostess" in a San Francisco bar reports:

In this one club, you sit around and wait for a waitress to tell you who to go and sit next to. You can't choose for yourself.... Even if the guy says he doesn't want any company, you're not allowed to leave.[4]

Management policies can also serve to undermine a sex worker's ability to negotiate what will be offered and for what fee. Jo Doezema states:

At a lot of clubs, clients don't give the money to you, they give it to the boss. And you're not allowed to ask for anything for extra services.... A lot of clients have the idea that their hour will be filled with sex of whatever sort they want. And because you can't say in the beginning, "If you want this, this and this, it's going to cost this much, and this I don't do," you are struggling the whole time to keep the client from doing things you don't want and trying to keep him satisfied at the same time.[5]

Sex workers who are self-employed face a different set of challenges in establishing control over clients and determining the limits of the erotic transaction. Here, class position, rather than employer policies, may dictate the right to choose. Licia Brussa of the migrant prostitutes' education project in Amsterdam argues that economically marginal workers are the most vulnerable to client demands for dangerous services:

In general, migrant prostitutes do all work with condoms. But in really tight times, during the winter for example, the pressure is on to take more risks. Everything is in such precarious balance for them that their priorities sometimes shift: first it's daily survival, then sending money home, then protecting yourself from the police who could deport you, and then maybe only after all these other things comes safe sex. In our interviews, everyone says it's super important. But when things aren't so steady, and survival's at stake, those other problems loom much larger.[6]

Sex workers with the greatest degree of class privilege, on the other hand, are in a far stronger position to exercise their right of discrimination. Carol Queen, an independent who works near the top of the wage scale in her profession, explains:

> I made a promise to myself when I started prostitution that if I couldn't find a spark of attraction or respect for a client, I was not obliged to be intimate with him.... Not everybody in this business is in a position to do that, but I do have a problem with women who are in a fairly privileged position as prostitutes, who make $200 an hour, who can always find another client around the corner somewhere, when those women agree to do things that they don't feel comfortable with and then blame prostitution.[7]

For sex workers for whom survival is not at stake, a carefully controlled client base may be preferable to increased income. Terry, a San Francisco call girl, suggests that this has been crucial to her positive experience in the trade:

> One of the reasons I think I can enjoy my work, is because I carefully screen my clients. I have no tolerance for any assholes. I'm providing a service to these men, and as far as I am concerned, they're privileged to have it. So they have to show me the proper respect. I deserve that respect. If they don't think so, then they should keep their cock in their pants and their money in their pocket. It means I make less money than I might otherwise, but my safety is worth it. People in more desperate circumstances have to put up with a lot more.[8]

Class position not only influences a worker's ability to screen out undesirable clients and to refuse dangerous services, but also determines the ease with which a woman will be able to transition out of sex work into other forms of employment. The archetypical "happy hooker" is in a position to generate substantial savings that can then be invested in a future outside of the trade. Underlying this expectation is the construction of the sex worker as young, single, educated, and white. Other less "happy" or, at least, less fortuitous sex workers may find themselves burdened with family responsibilities and restricted employment options. Licia Brussa notes that this is very much the case for migrant prostitutes:

> Migrant prostitutes unfortunately earn, or at least keep, less money in prostitution than other women. That's mostly due to the fact that they have such heavy responsibilities like supporting families while also taking care of their own basic necessities. If they are illegal, they can't make use of national health care or any other part of the social welfare state.[9]

In contrast, Carol Queen suggests that those in her community of independent call girls generate enough money to support themselves and to invest in their futures:

> Women who are call girls could turn around and be executive secretaries if not CEOs in two minutes if they could find somebody to hire them with the gap in their resumes. A lot of women in my circle are graduate students, law students, or women who have "straight" jobs that they supplement with work as prostitutes. I don't know too many women who are working full time at our level. And one of the reasons that is true is we don't have to work full time to make ends meet.[10]

The possibility of generating savings and moving from sex work into other forms of labor is a particularly critical concern in a profession based on youthful sexuality. Terry, an exotic dancer at the San Francisco Mitchell Brothers Theater reports:

> When you get hired, she [the manager] runs you through this long list of rules, which she reads to you as if you're illiterate. She gives you this talk about how much money you can make there, and how you should really invest in your future because this is not a lifetime gig. She tells you her little story about how she was a stripper for a while, and about how now she has a condo and a nice car.[11]

The operative model, in the words of one sex worker activist, is, "You get in, make the money, and get out."[12] While this appears to be the objective of workers at all levels of the sex industry, those most socially and economically marginal are least likely to be able to realize that goal and, at the same time, most likely to be held responsible for that "failure."

One San Francisco call girl, for example, acknowledges that not everyone is equally positioned to profit from prostitution, but insists that the most serious impediments to a sex worker's success are dysfunctional behavior and limited investment skills:

> I know not everyone has that choice [to get in, make the money, and get out] but that's not a problem with prostitution, its a problem with the welfare system. It doesn't teach people skills, and now you have a third generation of people with these checks coming in who have been brought up on welfare, and that means they don't develop the same work ethic as the rest of the population.[13]

The difference between those able to capitalize on prostitution as a profession and those who fail to do so, is understood, then, to be a "culture of poverty" not a structure of inequality.[14] But as adult film star Nina Hartley self-critically comments:

> I have to be careful. When I first got into this business, I had a lot of value judgements about some of the women: they smoked, they drank, they didn't wear their seat belts, they didn't eat their vegetables, and they didn't finish school. These were really street smart women, and I had to admit that I was having a tremendous classist reaction to them.[15]

Class differences among sex workers function not only to divide those within the trade, but also to create significantly different experiences in performing erotic labor. Sex workers with little class privilege working in positions of low status are generally afforded the least respect and are considered the most "deserving" of abuse by clients, the police, and the public. Jo Doezema states:

> I think that certain types of prostitution attract dangerous men, and that's the kind that's at the bottom of society's ladder. The message comes across very clearly that women who are at the bottom are the ones it's okay to abuse.[16]

Jan Visser of the Dutch research institute on prostitution, the de Graaf Foundation, concurs:

> When police deal with street prostitutes in a rough way and when the popular press describes them as "trash,"

then how are "normal citizens" going to treat them? …
it may not seem so bad to rob her or abuse her, to kick
her out of a car. After all, she's just a "disgraceful whore."[17]

Marianne, a former street prostitute, confirms:

In my experience, they [nice clients] were in a minority.
That might have had to do with the fact that I was …
just another dirty heroin whore. You had seen them in a
moment of vulnerability and so afterward they had to put
you in your place.[18]

Clearly, a worker's experience in the sex trade is heavily determined
by status position; but status is not exclusively a product of earned
income differences. As Jo Doezema reports:

With women working in the clubs, you can definitely
feel an awareness of hierarchy: at the bottom is the street,
then the windows, then the clubs. But it doesn't corre-
spond at all to the kind of money you make.[19]

A brothel worker may receive more from each client for services
rendered than the street or window worker, but because the intensity of labor is lower and the income divided with management, her
overall earnings may be substantially less. Nonetheless, as Doezema
points out, the brothel worker's status is generally higher than that
of more independent workers. Two factors help to account for this
apparent anomaly. First, status in the sex trade is assigned according
to the fee the client pays to be in the company of the sex worker not
the amount of money she actually receives. Secondly, those who are
most visibly and obviously selling sexual services carry the heaviest
burden of the "whore stigma."

Similar distinctions operate in venues featuring erotic performance.
In San Francisco, strip club workers with the highest status perform
at the Mitchell Brothers Theater, where admission fees are substantially higher than at other venues, such as the Century or Market
Street Cinemas. This is true despite the fact that workers in all three
theaters receive no portion of those admission fees; income is exclusively generated by tips. Still, as one dancer reports:

A lot of women who work at Mitchell Brothers tend to
think of themselves as "performers" or "entertainers"
and, therefore, above strippers. But when they get fired

> or they're not making any money, they swallow their
> pride and come over to Market Street to work. True,
> Mitchell Brothers is a much nicer environment, but the
> work comes down to exactly the same thing.[20]

While all sex workers struggle with the social stigma attached to the sale of sex, not all are equally burdened with the whore stigma. Those whose work most closely resembles non-commercial sexuality generally occupy a place of higher status than those engaged in less mystified forms of sex work. Peep-show workers who provide only a "tease" but no touch are less stigmatized than prostitutes who "go all the way." A dancer in a San Francisco peep show reports:

> At the Lusty Lady there was a big distinction made
> between what we did and prostitution. That's because
> there was no physical contact with the men. We felt like
> we were a special sort of sex worker: "the men never
> touch me and if they do I'll kill them." That made us bet-
> ter than the prostitutes who, it was assumed, handed
> themselves over lock, stock, and barrel to clients.[21]

For workers who do perform "hands-on" labor, a similar status distinction may exist between those who provide the illusion of a romantic "affair" and those who turn quick tricks involving less in the way of emotional labor. The high-class call girl may be seen as an "expensive date," while the street prostitute remains no more than a "whore." The illusion of affluence not only elevates a sex worker above the status of cheap whore, it also provides an acceptable justification for her involvement in the trade. For this reason, sex workers at all levels of the industry may feel the need to inflate reports of their income. Jo Doezema explains:

> It's not because prostitutes are liars by nature, it's
> because we have to justify what we're doing. If you say
> "I'm a prostitute and I'm working five days a week, twelve
> hours a day, and I earn fl. 1,000 a week," people are going
> to say, "Well, that's not much more than I'm making on
> my job. How can you do it?" So it's got to be at least fl.
> 5,000 a week. That's your one justification for being a
> prostitute: you earn good money. If you say it's because
> you like having sex with people and getting paid for it, or

you do it because you like rebelling against society, those are unacceptable reasons. The only reason that is even slightly acceptable is that you want to become filthy rich.[22]

Differences of class and status are only two of the more important factors producing conflicting experiences of erotic labor. A worker's position in other social hierarchies such as race, age, and physical appearance can also heavily influence a woman's relationship to the sex trade. One erotic dancer in San Francisco reports:

They [club management] were fucked in that they would hire only white girls mostly. There were two Black girls, one or two Latinas, and two Asian girls, out of about a hundred and fifty dancers. I would watch the auditions and if you were a Black woman who danced to rap music or soul, or if you were "too dark," you wouldn't be selected.[23]

An African American sex worker, Cheyenne, confirms:

One of the things I've learned from the sex industry is that when people hear you're Black, they have all these preconceptions and stereotypes. Most guys just don't want to hear that. Their ideal exactly matches what's presented to them in the media: a white or white-looking woman. So I give them what they want. Over the phone, I describe myself as half Native American and half Black. That way I appeal to the guys who want something "exotic" but want it packaged more like the girl next door. When I just say I'm Black, I get skipped over again and again. Look, I'm not saying I want it to be this way, I'm just telling you what I've had to learn about packaging myself for this market.[24]

Similarly, Theodora, who has worked as a prostitute for over twenty years notes:

I'm 46 now, though I tell people on the phone that I'm in my thirties. Men have a different mental image if you say late thirties or mid forties. I think that's going to shift as we see more and more women claiming their bodies as they move into their forties and fifties. But I'm still shy about saying my age because I feel that there's an onus on that. Basically when people call they want to know the price, what do I get for it and what do you look like. And I'm very honest about all that, except for my age.[25]

105

Pressure to create a more "acceptable"—and therefore more marketable— image cannot always be adequately addressed by strategic lies. Some sex workers also employ more invasive and permanent techniques. Terry, a dancer at an upscale San Francisco sex theater, notes:

> The women who get hired at Mitchell Brothers really make an investment in their product, that is in themselves. I mean they have tanning booths in their garages, they get hair extensions, and fake tits, and expensive jewelry, and elaborate cheesy costumes. And women who are older are constantly terrified they are going to be fired.[26]

Her colleague, Jane, confirms:

> Men really do buy into that shit. If you've got bigger tits, it's worth a couple of hundred more at least. I'm telling you, there's a reason why so many of those women have tit jobs.[27]

In short, women working in the sex industry operate within the constraints of social prejudice and unequal privilege. Not surprisingly, these differences of location produce dramatically different experiences of sex work. As a consequence, reforms directed at the sex trade itself will only partially address the problems sex workers face. The far greater challenge lies in tackling structural inequalities reflected in the industry but rooted in society at large.

▼ ▼ ▼

Candye Kane, *adult magazine model and blues musician*
San Diego, CA, 1995

I grew up in East L.A. and the way me and my friends got emancipated was to have a baby. Everybody thought that if we got married and had a baby, we'd be independent. We'd get to move out of our parent's house and have our own welfare check. It says a lot about the economics of East L.A. that we looked forward to a welfare check, not a job.

So at seventeen I got pregnant on purpose to get this guy to marry me—which didn't happen. He left, thank god, cause it would have been horrible if I had married him. But the result was that there I was dealing with motherhood and trying to make ends meet. I did get the welfare check but it wasn't enough. It never is.

Then I saw an ad in the *L.A. Weekly:* "Make $500 a week from your own home. Must be attractive." It turned out to be a phone sex company. I went in for an interview and right away this guy says that I'm too fat for the job. Even though it was phone sex, you had to look good because the company sent custom-posed polaroids of the girls to the customers.

But I really wanted that job, so I kept hounding him, telling him, "I know I can do this. I know big-tit fans will love me." And I finally convinced him. The work was actually kind of fun but the really big money was made by the porn stars who worked for the company. For a call with them, it was like $60 whereas for a call with me, it was only $35. I really wanted to make more money so I decided to get into print and video, too.

When my first cover came out, I was at the liquor store where I used to always cash my welfare checks. There I was on the cover of *Jugs*, looking so pretty. I was so happy to see myself on that cover. I felt famous. The guy at the liquor store even had me autograph his copy and gave me a tab at the store. I thought I had really hit the big time. I grabbed the magazine and raced home to show it to my mother. It was a strange moment when I realized that she wasn't as excited as I was. I mean, I was the first celebrity in our family.

Sometimes now I wonder about getting my self-esteem that way. It seems like I should have been able to feel good about myself no matter what. But it's really nice to get some external validation; that doesn't happen enough, especially for fat women. I don't mean to say that every big woman has to pose nude to feel good about herself. But it really worked for me.

All of my life, I had been fucked with for being fat. People would call me "fatty" and nobody would do a thing; they'd just stand there and let it happen. And then, suddenly, there I was, on the cover of a

Candye Kane © *Jill Posener*

glossy sex magazine looking beautiful. Seeing myself in those magazines meant that I could never again be told that I wasn't sexy or that
I was too fat for anything. I mean, I'm still told that all the time, but
the difference is I just don't believe it so much. I have so many beautiful, glamorous pictures to look at to reinforce that I am attractive,
and fuck them if they say otherwise.

I know a lot of women think that the sex business is responsible
for things like the idea of the perfect body. And, in some ways, I can
see that. But where else in our culture do you see a lot of big women
on the cover of magazines? I sure didn't see myself in *Cosmo*, I didn't
see myself in *Vanity Fair*, I only saw myself in *Melons and Mounds*, and
Jugs. There was a place for me in the sex business. My body wasn't
"perfect" but there were plenty of people out there who wanted to see
it. That was good for me to find out.

Of course I also have to say that I faced a lot of discrimination in
the sex business for being big. Sometimes I'd go to a set where I was
supposed to star in a video, and once they saw how big I was, they'd
just put me in at the end of the film or something. The worst was
when I did live strip shows. I was never very good at those but it was
a thrill to get on an airplane and go some place. I had never been on
an airplane before, and suddenly I was getting to go to places like
New York and Canada and Hawaii. And I was getting paid lots of
money to be there. But there was this one club in Hawaii where the
guy said, "You're way fatter in person than your pictures," and he
wouldn't give me any advance. He sent me back early. The same
thing happened once in Canada.

On the other hand, I don't remember the crowd ever being mean.
There were a lot of guys who just really appreciated big boobs.
Sometimes, I'd even get an audience who had come especially to see
me because they were Candye Kane fans and that was great. But no
matter how things went, after I got my money, I'd go to a really
expensive restaurant with white linen tablecloths and Italian waiters
cooing over me. And I'd be treated really good, just like the movie
stars in the place. That was cleansing; I'd feel classy again.

Now I just concentrate on my music. But actually, in a lot of ways,
I don't think that what I do now is that different than what I did

before. When I'm on stage with my band, I'm still really out there with my body and my sexuality. A lot of my show is about "Sister Candye" trying to give the audience a crash course in body empowerment.

I finally stopped stripping after a particularly bad scene at the Market Street Cinema in San Francisco. I was doing a lot of music by then, so I decided to try adding some to my act. I took out a guitar and stood there in my g-string trying to play a song. The crowd was really astonished but it was management that was yelling at me over the loud speaker: "Put that guitar down, take that off, put that guitar down." I'm a really good singer, but it didn't matter at all. I never did a live strip again. The whole thing still really bothers me. Strippers should be able to do whatever the fuck they want during their time on stage.

Maybe if strippers unionized or had some kind of mobilization, then things would be different. I'm the first to say that there are a world of changes needed in the sex business. That's why I get so mad when feminists throw rocks at us; we could really use some support. A lot of strippers don't think feminism has anything to do with them. I know because I was like that. I didn't think I could be a feminist because I was a stripper, and I was married, and I made dinner for my husband and two kids. I figured I wouldn't fit in. Then I took a Women's Studies course and I decided that maybe those women throwing rocks just weren't my kind of feminists.

▼

Julia, *phone sex worker*
New York, 1994

By the time I was nineteen, I had been sexually harassed in just about every job I'd ever had by people who we're supposed to be my mentors. I guess I just figured that if the exchange were more explicit, I would have more control. I thought escort work would be too dangerous, so I thought I'd try phone sex. I got a really interesting introduction to the business when I went in for an interview. If you've ever worked live phone sex lines, you know that the vast majority of calls are crank calls. As soon as you pick up the phone, before you can even get a credit card number, someone's trying to get off on your voice and you have to hang up on them. The more you work, the faster you get at recognizing the cranks, and slamming the phone down. So there we were having this interview and the other woman is constantly picking up the phone and slamming it down. At first I worked as a credit card checker, taking numbers and passing the calls on to women working at home. Most of the people who worked for that company were poor women or disabled or mothers with kids at home.

The job proved to me that the majority of men out there have sexual imaginations of grasshoppers. Ninety percent of the men who called wanted "blondes with big tits." I would always describe different acts, different types of women, and ask them what they were interested in. I'd say, "There's one woman who really loves coming with guys who want to make noise and another who loves to give head." But it was always, "Give me a blonde with big tits."

After a while I started taking calls myself. The first call I did, I was terrible. I hadn't yet heard anyone actually do a call so I just did what I thought someone would want for phone sex. I described everything in physical terms like, "Now you're getting hard, you can see the blood rushing to the ends of your fingers, you're sweaty, your heart is beating, you want to hump your body against another body ..." Finally the guy told me he had come—I didn't even notice—so I asked, "How was that for you?" He's like, "Well, it was interesting." It clearly wasn't what he was expecting. I found out that what they really want is "huh, huh, huh, uhhh"—making noises in a high-pitched voice and saying things like "Give me your big dick." No, actually it wasn't "dick," it's always "cock," "cock" and "pussy." The words are very specific. One woman told me the first time she took a call, she used the word "penis." The guy went, "Come on, lady. You're not a fucking nurse." You catch on pretty fast.

After about six months, I quit. I was losing my boundaries; like there was this one guy who'd call and we'd have quasi-intellectual conversations which he, of course, found sexually satisfying. At some point, I actually gave him my home number. He called me at home for a while and I always tried to keep everything very non-sexual. I wasn't getting paid; this wasn't supposed to be about sex. But I wasn't in control anymore and it scared me. I couldn't leave the work behind. I'd walk down the street and look at guys and think, "What's your fantasy? Another blonde with big tits?"

▼

Ans, *window prostitute*
Amsterdam, 1993

About nine years ago, I had the opportunity to move into an apartment in the middle of the Red Light district. I remember it was exciting in a way, but I was also a little scared. The very first time I had ever been in the Red Light district, a few years before, had been pretty disturbing to me. I had been out on a date with a guy who dragged me along because he wanted to check out a porn theater. I wasn't really thrilled to go in the first place, and then once we got there I felt completely trapped because I didn't think I could just walk away on my own. I guess I was around seventeen at the time and came from a really sheltered background. For me, the Red Light district was only someplace you went with the Salvation Army.

But then, just a few years later, there I was moving into the neighborhood. In the beginning, the most difficult thing was trying to figure out how to walk past the prostitutes working behind the windows. I didn't know if I should look in or not. I didn't want to give them the impression that as a woman I was staring at them like monkeys in a cage. On the other hand, it also seemed strange not to look. After I'd lived there for a while, I started to feel less panicked just walking down the street. I'd sometimes find myself meeting the gaze of a woman who was working and I'd smile and she'd smile. It was just nice human contact like you might or might not have with anyone on the street. It all started to be part of the landscape, instead of something I was so focused on.

About the same time, I was working for a feminist newspaper and was asked to review a book on prostitution. I think it was the first time I'd ever heard whores themselves talking about their work and it shook me up. I used to look at them and just see "a prostitute," but after reading that book I thought, "That could be me." I mean, I had already had some minimal contact with the women who worked on my street, and one of my neighbors ran a brothel. But they all kept their work out of their conversations with me. One time they were all standing around talking about a bad client, when the woman who ran the brothel actually stopped them saying, "This is a decent woman. Don't talk about that kind of stuff in front of her."

Still, whenever I really needed money, I'd ask myself if I could do it, too. But for as long as I lived in the neighborhood it just felt too close. I mean, what if it turned out to be a bad experience and then there I'd be stuck living in the midst of it all? This year, though, I finally decided to do it. First of all, I don't live in that area anymore and I needed some extra money in a hurry. Plus I had developed some kind of fantasy about the work after all those years and I thought I should check out the reality.

I only did it very briefly, just a few days. I think it's safe to say that I stayed a kind of tourist in the trade. But even those few days were really important. It's only been since I worked behind the windows myself, that I finally feel comfortable looking in from outside. I had to sit there myself to discover that, at least for me, it didn't seem annoying at all if women looked in at me; in fact, I found it more disturbing if they sped past looking straight ahead as if I didn't exist. I think each woman's feelings about it are probably a little different. It depends on your own personality, how you feel about your work, how you relate to other women. But probably most important of all, it depends on how the woman walking by looks at you. You can really tell what she thinks about what you are doing.

When I decided to do it, one of my friends decided to do it, too, which really helped. I also knew someone who worked at the Red Thread so it was easy to get advice. She told me that to earn quick money, it was better to work behind the windows than in the clubs where you don't earn enough and you are more exploited. She even gave me the address of the window she had worked out of. My friend and I went to check it out, but the owner wasn't there. The woman who was working gave us a couple of other addresses. It was that easy; I hadn't expected that. We assumed we would be given a hard time because everyone would be able to tell immediately that we had never done it before and that we were outsiders. But you know, I don't really think it works like that. There aren't "insiders" and "outsiders." Once you decide to work, you are just another prostitute.

From the outside you think only certain kinds of people do prostitution and that they belong to their own club. Like they all know each other, and you have to work your way in. But it's not like that at all. The woman who rented us the window asked if we'd ever worked before. When we honestly told her that we hadn't, she just gave us a few tips. Some of her suggestions were pretty racist, but others were actually very helpful. She told us, for instance, to avoid having to tell anyone "no" once they came all the way up to your window. You can get into an ugly situation like that, "What do you mean 'no', I have money. What's wrong with my money?" She suggested instead that we just not acknowledge the guys that we weren't interested in in the first place. You have mirrors that allow you to see them approaching. Often they'd walk up and down the street three or four times. If I saw a man that I thought, "Oh no, not him," then I would bend forward to light up a cigarette, or I'd turn around and put on some more lipstick, or go to the back of the room and change the cassette. Or sometimes I'd just look straight ahead with an unpleasant expression on my face. That worked fine. I mean, look, most of these guys need some kind of encouragement themselves to take the step. You really do have to seduce them inside. After all, there's another woman in the window next to you, and one on the other side of the street and so on. If you don't seem interested, there's always someone else who will be.

I never had to directly say "no" to anybody, except to some of the things they wanted to do. There was one guy who wanted to fuck without a condom; naturally I said I wouldn't. And there was another who wanted to do it for fl. 35. I said no to that, too; I wasn't about to undercut the price. And there was someone who wanted to have anal sex, and I wasn't interested in doing that either. I had been told in advance that the going rate was fifty guilders for a fifteen-minute trick, and you were supposed to get the guy out the door in ten. That was hard in the beginning, but you figure it out pretty fast. Fifty guilders is nothing, so you just get them in and out as quick as possible. I was also told that if the guy was having a good time and seemed like he might want to stay longer, to just ask for more money. I got good at that.

There are women who work for less than the going rate. That man who offered me thirty-five guilders didn't just dream it up. And there are also women who will do more for the money like give the guy a blow job or a hand job in addition to fucking him. I was willing to add in a bit of a hand job, but only to keep the fucking to a minimum and only within the fifteen minutes. Otherwise I wanted more money. It all depends on the woman, and on her sense of the market. The woman next to me did a lot more for fifty or sixty guilders than I did for seventy-five. And she did get more clients. But, see, I wasn't dependent on the work; she was. I was able to determine for myself what it was I was willing to do and to demand what I thought was reasonable payment for it. For a lot of women, that may be a luxury. If you are really dependent on the work, you probably develop more flexible limits if you notice that you aren't getting enough clients.

I think that one of the most surprising things is that before you do it, you think, "If I'm going to sell it, I better be paid well for it." But once I actually did it, it just wasn't that big of a deal. I didn't feel like I was selling something all that precious. On the other hand, I did find that I was working really hard and I wanted to be well paid for that. And I have to say that I did find the money a kick, the fact that you got paid for it.

Of course it's important to remember that I only worked for a few days, so I didn't have that many clients. I don't know what it's like to do this for years and years. And I'm pretty sure I couldn't do the work in a way that would make me a lot of money. After about five clients in a day, I'd had enough and you don't get rich that way. I only worked mornings, my friend worked the afternoons and we split the rent on the window. That meant we each only had to pay about sixty-five guilders a day, which you could cover in one trick. I was always really glad I didn't have to work more than those few hours. The result, though, was that I didn't earn that much. I had to buy a wig and all sort of lingerie in addition to the rent on the room. So I made all my expenses back and a few hundred guilders more, that's all.

For me, the heaviest part of the job was making contact with each new client, making him feel comfortable, giving him my attention. Doing that with people I didn't know and couldn't care less about was hard work. Normally, I wouldn't have had anything to do with those guys, and I didn't really care about the stuff they wanted to talk about. But while I was there, in my blonde wig and lingerie, it was okay, I was really able to give them my attention. I felt like they weren't really talking to me, they were talking to the woman they saw in front of them. No, that's not quite right; it was a part of me, of course, the wig didn't create it. But it was useful that I looked totally different when I was working, otherwise I would have felt much more naked. I don't think that any whore totally reveals herself in her work. You just show a part of yourself, the part they can have sex with, but you keep the rest for yourself.

There was a kind of power play in the whole transaction that I enjoyed. I lured the men in and I controlled most of what happened once they were inside. What I didn't want to have happen, didn't happen. That was different than having sex with men in my private life. And sitting behind the window itself was fabulous. Still, I don't want to do exactly that kind of work again because I don't want to have to fuck like that anymore. I had a bad scare, really bad luck, right at the very beginning. With my second client on my first day, a condom burst. After that, I couldn't shake the anxiety for the rest of the time I worked. It was really shitty. I try not to think about it that much, because there's nothing to do about it at this point. It hasn't been six months, so an AIDS test is no use. That experience took a lot of the fun out of the whole thing. The worst part of it was that the guy was so fucking unconcerned—he just laughed and said I was a good fuck. I was furious. But I guess that's the risk of this kind of work. It happens to every prostitute sometime, I bet.

Still, I just can't get beyond it. Of course, if I were dependent on prostitution, I would just have to get over it. Or at least I'd have to get more skilled at preventing it from happening again. I noticed that the other women all have ways to convince themselves that the risks aren't really so high. Right after it happened, I went to the woman who had rented me the room and said, "God damn it, I just had a rubber break on me …" She was so sweet: "Let's call the doctor right away and get you the morning-after pill." "I'm actually a lot more worried about AIDS than pregnancy," I said. And immediately she and this other whore started telling me, "Oh, you don't have to worry about that. That's not such a problem here. You're not working on the streets or something." Like if you work the streets you get AIDS but if you work behind the windows you don't. Right.

▼

Jo Doezema, *staff worker at the Red Thread*
Amsterdam, 1993

I started working in prostitution when I was about twenty-five in a brothel in Amsterdam. After a few months, I left that brothel to try another brothel, because at the time I wasn't aware that all brothels are actually shit. There are so many stories going around in the whore world about "you can earn so much money at this other place" or "you should go work there because it's so chic." I really thought I was going to find it: the fabulous brothel where you really made a lot of money. So I started working in a really chic place where the guys paid fl. 400 for the hour with you. Of course, you got less than half, and it was really, really slow—almost no clients. And the place was so incredibly pretentious. The women who worked there weren't whores, they were "glamour girls." The clubs purposely look for women like that: women who don't have any kind of whore consciousness. Those are the women that are easy to exploit, women who are terrified of anyone finding out what they do, who will give up everything—including more than half of their earnings and a lot of their freedom—for the anonymity that a club offers.

It's also their marketing strategy to attract clients: "These aren't real whores, these are just kind of nice girls that happen to be sitting in a bar." A lot of women start working in the clubs and then move on to do escort or to working behind the windows. But it's a common place to start because it gives this illusion of safety. Everybody—including most beginning prostitutes—think that the clients are really violent and scary and you'll face a lot of risks. So the clubs seem safe because there are people around and there's maybe a little bell next to the bed in case of trouble. And because the clubs have a chic image, they give you the idea that the clients that come in are of "the better sort," which is bullshit.

Jo Doezema   © Gon Buurman

In fact, in many ways I think club work is a lot more unsafe. In a club the clients drink and most times so do you because you make money getting drinks. It's also very difficult to refuse a client. Most clubs won't come right out and say "you have to go with everybody that wants you," but they put a lot of pressure on you. Some of those guys running the clubs are real bastards. Mostly they're men, though there are some women. But having a woman boss is no guarantee that anything will be any better. The really good bosses are women, that's true, but it's not the case that every woman is a good boss. There are a lot of Madames out there, the woman who started out herself as a prostitute, worked her way up and is determined to exploit the hell out of everybody who's working for her.

The people who run the brothels are definitely bosses, not colleagues. But don't call them "pimps," they get so pissed off if you say that. They're just businessmen and women offering a service, for which they ask a reasonable price. I guess what pisses me off is the way they run their businesses. The way they think about the women who work in their clubs and the way they treat them is full of 17th century paternalism. There's "papa," the sex club owner, and "*zijn meisjes*," they all say it, "my girls," not "the girls," certainly not "the women," but "my girls." But at the same time, "papa" isn't shouldering any of the responsibilities of a boss under Dutch law, such as making sure that workers are insured, paying national health care premiums, that kind of thing.

Another problem with the clubs is that it's always a struggle with a client because it's not clear what your roles are. Behind the windows it's clear—you're a whore, he's a client. But that whole kind of fake romanticism around the club means that he doesn't want to think you're a whore and he doesn't want to see himself as a client. Not all clients are like that, some are very well aware. And they are usually the good ones. But there are no set agreements about what's going to happen once you get in the room. A lot of clients have the idea that their hour will be filled with sex of whatever sort they want. And because you can't say in the beginning, "If you want this, this, and this, its going to cost this much, and this I don't do," you are kind of struggling the whole time to keep the client from doing things you don't want and trying to keep him satisfied at the same time. I've worked in some private houses where the men pay fl. 100, the women get half, and the clients expect to come *twice*. Unbelievable.

I did escort work for a while, too, but escort is only a little better than clubs. Really the only improvement is that you don't have to drink and you don't have to sit around there all day. But the only way to make good money in escort is to be available to be beeped for work all the time, twenty-four hours a day, seven days a week. You can go for days without any work and suddenly they beep you at three in the morning or in the middle of dinner with friends. And if you don't say "yes" you don't make any money and they probably won't call you again.

And another thing is, you have no sense of the client when you agree to go out on a job. You have to trust the escort bureau that they aren't sending you into a dangerous situation, and they are so unscrupulous. They don't care about you. I had them send me out to a guy who was really drunk.... That's the thing with escort work. You know that you shouldn't be going with this client because he is too drunk or you don't like the way he looks or whatever. But because it is the middle of the night, and you've already spent at least an hour of your time getting to the client, it's hard to have wasted a couple of hours and not get any money for it. So you tend to take more risks than you should.

This guy was really really drunk and a little bit crazy and.... I don't think about it a lot actually. I managed to get myself out from under him, told him that it wasn't working for me. I don't know if anything really horrendous would have happened but it was an uncomfortable situation. I think this is the first time I've ever told anyone about this because I'm sure all my friends would have flipped out if I would have told them. They would have said, "You are stopping: don't ever do this again." I didn't want to stop, so I never dared tell anybody. I think for almost everybody I make it more positive than it is, because everybody has such a negative idea about it already. So you tend to only talk about the good things or the funny things. With most jobs, if you have a shitty day or a bad client or something, people don't immediately say that it's because of the kind of work you do and that you must stop right away. But with prostitution, I've always felt that if I didn't convince everybody that this work was fantastic for me and that I really loved it that they would all be on my back to quit.

Anytime something negative happens in your work, it just confirms peoples' worst suspicions. They are already convinced that prostitution is going to destroy you. I think it's ridiculous that people think if you have sex for any reason other than to satisfy your own desire you will be destroyed. Didn't it used to be that sex without "love" would deeply damage a woman? And before love, it was understood that sex outside of marriage would destroy her—look at Anna Karenina or Madame Bovary. And now it's sex outside of desire that'll destroy us. Look, we've already survived sex outside of marriage and sex without love so it's likely we can survive sex outside of desire, too.

Now it is true that there are parts of myself that I don't want to share with my clients. But drawing boundaries in my work doesn't mean that I am in danger of being destroyed by it. The way you deal with clients is different than the way you deal with friends or sweethearts. It's always used so negatively that you've got to separate your work from your private life, as if that's unique to prostitution, and as if you actually found it so disgusting what you were doing in your work that you had to put up this kind of barrier so that you wouldn't be destroyed. I think that's how people understand it if I say that I don't kiss during my work. They think that I've got to save some part of myself from being horribly degraded by the transaction of money for sex with a client.

For me personally, I don't like kissing someone if I'm not attracted to them. Also part of it is the professional code, the whole idea of prostitutes don't kiss. I think, "Well, okay we won't." Kissing is also very unhygienic; if you're having sex you use a condom, so the chance of catching anything, even his cold, stays pretty remote. But not if you're kissing. Besides, for me kissing is very intimate. It's a kind of intimacy I don't want to share with my clients. But that doesn't mean that the rest of what I am doing with my clients is disgusting or damaging to me.

So there are parts of my life I don't want to share at work. So what? Do I have to give all of myself and not hold anything back in order to legitimately be able to say that I like my work? Sure, there are still times when I put up with something from a client that I don't want to have happen, either because I'm too tired, or I don't know how to say that I don't want it. But I have learned now to deal with that; instead of thinking, "Oh, I'm the worst whore in the world," I just think, "Okay, next time better." And it's not like if a client touches my breasts and I don't feel like it that I am going to be emotionally and sexually damaged for the rest of my life. Just next time better.

I won't say it isn't true that some women in prostitution are emotional wrecks. But does that come from prostitution or from internalized self-hatred about being a whore? Does it come from the stigma because people found out and never wanted to talk to you again? Or does it come from something completely outside their work? I know that some women really shouldn't be doing the work and should get out. The problem is that those are the only admissible stories. The other stories of prostitutes who say, "I like what I'm doing, or even if I don't like it, it's not destroying me," are dismissed. We apparently just don't realize that we're being destroyed.

Not too long ago, the Red Thread did an action in Amsterdam around street prostitution, and two French journalists came with us to cover the story. They did long interviews, we gave them a lot of our time, and I actually thought they would produce a good article. When the piece appeared, they sent us a copy. It started "Jo and Margot and Laurens all seem really happy and well-adjusted and insist that prostitution has not damaged them. But behind all this there is a sort of quiet desperation." I thought, "What? How dare they!" And they had the nerve to send it to us! What can you say in response to that? Everybody wants to believe it already way too much. I'm certain there wasn't any quiet desperation, they just made it up, because it had to be there.

▼

Sandy, *former teenage street prostitute*
San Francisco, CA, 1993

I grew up in a big working-class Catholic family. My parents and my grandparents all grew up in the same part of Chicago. I didn't know what a slum we lived in until I left it, even though we constantly had to deal with things like social workers and community centers. My father and mother were not people who should have been parents. I am the second oldest, and they ended up with seven kids, each fourteen months apart—except for one break of about a year and a half when my father was in a mental hospital. My dad was an alcoholic with serious mental problems. He was always violent toward my mother and had trouble keeping a job; he started sexually abusing me when I was still in diapers.

I always had bruises. That's how I lost part of my hearing. I don't know which of my parents it was because, when I was in the fifth grade, within one week my father had knocked me down and kicked me across the floor and, a few days later, my mother got mad at me for mouthing off and knocked my head up against a wall. And then for years they denied I had the hearing problem. I haven't always had this hearing aid because they always told me it wouldn't help.

During my sophomore year, my father got me pregnant. That was the only time my mother had to acknowledge the abuse because she was the one who set up the abortion. At a certain level, I had totally shut off from the sexual abuse. I would tell the nuns about the physical violence, the alcoholism, that stuff, but I didn't talk about the sexual abuse. But finally, after I got pregnant, I told a nun about it. My mother was called to the school and she denied everything: "Sandy's crazy." And when the nun believed her, I just didn't know what to do. My father was getting more violent all the time, and I could see what it was doing to the little kids. I really wanted to get out. I thought if I got a job, maybe I could make enough money to leave. But then I thought, "No, I can't leave my sisters. I can't leave them." So I decided I needed to get enough money together to take my sisters, too.

I was already out of the house almost every night by then doing these babysitting jobs and going to school meetings. So a couple of nights, when I was supposed to be babysitting, I just kind of scouted the area where a lot of prostitutes hung out in my neighborhood. I had seen it my whole life, so I knew it was there. But still it was a little like: What do you really do? So I hung out in a coffeeshop and watched through the window. Okay, I'm getting it, I'm getting it now. I figured out how much to charge by watching conversations; I could read lips.

It was pretty clear what was done where: if you went south of North Avenue you could get picked up by white or black guys. And that was where all the black girls were, and the white girls who would go with blacks. And if you were north of North Avenue, none of the black guys would go there. So I went south of North Avenue; I mean, come on. Besides, I was really fired up about the civil rights move-ment, so it was kind of a political decision, too. I got a really sexy out-fit with a short, short skirt and high heels, and I did that look some-times. But other times, I wore pieces of my Catholic school uniform, and that made me look really young and innocent. Looking young worked really well, too.

Once I was out there and did the first couple of tricks, I started talk-ing to the other girls a bit. We all would kind of keep an eye on each other because this was not fancy "take-me-to-a-nice-hotel" hooking. This was like, "Let's go back in the alley here and do a quicky," or "Get in the car and we'll pull over and do a blow job." I thought the guys were so stupid. If you played like you liked it, you'd get more money from them. Half of them were drunk and couldn't even get it up, but they were acting like they were getting off and paying me for it.

I was already familiar with Marx and Freud by that age, and I would stand there and have conversations with myself about what I was doing, trying to understand it: "What's the surplus value here?" "Am I selling myself or what?" That felt scary, to sell your whole self. "No, I'm just acting." I wondered about what was being exchanged, what the commodity was. It was kind of a way to be there but to be think-ing my own thoughts. I knew I couldn't daydream; it was too dan-gerous for that. But, with those kind of thoughts, I could keep my mind on what was happening and still distance myself from it.

One night, this car stopped with a man driving. At least, it looked like a man. I got in the car and someone spoke from the backseat and I got really scared. The voice from the back seat was really deep, but it was female. "Hey wait a minute, I didn't say nothing about doing a double. We got to slow this down. Don't be driving away." And these women were like, "Gee, we didn't mean to scare you …" I had done only one other trick with a woman and that had been really weird because she didn't want to pay me. Deciding to go with these women really broke all my rules. I even let them take me to their house which was right near there. These were what we used to call the "lizzies."

The one woman, Bud, she passed almost all the time for a man. And her partner, Pat, passed sometimes, but it was harder for her. When I started doing the thing with them it was like all of a sudden it was different. My body had moved with the men, and I knew the feeling of release and stuff. But this was like, "Wow, women." And then I got scared: "Oh, my god, what am I?" But they were really cool. They didn't try to mess with me. They paid me right away and then they said, "Do you need to make more money tonight or are you going to sit down and talk to us?"

So we all sat at this table, and they started talking. They really identified with being a third sex. They showed me some old magazines and, later, they introduced me to some of their friends. I worked a little bit doing tricks with all of them. I noticed even at sixteen that with women it was harder. If you acted like you liked it, that was when they tried to stiff you. With men, if you acted like you liked it they gave you a couple of extra bucks. But with some women if you acted like you liked it they thought that meant they didn't have to pay. You know, it seems like nobody wants to hear about lesbians and prostitutes, not the good stuff and certainly not the bad stuff. A couple of the women I worked with got beat up once by a gang of dykes they were doing an inside show for. Raped by them. I mean they stuck coke bottles up their ass all night. No one wants to hear about it.

It was different, though, with Pat and Bud and some of their friends. I mean the cool thing was that I would turn tricks with them but they would also invite me to their parties and just let me be with them. I didn't really know what to do with the third sex stuff, but I knew that there was something there for me. One of the good things was that they had all these catalogues and stuff lying around, and that's when I first saw things like dildos. I immediately thought, "Shit, I could pass." I mean it's fucking cold in Chicago in the winter. I didn't want to be standing out there in a miniskirt. Even the school girl outfit was cold.

So I went over to where all the gay guys went and I became a little transvestite. I just did blow jobs; all they wanted to do was to feel it, so I wore a dildo. They just wanted a little boy-looking thing. I did let a couple of them do anal, but even then, they didn't figure it out. It was the mid-60s and, for the guys that came to that area, it was all so fast and secretive. It wasn't like they were even going to park the car; they'd just sneak into this corner alley and get going. For me, the big thing was that I could wear my jeans and not fucking freeze, it was fucking winter.

But then this one night—I was being a girl that night—I was talking with this guy, making the deal, and suddenly he pulls out his badge. Oh, shit, this is not cool. So I get taken down to the city station. I was totally freaked. My parents were going to kill me. I had no doubt that they would literally kill me.

Then one of the cops recognized me. This guy worked with the equivalent of "gang prevention" and he knew both of my brothers who had already been getting into a lot of trouble. He told me he was going to take me to the juvenile jail but, once we got in the cop car, I realized he wasn't going the right way. "Oh, shit, he is going to make me give him a blow job on the way there." But, instead, he stops the car, goes into a restaurant, and comes out with two cups of coffee. Then he says, "I know your dad's a drunk." "Yeah he is. He's going to kill me. And if he doesn't my mother will." "Yeah, I know," he says. "You've been a good kid; you've never got into any trouble. What are you doing?" So I told him; I said I had to do it, I had to get my sisters out of there. He was great. He said, "This is going to sound awful, but you have to take care of yourself. You are not their mother. They are not your responsibility." That was the hardest thing for me to believe. But finally the moment I turned eighteen, I got out.

So as a teenager, I only did prostitution for a few months. But when I needed to do it again later, I found that I had learned some stuff. That time, I decided to form a support group. We were exclusively street prostitutes; no strippers, no call girls. We needed to protect ourselves from their attitude. They could be really snooty toward the street whores. Sorry, but that's what we were, and they were totally disrespectful. They would talk about the glamour of what they were doing, which is fine. Maybe what they were doing was glamorous. But they acted like their experience spoke for us all. Well, for the people in my group, it was not glamour. They also had this weird line about how such a small percentage of whores worked the streets. Whereas, as far as I could see, street prostitution was the main thing. I've noticed that COYOTE [prostitutes' rights organization] still gives off this attitude of "It's only about ten percent of these women that are on the streets, and that's a bad image of the whore." Well, first of all it's a real image and I just can't quite believe that it's only 10%. I have to admit that some of my condemnation of call girls is internalized class stuff. I just don't like middle-class women a lot of the time. You know, when I read some of the stuff written by so-called "feminist allies," it feels like they are fighting over our bodies. Some of them say they are "pro-prostitution," as if it could be that easy. Then there are the others who say that prostitution is evil because it contributes to violence against women and they'll have their "Take Back the Night" marches right through the Red Light district without even dealing with the sex workers as other women. It's like prostitutes are just these bodies who are somehow connected to something bad and evil or something good and on the cutting edge of revolution. They just turn us into symbols.

▼

SECTION III
STRATEGIC RESPONSES

Chapter 5
Prohibition and Informal Tolerance

Women's experience performing erotic labor is highly determined by the conditions under which the work is performed. Under some circumstances, a worker's control may be so radically diminished as to approximate slavery or indentured servitude. For abolitionist critics of prostitution, such cases serve as compelling evidence that the commercialization of sex is an inherently abusive transaction. From the perspective of prostitutes' rights advocates, on the other hand, what makes prostitution abusive in some but not all instances is a question of the conditions under which the *work* takes place (the relations of production) rather than the terms under which the *sex* takes place (for money, love, or pleasure). These two very different perspectives have produced opposing strategic responses.

Those who view prostitution as an inherently abusive practice generally support prohibition of the act and punishment of some or all parties involved. In contrast, those who view prostitution as a form of labor tend to advocate policies designed to enhance worker control through decriminalization, regulation, and worker self-organizing. These competing perspectives have been advanced not only by those located comfortably outside the trade (such as academics, social activists, politicians, and policy advisors) but also increasingly by current and former prostitutes.[1]

The United States offers a useful example of the difficulties of achieving the abolition of prostitution through policies of prohibition. In the U.S., almost all forms of prostitution are currently illegal, but prostitution remains widely practiced throughout the country.[2] Efforts to eradicate the sale of sex have proved to be as expensive as they are ineffective. In one recent study of American prostitution policies, legal scholar Julie Pearl uncovered the disturbing fact that in the 1980s, many of America's largest cities spent more on enforcing prostitution laws than on education, public welfare, health care, and hospitals.[3] The city of Los Angeles, for example, spent thirteen times as much on controlling prostitution as it did on health-related services.[4] These expensive attempts to control commercial sex through prohibition have been also highly inefficient in curbing the practice: fully eighty percent of those arrested for prostitution in large U.S. cities are not held for prosecution, and only half of those brought to trial are found guilty.[5] In other words, despite large investments of police time and resources in the entrapment and arrest of sex workers, very few are even temporarily removed from the streets.[6]

Police officials interviewed in Pearl's study expressed serious doubt that "even a tripling of current law enforcement efforts could make a dent in the prostitution problems of their respective cities."[7] Nonetheless, they generally continued to support prohibitionist policies. Law enforcement's enthusiasm for prohibition, then, appears relatively unrelated to its effectiveness in actually eliminating or even controlling prostitution. One California District Attorney suggests that while criminalization of prostitution may not work to abolish the practice, it plays an important role in creating a general climate of law and order:

> When you talk about legalization, the overall problem is how you see the community and what kind of direction it will go in. Legalization is the first step in my mind to bringing other activities with it, where people will say, "Well, if prostitution is okay, then everything is relative." You can then rationalize just about every kind of behavior even if it's dangerous.[8]

Snowball

watershed

In addition to any symbolic moral function it may play, prostitution prohibition also has a direct payoff for police. Prostitution arrests are relatively safe and easy to make and can improve the image of law enforcement in communities beset by crime. In the United States, in the 1980s, the majority (over seventy percent) of violent crimes committed in large cities did not result in arrest.[9] This dismal crime-to-arrest ratio was improved, at least on paper, by cracking down on "victimless" crimes such as prostitution. During the same period in the same areas, arrests of prostitutes rose by one hundred and thirty-five percent.[10] Energetic enforcement of prostitution laws thus served to create the impression of an active and efficient police presence even as it diverted scarce resources away from the control and prosecution of violent crime. As Pearl notes:

> Prostitution cases raise the "closed by arrest rate" for total crime indices. Prostitution is one of the only offenses for which nearly one hundred percent of "reported incidences" result in arrest. To the extent that total arrest rate indices are elevated by the inclusion of this high percentage for prostitution, they engender a false account of overall police protection.[11]

An even more serious indictment of prohibitionist policies lies in their negative effect on the very population the laws ostensibly were created to protect: women understood to be "trapped" in the trade. Prohibitionist policies in the United States, as elsewhere, are the product of social purity and anti-trafficking campaigns, and were designed to prevent the exploitation of women in prostitution. However, efforts to protect workers by abolishing their places of employment or by arresting them (and their clients) have not served to enhance their general safety or well-being. Indeed, once prostitution has been criminalized, those charged with "protecting" prostitutes—the police—become a problem to be avoided instead of a resource upon which to draw. The resulting antagonistic relationship between prostitutes and police is a particularly serious problem in a profession in which participants face extremely high rates of violence.[12] Fear of arrest also encourages hasty and euphemistic negotiations between prostitutes and clients which can undermine a worker's authority and thereby her ability to protect herself. And, finally, laws against prostitution and "pandering" complicate workers' efforts to share crucial information about safer working methods and dangerous customers. One member of the Prostitution Task Force of the California National Organization for Women argues:

> Fear of the pandering law works to the detriment of prostitutes, as it discourages them from sharing information openly which may help them work more safely, to tell others of a safer, more pleasant place to work, or to educate each other or the public about their work in a manner which differs from its usual negative connotation.[13]

For these reasons, the California chapter of NOW passed a resolution in 1994 supporting decriminalization of the sex trade. The organization concluded: "Laws prohibiting prostitution are a prime factor in perpetuating violence against prostitutes."[14]

This recognition that prohibitionist policies can threaten the safety and well-being of prostitutes has led some abolitionist activists to emphasize strategies targeting clients and third parties (business owners, landlords, and pimps) rather than workers. Cecilie Hoigard and Liv Finstad, for example, argue that because prostitution is a form of sexual violence, criminalizing the clients must be a priority:

> Prostitution is like a piecemeal rape of women. Therefore, it is our view that prostitution should be defined as a crime of violence.... The demand can be ... restricted by criminalizing those who represent the demand-side of the purchase.[15]

Over the past decade, this strategy has become increasingly popular in abolitionist countries such as the United States.[16] In the 1980s, many U.S. cities passed laws allowing for the seizure of cars used in prostitution offenses.[17] The intent was not simply to shift the burden of punishment from worker to client, but also to discourage prostitution through the public humiliation of those paying for sexual services. In Portland, Oregon, for example, motorists whose cars had been seized were not only obliged to pay fines of about $300, but were also required to have all parties on the vehicle registration—including wives or employers—sign off before a car could be released. The intent of this provision was made clear by one Portland police officer: "If you choose to use your car in this type of activity, you're going to have a lot of explaining to do at home."[18] Over four hundred cars were seized in that city in a single year.[19] In Washington, D.C., where similar laws are in force, a city council spokesperson complained that the law was so effective that the police "say they don't have enough space to store the cars."[20] Of the 124 cars which were seized in that city in 1992, about half were simply forfeited, suggesting how serious the problem of stigmatization is for many clients.

Humiliation is also the explicit objective in many neighborhood vigilante efforts at curbing prostitution. One member of a San

Francisco neighborhood group opposed to prostitution proudly reported, "I have personally called employers if there's a logo on a company car or truck circling the block in search of women.... In two cases I know of, the men have been fired."[21] Through such efforts, punishment precedes not only (eventual) conviction but even arrest. Working prostitutes typically oppose these strategies. As a delegate to the First World Whores Conference argued:

> First of all, arresting johns is bad for business. Secondly, it pushes us further underground where we're more vulnerable. And thirdly, it misses the point: we want as much right to sell sex as men have to buy it; we don't want punishment for *them*—we want rights for *us*.[22]

While prostitutes and johns are the primary-targets of prohibitionist policies, other parties involved in commercial sex, such as landlords and business owners, also have been the object of public harassment and legal action. In the past few years, U.S. law enforcement officials increasingly have been employing so-called "Red Light Abatement" procedures (involving the seizure of property rather than the arrest of participants) to close commercial sex establishments. Police have found that the simple threat of loss of property often inspires landlords to take swift action in evicting tenants suspected of running brothels or engaging in other forms of illegal sexual commerce. Whether the procedure is effective in curtailing prostitution, however, is less clear. Shortly after the strategy was employed in one California city, the local paper reported:

> Workers are neither leaving Santa Cruz, nor leaving the sex business because of the crackdown. They're just going into less conspicuous, independent work. "They're not rooting us out," elaborated one woman, "they're driving us underground, where it's more dangerous."[23]

As the U.S. example suggests, policies of prohibition appear to be ineffective as well as costly, and compromise the safety of those working in the trade. As a result, other countries increasingly are moving in the direction of legalization or decriminalization of the sex trade. No country has so fully embraced informal alternatives to prohibition as the Netherlands. While prostitution itself is legal in that country, third-party sexual commerce (such as brothel prostitution) is formally prohibited but informally tolerated.[24] This "tolerance policy" (*gedoog beleid*) has resulted from coalition governments composed of Socialist, Christian Democratic, and Liberal (fiscally conservative) parties with radically differing views on "social problems" such as drugs and prostitution. Socialists and Liberals increasingly have embraced policies of formal decriminalization and regulation, while the Christian Democrats have held firm to an abolitionist morality without insisting on prohibitionist policies. The resulting strategy of tolerance has allowed the state to formally condemn prostitution and drug use while investing few resources in their prohibition and has ensured the survival of coalition governments across ideological differences.

The de Graaf Foundation, a Dutch research and documentation center on prostitution, notes that such tolerance policies have been relatively successful in controlling the Dutch sex trade, but they also have required authorities to make "creative use of roundabout methods or else operate in outright opposition to the legal code.... As long as no one went to the courts to stop it, a great deal could fall under the concept of 'tolerance.'"[25] Zoning policies, for instance, have been used to informally concentrate sexual commerce. Disgruntled residents of impacted areas have been offered state subsidies to relocate should they so desire.

But, as the de Graaf Foundation suggests, informal decriminalization requires not only the cooperation of authorities, neighbors, and businesses, it also depends on a willingness of all parties to turn a blind eye to the formal legal prohibitions on organized prostitution. In one Dutch city, Rotterdam, where residents could not agree on an area to serve as the designated Red Light district, municipal authorities found themselves stymied in their efforts to concentrate and control sexual commerce. The preferred solution—moving the sex trade onto "sex boats" in the Rotterdam harbor—was thwarted by penal code provisions prohibiting the organization of brothels. The result was that, by the late 1970s, informally zoned window prostitution had disappeared entirely from Rotterdam replaced by widely dispersed and unregulated street prostitution and more hidden forms of the indoor trade including brothel, sex club, and home-based work. The net result was a loss of control by local authorities over the sex trade in that city.

For this reason, successive Dutch governments over the past twenty years repeatedly have attempted to revise prostitution law to allow for more direct and formal regulation and municipal control of the sex industry. Such efforts have been justified as a means to better protect the rights and interests of local residents and—rather incidentally—those of sex workers. This bias toward the interests of residents over workers has been a consistent feature of all discussions of legalization of the Dutch sex trade. Already in 1977, when the first government taskforce was established to study possible revisions in prostitution law, the commission understood its task as an investigation into whether "the unrest and public nuisance that prostitution had occasioned in Rotterdam might be more actively addressed by the state through the creation of a so-called 'eros centre' elsewhere in the city."[26] The commission specifically expressed concern about the impact of prostitution on the legitimate rights of neighborhood residents: "If prostitution takes forms that create unrest and disturbance for the surroundings, then this certainly is a case of the violation of the reasonable interests of third parties; the government has a responsibility to work against this."[27] Missing from this assessment of the shortcomings of formal prohibition and informal decriminalization was any mention of the problems "tolerance" policies might pose for women working in the Dutch sex trades.

While informal decriminalization does offer workers some advantages over outright prohibition (allowing for a more normalized relationship between sex workers and police, for example), tolerance policies still leave sex workers more vulnerable than any other party in the commercial sexual transaction. Under the current system of tolerance, municipal authorities generally have been able to exercise a relatively high degree of control over sexual commerce in the Netherlands. Business operators, too, have found tolerance policies to serve their needs. Under the current system, the brothel owner has "his personnel, his contacts with the police, the city, the neighborhood association, and the tax office.... Of course, he doesn't pay health insurance premiums, because, after all, the girls are 'independent contractors.' But he does dictate their work hours, how they have to dress, and how much they can charge each client."[28]

Indeed, as this description suggests, informal decriminalization actually is advantageous to sex business owners because it allows them to avoid obligations borne by legal businesses. Prostitutes employed in these clubs and brothels, on the other hand, have few such advantages. They are already saddled with a number of obligations, such as registering with the police and paying taxes on their income, with no corresponding rights as workers. One Dutch researcher, Lucie van Mens, notes that working conditions vary dramatically under policies of informal decriminalization. While some business owners do understand their function to be that of providing a venue for workers to operate as truly independent contractors, more common are businesses where workers are "independent" in name only. Van Mens concludes:

> The crazy thing is that the sex trade is becoming increasingly modern, more commercial and market-oriented, but the working conditions of the prostitutes still resemble the 19th century.... [with the failure to repeal the law formally prohibiting brothels, 250-bis] there continues to be no control over the well-being of the prostitute.[29]

Because their places of employment remain formally illegal, sex workers employed by Dutch brothels, sex clubs, and escort agencies have been unable to demand any of the benefits that normally accrue to workers in the Netherlands, such as unemployment insurance, sick leave, retirement benefits, vacation pay, and collective contract negotiations. The prohibitionist legacy of Dutch penal code 250-bis also serves to effectively thwart efforts by municipalities to set minimum standards of workplace safety and hygiene.

Prostitutes' rights advocates insist that sex workers' concerns must be at the forefront of any revision in this prostitution law. From the perspective of the prostitutes' association, Red Thread, an adequate prostitution policy "should strive to establish a balance between the different interests: those of the prostitutes, those of sound prostitution businesses, and those of the neighborhoods where prostitution is practiced."[30] While the Red Thread thus acknowledges the legitimate concerns of neighborhood groups, they urge a distinction be made between actual public nuisance problems (such as noise or traffic) and opposition to prostitution on moral grounds (for example, concerns about an "image problem" the sex trade might create for a neighborhood).

Policies developed to address only such moral concerns, they argue, generally attempt to conceal prostitution with the result that "prostitution is pushed, both in a literal and a figurative sense, toward the edge of society. Such a policy will not promote the acceptance of prostitution in any way."[31] Furthermore, the Red Thread points out that policies designed to conceal prostitution have no positive effect on abuses within the trade: "This type of policy hardly sets any conditions to the conduct of business as long as there is no question of public annoyance. Therefore, it is not concerned with the situation of prostitutes, either as employees or as self-employed persons."[32] The Red Thread concludes that "in addition to addressing the causes of public annoyance, improving the situation of prostitutes must be included among the new demands [for revising prostitution law, 250-bis]."[33]

Such efforts to redirect attention to the rights and concerns of sex workers have been an ongoing struggle in Dutch prostitution policy debates. Most recently, in 1993, the Justice Department (in Christian Democratic hands) submitted a proposal to revise Dutch prostitution law with no specific mention of improving the position of those working in the trade. Indeed, the proposed changes would have seriously disadvantaged the majority of sex workers in most large Dutch cities. Under the 1993 proposal, municipalities would have been individually empowered to either prohibit, decriminalize, or regulate organized prostitution. The possibility that laws would differ radically from municipality to municipality served in large part to defeat the measure. But a more serious concern for sex workers was a provision in the proposed legislation that would have restricted employment in the Dutch sex trade to legal residents of the Netherlands and other European Community countries. Because the majority of sex workers in many Dutch cities come from Latin America, Asia, Africa, and Eastern Europe, the proposed law would have had the effect of criminalizing many of those currently employed in the sex trade. Prostitutes' rights advocates, including the Red Thread and the Dutch Foundation Against Trafficking in Women, condemned the proposed law noting that a "commitment to the improvement in the position of prostitutes has completely disap-peared from the discussion."[34] Without placing sex workers' con-cerns at the center of proposed policy revisions, movement toward legalization will no better safeguard prostitutes' rights than has pro-hibition.

▼ ▼ ▼

© *Annie Sprinkle*

Battling Thugs in Miniskirts:
Prohibition in San Francisco

A key argument for the prohibition of prostitution is the negative effects it is presumed to have on the broader community in which it is practiced. One study of business, neighborhood, and police groups in Boston, Massachusetts, for example, showed that eighty-five percent of those sampled thought "prostitution breeds crime where it is concentrated; seventy percent thought it contributes significantly to the spread of VD; and seventy-seven percent believed it is often accompanied by muggings and violent crimes."[35] Similarly, in a special report on prostitution in the United States, *The Congressional Quarterly Researcher* describes a new mobilization against prostitution among neighborhood groups who believe that "street prostitution brings noise, declining property values, a bad environment for children and a health threat evidenced by the used condoms and drug paraphernalia littering city sidewalks."[36] These negative social "effects" of prostitution are used to justify criminalizing its participants in an effort to abolish the practice.

The perception that prostitution leads to an increase in crime becomes a truism if prostitution has been criminalized. However, the fact that laws have made criminals out of sex workers and their clients is not generally understood to be the source of the problem. Instead, commercial sex itself is held responsible for rising urban crime and violence.[37]

In language reminiscent of that historically used against other marginal groups such as foreigners, Jews, and homosexuals,[38] prostitutes are depicted as "a menacing flood" of filthy and contaminating outsiders who have usurped control of city streets from their rightful occupants: "What we're doing," explained a member of one San Francisco anti-prostitution group, "is taking back our neighborhood from the prostitutes and the johns who took it from us."[39] Similarly, the San Francisco "Downtown Vigilance Committee" explains they are just attempting to reclaim downtown "from the hordes of prostitutes who are destroying the neighborhood ... we community members want them out of our neighborhood."[40]

What distinguishes the prostitute from other menacing "out-siders" is the fact that sex workers generally are understood to be working-class females and thus both vulnerable "victims" as well as dangerous "thugs." In an article on "reformed prostitutes," one San Francisco reporter concluded: "While law enforcement agencies and citizen groups argue that prostitution fosters drug trafficking, theft, the spread of AIDS and the deterioration of neighborhoods, possibly the biggest victim of the business is the prostitute herself."[41]

Whether hapless victim or conscious criminal, prostitutes are seen by many anti-prostitution forces (including law enforcement in countries where prostitution is illegal) as key contributors to a crumbling social and moral order. For instance, attorney Dan McIlroy, who is in charge of prosecuting obscenity cases against video dealers and "live sex performers" in Maricopa County, Arizona, declares: "Obscenity is as dangerous as any crime out there. You're polluting the moral stream of the community and it affects children, women and families."[42]

In San Francisco, the absence of a moral consensus on the dangers of "obscenity," commercial sex, and sexual "deviance" in general means that law enforcement and community groups must package their opposition to prostitution in terms of a more concrete threat to health, safety, and property values. As conservative San Francisco Supervisor Bill Maher, notes: "There's this notion that we no longer can say, 'You will not engage in this type of conduct.' We don't seem to have the concept that we can ethically influence anti-social behav-ior."[43] San Francisco Assistant District Attorney Mark Donohue, responsible for prosecuting "red-light abatement actions" in San Francisco since 1982, asserts: "San Francisco is a place where adults come feeling they can do adult things without the consequences. Now we're seeing the consequences."[44] Donohue's euphemistic sug-gestion that "adult things" are producing serious problems for San Francisco in the 1990s, reflects the belief that AIDS and urban decay are the responsibility of marginal social groups such as homosexuals and prostitutes.

This theme was taken up with a vengeance in a 1992 *San Francisco Examiner* story which proclaimed in front page banner headlines: "Playground for Prostitutes, nuisance for a neighborhood: downtown

San Franciscans fearful but fed up, declare war on 'thugs in miniskirts.'"[45] In the paper's choice of the term "playground," prostitutes are depicted as children and denied the status of worker. The streets become a place of recreation, not merely for clients, but *for* prostitutes themselves. Still, these childlike delinquents should not be understood as benign. The paper reports: "Prostitutes are overrunning a large portion of downtown San Francisco, terrorizing residents and destroying property values, while city government looks on helplessly, an *Examiner* investigation shows."[46]

In the article, sex workers are depicted as filthy and contaminating, littering the area with "condoms and hypodermic needles" and even "smearing the sidewalks with human waste." Prostitution is thus seen to be literally fertilizing the ground for other urban social ills. In the words of the chairman of the San Francisco "Downtown Vigilance Committee," (described in the paper as a "group of anti-hooker crusaders"): "It's the drugs, the street thugs, the muggings, the purse snatchings, the noise, the violence. As the number of prostitutes escalates, so does everything else. They are tearing the neighborhood apart."[47]

The problems of urban life in post-Reagan/Bush America—an "ordeal marked by noise, filth and violence"[48]—are revealed in this "investigation" to be the result not of increasing poverty and a disappearing social welfare net, but rather, to the presence of some "80 to 100 hookers and pimps" working a 35-square block area of downtown San Francisco.[49] These few dozen interlopers are powerful far beyond their numbers, holding the city hostage while "government looks on helplessly." San Francisco Supervisor Bill Maher attributes this to the overwhelming power of civil and prostitutes' rights groups: "There's an attitude that there's not much we can do with the Tenderloin. There's this real sense of fear that the ACLU and COYOTE will be picketing the death out of me."[50]

Former San Francisco Police Chief Richard Hongisto confirms the perception that prostitutes' power goes unchallenged despite the terror they are inflicting on the citizenry: "All the lowlife laugh it up and normal people become afraid. Every hooker in the United States knows that if you come to San Francisco … nothing will happen, absolutely nothing."[51] In actuality, during 1992 when the article was written, arrests of San Francisco street prostitutes was not only a common occurrence but was steeply on the rise. In 1989, 150 prostitutes were arrested in one month; a year later, arrests averaged 211 a month, and by late 1992, the average was 357 a month.[52]

Despite the facts, comments such as Maher's and Hongisto's contribute to a community perception that it is law-abiding citizens, not socially marginal prostitutes, who are persecuted and at risk. In the words of one resident: "San Francisco cares more about people who are deranged than people who work nine to five and want to have a peaceful existence.... Rather than pay attention to the people who actually contribute to the system—the taxpayers—they pay attention to people who hassle other people on the streets."[53]

Attention is thus shifted away from the abusive conditions experienced by the most socially marginal to the threat posed to the rights of the middle class to enjoy a comfortable "quality of life" on increasingly impoverished city streets. In a discussion of "the epidemic of prostitution" in San Francisco, one member of the District Attorney's office concludes: "I sense the quality of life deteriorating on a daily basis. What's bothering citizens is walking down the street and not knowing what they'll encounter. It's the fear of being unable to predict what a whole class of disorderly citizens will do."[54]

The suggestion that the class creating the "bother" might also be composed of "citizens" with both rights and a reason to be disorderly is almost entirely missing from the *San Francisco Examiner* investigation of the conflict. Winokur's article, which covers both a portion of the front page and two full inside pages, contains precisely three comments by "hookers." Two of the women are discredited even before they speak: "Two nineteen-year-old hookers ... stepped into a corner grocery on Geary and shoplifted soft drinks, as a reporter looked on." They are then quizzed on their attitude toward local residents who, they are told, "bitterly resent" their presence. One woman expresses sympathy for the neighbors, while the other responds "They can basically go to hell as far as I'm concerned."[55]

The only analysis attributed to a prostitute in the article is by Carol Leigh, described as "a self-styled 'sex worker.'" (Winokur apparently feels compelled to put "sex worker" in quotes despite his frequent use of the term *hooker* free of quotation marks.) Leigh is the only respondent to suggest that the "real issue is women's poverty," a dimension of the problem explored no further in the article. Leigh goes on to express concern about the rights of women working in the streets (she is the only person to do so): "Just because there's a problem doesn't mean you can take rights away."[56] This observation is subsequently dismissed or, at best, ignored; directly following Leigh's comments is a quote by San Francisco Mayor Frank Jordan expressing sympathy for the plight of *residents* and boasting of a recent surge in arrests of street workers during his administration.

The rights and concerns of sex workers disappear in the depiction of the problem as a war between victimized citizens and dangerous and diseased criminals. In a letter to the editor appearing some two weeks after the *Examiner's* "Playground" investigation, one reader complained: "Apologists like to call prostitution a victimless crime, but as practiced on the sidewalks of the Tenderloin, it is very much a crime with victims: the people who live and visit here and have a regard for the health and safety of the area.... Whores peddling their wares ... [bring with them] pimps, followed by the drug dealers, and ... lurking like hyenas in the jungle that's been created, are the muggers." The reader acknowledges that the women may have problems of their own, but "hundreds of young women who have two strikes against them can still find the determination to improve their lives. Why should our hearts bleed for these bums...." He concludes by justifying a vigilante response: "If residents do resort to bullying it will be because the trash whose cause [some people] espouse turned this place into a combat zone."[57]

From this perspective, the real victims of the class conflict between those forced to live or work on the streets and those residents who "pay taxes," are clearly those with homes and legal employment. It is *their* rights which are threatened. In the words of one disgruntled downtown resident, "Our human rights are being violated and destroyed [by the prostitutes]."[58] Prostitution is thus made to bear the weight of citizen concerns about urban crime and violence in a time of economic crisis, as well as fears for public health and safety in a time of epidemic disease. A proposed billboard campaign for the city of San Francisco summarizes the attitude with admirable brevity: "Prostitution is not only illegal but a threat to health and safety."[59]

Epidemic disease and high rates of criminal violence are realities in many American urban areas of the 1990s. But there is compelling evidence to suggest that prostitution itself has no necessary or causal relationship to these problems. Cities with much more widespread and public prostitution, such as Amsterdam, have significantly lower rates of crime, violence, and HIV disease than comparably sized U.S. cities such as San Francisco. Furthermore, residents living directly in Amsterdam's flourishing, but decriminalized, Red Light district report a high level of satisfaction with their neighborhood. In a 1994 police study in which Amsterdam residents were asked to rate their satisfaction with their neighborhoods on a scale of one to ten, residents of the Red Light district (district two), awarded their area a 7.5 compared to a city-wide average of 7.6.[60] One reason for this high level of satisfaction may be related to the fact that, unlike residents of major U.S. cities, the vast majority of those inhabiting Amsterdam's Red Light district feel safe.[61] District two residents also reported overwhelmingly (eighty-nine percent of respondents) that they believed their neighborhood to be "as safe or safer than the preceding year."[62]

Neighborhood safety and satisfaction appear to have very little relationship to the presence of prostitution in urban Dutch neighborhoods. Far more significant may be Dutch laws and social policies that ensure low rates of homelessness, provide comprehensive national health insurance, restrict gun ownership, and redirect law enforcement efforts toward safety on the streets and away from victimless crimes such as prostitution and drug use. In countries such as the United States, however, it appears easier to blame sex workers for urban collapse than to raise taxes, ban guns, provide health care, and offer real alternatives for those currently living and working on the streets.

▼

Al Noren, *Sheriff*
Santa Cruz, CA, 1988

Al Noren: I don't think that it's any revelation that you get an unhealthy type of climate that surrounds prostitution. It's just an industry that begs other criminal activity, I don't know any other way to put it. It just creates an atmosphere where too many things are going on and people are taken advantage of and it just is not right. And if some of these gals in the business want to portray themselves as something else, if they feel good about it, that's fine, I don't care. I'm just saying I have an obligation to the whole public out there to see that we don't become a cess pool for the Silicon Valley.[63]

I am no great moralist but historically, as restrictions in terms of our sexual mores have lessened and we have become more "liberal" in our thinking, we have seen a tremendous increase in sex crimes. Now if you believe the tripe that people are putting out that all the sex workers are providing this wonderful treatment or therapy, then one wonders why every year we are getting an increase in violence against women, children, and so forth.

I've been in this Sheriff's office—including the military—for thirty-two years. And where society is more permissive, people just tend to go a little farther. There is always someone who doesn't play by the rules of society. And as we lower our restrictions as a society, there seems to be a tendency to go farther and farther beyond. The greatest restriction on criminal behavior is society itself and how it responds. It's most effective if the community says, "We don't tolerate this sort of behavior."

And let's face it, not a great deal of thrust is put forward by the Santa Cruz City Council or the County Board of Supervisors in terms of law enforcement. They are more interested in what color you paint your house and a few other things. There's not a strong belief in law enforcement. So as pressure is put on in other places, Santa Cruz becomes ripe for criminal activity. We live close to a million and a half people in Silicon Valley; its a hop, skip, and a jump. So they crack down in San Jose, and people move over here and set up business. The emphasis over here seems to be one of "do your own thing" and "being mellow yellow" or whatever. Then it gets beyond our limited resources to even deal with. Because there is no message being sent out that "we don't tolerate miscreant behavior." And you know the old story: give them an inch and they take a mile. So it mushrooms to the point where people are wringing their hands and don't know what to do.

I have no visions of grandeur that we are going to be able to eliminate prostitution anymore than we are going to eliminate homicide, petty theft, shop lifting, drug use, or what have you. But we are obligated to try. Basically what we are doing is to try to keep objectionable behavior down to a point where people can go about in the community and enjoy themselves without being put upon by unwanted activities. Some of my officers went back to New York, and said they couldn't believe the activity that went on unheeded in the streets. All these hookers plying their trade, all these dope deals going on and people just accept it, even the policemen accept it. And that's kind of sick in the sense that very few people are safe in many of those areas. That's the way it is with prostitution; you see all this other illegal activity taking place. You can say what you want, but this county just spent close to half a million dollars prosecuting a case where an out-call massage ended up in a homicide. Maybe the guy would have killed somebody else. But there's a whole lot of activity that surrounds prostitution. There's no escaping that fact.

I don't think you are ever going to get society to accept prostitution. It's like a lot of other things that go on: the pillar of the church carrying on with one of the elders or something. People know about these things and kind of wink and look away but they aren't going to come out and condone it. Now if society thought it was so wonderful it would seem like they would make it legal. And society hasn't chosen to do that. So in the meanwhile it's illegal and we're going to try to stop it.

The nice thing about the civil procedure is that if a woman owns her house that she is working out of, we don't have the same burden of proof we have in a criminal case. If the case progresses we can simply padlock her house if she owns it. Landlords, unless they are totally blind, know that some type of illicit activity is going on in their rentals. So we'll shut down their property, just put a padlock on it. If they want to take that chance it's up to them. It's a free society, you can do what you want until you reach a certain point and get caught at it and then you pay the price.

Wendy Chapkis: Some of the women I've spoken to who work in prostitution worry that this makes their lives more dangerous by making their work even more clandestine. And they also now feel even less free to call on law enforcement if they have a problem.

AN: That is a perception on their part. If one of them is robbed or beaten up, I don't see why they would have any great reluctance to report it now. Because we are not going after them criminally. Before this "crackdown" as you call it, the cases we brought were criminal cases. Now we are not doing that at all. But you're claiming that they say, "We are afraid to report getting beaten up because they could go after us civilly"?

WC: You mentioned putting a padlock on someone's home …

AN: They don't own their own homes. How many of them own their own homes? How many of them do you really believe are independent? There may be a few but I would be willing to bet you that they are supporting some guy. We had a university student here who would go out and hook for six months to support her boyfriend. Now I'm sure she didn't consider him her pimp, but I don't know what the hell else you'd call him. That's the definition if you look it up in the dictionary.

These gals either have a pimp or they are paying some guy to operate a parlor and he's collecting an outrageous fee. These guys who run these places, if you think they are some kind of futurist thinking people trying to provide therapy for the world, you're crazier than … that just ain't so. Some of the women run around and say, "I don't have a pimp, I just work at this establishment." But somebody is getting a hell of a big cut of their labors for not doing anything.

So you can call them what you like, and use all sorts of nice terms but it doesn't change anything. It's like in interrogation where you say, "Why do you take things?" you don't say, "Why do you steal?" "Steal" shocks the conscience so you minimize the language. That's all you're doing by calling people "sex workers." It may minimize it in somebody's eyes and they can say, "I'm doing this wonderful job," but they're charging outrageous prices.

WC: The women?

AN: Sure. I mean if they are really that benevolent, why would they charge such outrageous prices for their service?

WC: Of course you could ask that of a lot of professionals. Psychotherapists charge a lot of money too, and we assume they are benevolent.

AN: Yes, but at least they have some schooling and training, and there's some science behind it. I don't know that there's any great science behind what they're doing at the massage parlors. Calling it a profession is a bunch of crap. I think most people define as professional where study and effort are put forth. Having sex is no great accomplishment I don't think. It's like saying when you have breakfast that you are a professional breakfast eater.

WC: But you might be called a professional cook if what you do is to cook breakfast for someone else.

AN: No, no, but just eating breakfast would make you a professional.

WC: I don't think that sex workers are just "having sex," they are performing sex, they're doing something. You don't think that that's true?

AN: (short laugh) No. Do you? No.

▼

Fons Bierens, *North Holland Police Academy Instructor*
Amsterdam, 1994

Prostitution exists in all major cities, but in many places it's treated like an open secret and turned into a criminal offense. In my opinion, that approach only creates more problems which can't be solved using the criminal code. What we've done in the Netherlands is to develop a policy where prostitution is accepted but more or less restricted to certain areas. In Amsterdam, the Red Light district, "the Wallen," has historically been located near the harbor. The problem is that according to the law, a city government is absolutely not allowed to stimulate prostitution so even accepting it through a policy of toleration borders on stimulating it in a way. After all, if we say it's allowed here, but it's not allowed there, then we stimulate it in the area where it is tolerated.

Another problem is that as Amsterdam grows, the Red Light district grows too, and it's spreading well beyond the Wallen to other residential areas. Residents then start complaining about the noise, the cars, the honking horns, the inconvenience of not being able to find a place to park, that sort of thing. Prostitution just gives a neighborhood a bad name; people don't want to live in a neighborhood of whores.

The interesting thing is that despite the negative reputation, in general, neighborhoods in this city with a high concentration of prostitutes are pretty safe. The crime that does exist—and its mostly theft—is connected to the tourist trade, not particularly to prostitution. Of course there is some kind of relationship since prostitution attracts tourists, and tourists attract a certain kind of crime. But what tends to happen is that a direct line is drawn between prostitution and crime, and that's just wrong. The same kind of mistake is made when people try to make a clear link between drugs and prostitution. It's true that some prostitutes work to earn money for drugs, like heroin whores. But they represent only about two or three percent of all prostitutes in this city.

I live right near the Red Light district myself, so I know what I'm talking about when I say that it's a comfortable and safe area. It's a real neighborhood with people just going about their business. We're very committed to keeping the Red Light district from becoming forbidding or dangerous. There are even a couple of police stations right in the middle of that part of Amsterdam.

Of course, the relationships between the police and the Red Light district would be very different if prostitution were illegal here. But in the Netherlands, the only thing that's prohibited is profiting from the prostitution of another, like pimping. And even that is only selectively enforced. The sex clubs in Amsterdam that appeal to men with lots of money obviously profit from prostitution but they aren't the target of police action. Our attention in law enforcement is on the underside of the trade—drug prostitution, for example. The fact is that high-priced club prostitution takes place behind closed doors and therefore doesn't disturb the public. Since it's more or less invisible, it's not perceived as a law enforcement problem despite the fact that in many ways the clubs probably represent the ultimate in pimping.

But if prostitution takes place indoors and out of sight, it's usually not a problem. If an individual wants to hang up a red light in her window and work out of her home, she probably won't run into any trouble. But if more women in the same area start to do the same thing, neighbors might get nervous and the police might be asked to intervene. In general, though, and I emphasize in general, the relationship between the police and the prostitutes working in the Red Light district is pretty good. We even have a special person appointed to deal with complaints filed against police officers by members of the community. Believe me, those complaints are taken very seriously, including those filed by prostitutes. It's all part of a policy of increased sensitivity to sexual discrimination and sexual harassment.

Several years ago, I was asked to create a course at the police academy dealing with social issues like drug addiction, sexuality, and social minorities. Of those subjects, sexuality has been the most difficult to deal with in the classroom. Part of the problem is that my classes are about seventy percent men and thirty percent women. Sometimes the percentages are even lower; in one class I had just one girl. Sexuality makes everyone really uneasy, it hits so close to home. Some of the girls have experienced terrible things like rape and incest. And the guys try to cover any anxiety they have with nervous jokes and comments.

When we talk about prostitution, the conflicts are really clear. Most of the students will say, for example, that they think prostitution is dirty, but at least half of the male recruits have a poster of a naked woman in their room. Remember, I'm dealing with a very particular public here. People who pursue a career with the police have a certain sense of ethics. It's not only the adventure of the job and the unpredictability of the work that attracts them, it's also a commitment to right and wrong, and to power. The tendency to criticize and label things according to whether they are "good" or "bad" is intensified in police training. That's the basis of a profession where they are constantly asked to distinguish the good from the bad and to punish the bad. Added to that is the fact that they are often very young, say nineteen or twenty, and may come from small towns and protected backgrounds.

Their attitudes about sex can really affect how they do their job. After all, at some point they are going to get an order to pick up a bunch of street prostitutes who are working somewhere where they're not supposed to be working. Maybe some neighbors complained to the city and the police are called in to "clean up" the area. It's no more than a temporary solution because the prostitutes just move someplace else for awhile. But at least it gives the neighborhood the idea that their concerns are being heard.

In any case, a clean-up operation like that is the kind of work a lot of police officers really like to do. First of all, it isn't dangerous compared to responding to a robbery or something where you could get shot. Plus the girls are prostitutes, and that's something the guys always find exciting. It's my job to get them to look at that, to point out that yes, they are just doing their job, but that they are also enjoying it. The students categorically deny this, but I always bring in a few complaint reports filed by prostitutes and read them aloud. It's not only the men in the class who have conflicted ideas about prostitution. For several years now, I have been inviting women from the Red Thread [the Dutch prostitutes' rights organization] to speak to my classes about their experiences. The last time a prostitute visited the class, she came up to me afterwards and complained about the denigrating looks she received from one of the female students. I had noticed it, too. In fact, in general I think the women are often more critical than the men; I guess it's closer to them in some ways.

I have a lot of respect for the women who come speak to my class. It's no small thing to stand up there talking about your experiences as a prostitute in front of a roomful of people in uniform. They really have an impact, too. I've lived in Amsterdam my whole life, and prostitution has always been part of the landscape, but I've really learned a lot from the women who visit my class. I remember one of them saying, "Men have all the power in society but from the moment one of them becomes my client, I determine everything— the time, the price, and what will and will not happen. If he doesn't like it, he can just get out." She was pointing out that in a very intimate moment those women have power, but she was also saying that women still have a lot less power than men in general. The Red Thread has really changed my image of prostitution. I used to have a certain idea of what a prostitute looked like; you know, an attractive girl in a short skirt, teased-up hair, and lots of make up. The first time I walked into the Red Thread offices, I thought, "God, what nice girls." There are all kinds of prostitutes, everything from heroin whores to escort girls to women who occasionally turn a trick in their own homes to earn a little extra money.

When I was at the university, I remember being approached by a girl for something like that. It really threw me. There I was studying criminal law one night, preparing for an exam, and this girl says, "Fons, can I sleep with you tonight? It won't cost you much." I thought, "Oh, my god." I told her she could stay if she wanted but no thanks to the rest. I didn't like the idea at all. There's probably a lot of that kind of hidden prostitution; in fact, I wonder if you can even call that prostitution. I think of real prostitution as something you do to support yourself not just something you do occasionally to pick up an extra fl. 50 or fl. loo. On the other hand, there are so many different forms. Right now, we have lots of foreign prostitutes working in Amsterdam. Their relationship with the police isn't so good because most of them are here illegally.

For about a year, we've had a special working group within the police department—operating in conjunction with social workers—focusing on the problem of foreign prostitution. These women come to the Netherlands to work, but neither they nor their families know that they are really going to end up in prostitution. Then when they come in contact with the police, they're deported. It's a terrible thing that they've been deceived into coming here for a job that turns out not to exist and instead have to work in prostitution. Of course, the foreign police do have to deport them, but they also deserve extra protection.

▼

Chapter 6
Legalization, Regulation, and Licensing

Since the birth of the international prostitutes' rights movement in the 1970s, sex workers' rights advocates have consistently promoted strategies of decriminalization rather than legalization. While *decriminalization* entails only the removal of criminal penalties for sexual commerce, *legalization* implies state regulation of the trade. Sex workers' resistance to state policies of regulation reflects the fact that where such measures have been implemented, they have advanced the interests of clients and "innocent third parties" (such as neighbors), assisted in state surveillance of "deviant" populations, and ensured greater state control over sexual commerce. They have not, however, served to protect the rights and interests of sex workers themselves. In light of this, prostitutes are understandably suspicious of state intervention in the exercise and regulation of their profession.

Paradoxically, though, one problem for sex workers is precisely the unregulated status of the sex trade. A majority of prostitutes work not as true independents (whether in a criminalized or decriminalized context) but rather as pseudo-employees of brothels, parlors, clubs, houses, and escort agencies.[1] These workers rarely attain the status of employee because, with few exceptions, such businesses are formally prohibited throughout the world. Even where tolerance policies are in place, as they are in the Netherlands, prostitutes are not guaranteed workers' rights. This had led some advocates, such as the de Graaf Foundation, to conclude that "decriminalization is only the first step."[2] Decriminalization, they argue, must be followed by policies formally placing prostitution under standard employment laws and regulations: "Prostitutes work primarily in sex businesses, so the necessity remains to give them the same protection as other professionals, for example, welfare provisions, unemployment, and so forth."3 This process of "normalizing" relationships between employers and employees in sex businesses requires some form of regulation of the prostitution trade. Prostitutes' rights advocates, however, insist on the importance of distinguishing between policies intended to regulate prostitutes (which continue to be opposed) and those intended to regulate prostitution businesses (which receive tentative support).

This distinction between the regulation of prostitutes and the regulation of prostitution underlies many of the policy proposals advanced over the past twenty years by the international prostitutes' rights movement. The World Charter for Prostitutes' Rights, produced at the first World Whores Congress in Amsterdam in 1985, for example, demands both the *decriminalization* of prostitutes and the *regulation* of third parties according to standard business codes.4 In short, the Charter proposes regulating prostitution businesses not sex workers. Thus, policies aimed at controlling individual prostitutes such as registration or mandatory health examinations are rejected.

Regulation of Prostitutes

In countries where prostitution is either formally or informally decriminalized, authorities often attempt to maintain control over the sex trade through registration of prostitutes. But sex workers insist that registration can negatively affect their mobility, future employment options, and social status. Many countries, including the United States, include prostitution among a list of "moral turpitude" offenses which, when applied to aliens, allow for exclusion or deportation.5 In the final document of the second World Whores Congress in 1986, delegates addressed this problem noting that "police records [of prostitution] registered on computers at certain borders will prevent prostitutes from leaving or entering the country."6 Delegates further reported that "Prostitutes are denied job mobility by requirements for letters of good conduct which are granted only to those who can prove that they have not engaged in commercial sex for at least three years (for example, in Switzerland and Austria)."7 Thus, the final Congress document condemned registration arguing, "Forced or pressured registration with the police stigmatizes prostitutes and frequently violates their privacy and liberty to change professions if they so choose."[8]

Nonetheless, registration requirements continue to be a common form of state control over individual prostitutes. In Amsterdam, where such registration is still nominally optional, a special police team, the DCP (Decentrale Controle Prostitutie), was assembled in March of 1994 to encourage compliance. Police officer Ron Beekmeijer of the DCP explains: "The DCP is a response to the fact that vice couldn't keep up with it all … so good control over window prostitution and registration of prostitutes wasn't possible."[9] Beekmeijer defends registration in terms of its value to police, clients, and the sex workers themselves:

> [Once they're registered] it's easy if you ever want to contact them again, or need a follow up conversation. A lot of stuff happens in this area, and it's quite possible that someone will come to the station and tell us that, "I was at such and such a place seeing a prostitute and such and such happened," and he wants to know, "Who was she?" [WC: So if a client has a complaint against a prostitute, it's easier to track her down?] Well, also the other way around. It could just as easily happen that a prostitute has a complaint against a client. [WC: But what would the advantage be to her of being registered in that case?] Well, if she comes to the station, especially if she's a foreign prostitute—you know a lot of them are Spanish-speaking—who then tries to give us her particulars, she could be misunderstood, whereas if she is already registered, we'd already know all that information. And that's a big advantage so we know who she is.[10]

Perhaps sensing that this is a less than compelling argument, Beekmeijer adds that an additional advantage might be in rounding up colleagues as witnesses if anything happened to a registered sex worker:

> Things sometimes happen including the abuse of prostitutes. Then we can proceed more easily with an investigation—who worked in the area and did anyone see anything. That's a huge advantage to registration for the prostitutes themselves.[11]

The Dutch prostitutes' organization, the Red Thread, challenges the assertion that registration offers any advantage to sex workers: "[Despite police claims that] compulsory registration enhances the safety of prostitutes ... there is no evidence whatsoever that perpetrators of acts of violence have been more frequently tracked down or that there has been less violence."[12] Indeed, despite Beekmeijer's claims of "huge advantages" to prostitutes, the problems with registration seem to well outweigh the benefits. The Red Thread notes that "there will always be prostitutes who find it impossible to register, including those who are underage and those who stay here illegally, but also including those who want to work as a prostitute for a limited time and do not want to be known as such."[13]

While the Amsterdam DCP currently has an informal policy of not sharing information gathered during registration with other official agencies, there is no guarantee that such sharing of resources will not happen in the future. This is, as the Red Thread notes, a serious problem for foreign sex workers, many of whom are not in possession of legal residency or work permits.[14] Beekmeijer's reassurances do not go very far to alleviate those concerns:

> With the foreign girls, we do control whether they're working illegally, only we won't haul them away if they are.... That information doesn't go to the foreign police, we don't provide them a list of names to help them do a sweep. Because the idea of a registration system is a relationship of trust ...

He also explains:

> we don't at this time give any information to the tax authorities either, because I bet a whole lot of them don't pay taxes or report their income and if you suddenly give that information to the tax authorities, you might as well not go back to the streets the next day. You'd lose the trust.[15]

While the police may not "at this time" share potentially damaging information with their colleagues, there is no guarantee of confidentiality without formal protections. The Red Thread notes that they "have never yet received a written guarantee that information recorded by vice squads will not be passed on to third persons. We know of cases where data has been handed to an employer, to the social security office, or to the tax-collector's office."[16] The absence of privacy provisions in registration requirements makes it a policy that is perceived by sex workers to pose more risks than advantages.

While registration is generally understood by prostitutes' rights advocates to be a tool of state surveillance with little or no benefit to sex workers, "licensing" of individual prostitutes is embraced by some as an alternative to assist in "professionalization" and destigmatization of those in the trade. Feminist philosopher Laurie Shrage, for instance, proposes "a system where prostitutes would not be 'registered' ... but where prostitutes themselves would be licensed, much like other professionals and semi-professionals."[17] Shrage suggests that licensing would thus establish "sex providers" with credentials as skilled professionals equipped with special training. A commission, composed of "service providers, community leaders, educators, and legal and public health experts" would determine the requirements for obtaining a license:

> The standards these commissions impose [for licensing] should reflect the kinds of knowledge and skill required for the sex provider's work, and required to protect the society from any harm ensuing from her work. For example, candidates for this license could be expected to complete some number of college-level courses on human sexuality from the perspective of biology, psychology, history, medicine, and so on.[18]

There are a number of problems with Shrage's proposal to license sex workers. Despite her concern that "license boards must make sure that the personal and material costs of obtaining a license do not outweigh the risks of operating without it ... [and therefore ensure that] any required courses and tools must be available and affordable," the suggestion that "college-level courses" be required for licensing would eliminate many who are currently employed in the trade.[19] Prostitution is a survival option for many women with limited educational and economic resources. Requiring formal training at the college level would exclude these women and thereby create a two-tier system of prostitution dividing those who are licensed (and thus legal) from those who are not. Furthermore, licensing shares with registration the problem of public identification as a sex worker.

As the Red Thread notes, "As long as women and men are at a disadvantage if they admit working as prostitutes, it is only reasonable
that they should wish to remain anonymous."[20]

Regulation of Prostitution Businesses

Attempts to regulate prostitution through surveillance and control
of individual sex workers are clearly flawed. This does not mean,
however, that an absence of all regulatory mechanisms in the commercial sex trade necessarily benefits prostitutes. As the Dutch model
of informal decriminalization demonstrates, the party most seriously
disadvantaged by an absence of formal regulation of third-party prostitution is typically the sex worker herself. It is for this reason that
prostitutes' rights advocates often support regulatory measures
directed at businesses, intended to enforce fair and safe working conditions in organized prostitution.

Here, too, though, prostitutes have reason to be suspicious.
Existing regulatory schemes such as zoning and licensing of prostitution businesses traditionally have been implemented without attention to workers' interests, while protecting the interests of clients,
owners, and local municipalities. Zoning, for example, which involves
restrictions on the sale of sexual services to specified geographic areas
is often embraced by authorities as a tool to ensure police surveillance
of the sex trade and thereby to facilitate the control of "public nuisance" problems associated with unregulated prostitution. In places
where prostitution is fully criminalized, such as San Francisco, a sort
of reverse zoning has been proposed to combat street prostitution.
Once arrested, a prostitute would be "mapped" out of an area in
which she had been initially detained and prohibited from returning.
Thus, as a condition of plea bargaining or in exchange for a reduced
sentence, "prostitutes would be pressured to agree to stay out of certain bars or neighborhoods."[21]

Both mapping and zoning are policies intended to address neighborhood concerns rather than to enhance the safety or well-being of
those working the streets. Not surprisingly, sex workers have strenu-
ously resisted such policies. One German sex worker, for example,

denounced zoning as practiced in that country as a policy that only increases risks for working women:

> In Germany right now a certain percentage of each town is set aside where prostitutes can work, and the percentage depends on the size of the town. In Frankfurt it is eleven percent. But they gave us spots at the East Harbor and at the West Harbor. In those places there are no lights, no telephone booths, no houses, no shelter if it's raining or snowing. They are dumping places, next to water. It's too dangerous for a woman to work there. She can be killed and dumped and no one would ever find her. So they've given us spots where we're *allowed* to work, but where we *can't* work.[22]

Most major Dutch cities now, too, are moving toward the development of regulated zones for street prostitution. As in Germany, these zones are intentionally set away from densely inhabited areas. But in response to concerns raised by prostitutes' rights advocates, Dutch authorities are investing in the development of facilities for street prostitutes in these designated zones. In 1994, the city of Nijmegen, for example, committed about $75,000 toward improvements in a regulated street-prostitution zone including landscaping and creating dividers for work spaces.[23] Similarly, Amsterdam, which long had resisted any form of street prostitution, finally created a legal tolerance zone in the harbor area (de Oostelijke Handelskade) of that city in 1995. This somewhat isolated area, surrounded by wharfs, railroad lines, and storage depots, was made more attractive to street workers by creating an on-site service and relief center. In addition, four police agents have been assigned specifically to patrol the area to better ensure the safety of both prostitutes and neighborhood residents.

At the same time as government authorities appear to be making some limited movement toward addressing sex workers' concerns about zoning, prostitutes' rights advocates too appear to be softening in their once absolute opposition to the practice. While in 1985, the World Charter for Prostitutes' Rights rejected zoning as unacceptable ("There should be no law which implies systematic zoning of prostitution. Prostitutes should have the freedom to choose their place of work."[24]), a decade later, proposals are being circulated to revise the charter in order to allow for the practice *if* zoning policies are developed in collaboration with prostitutes and reflect their interests. The U.S. National Task Force on Prostitution and the Prostitutes of New York collective, for example, have proposed the following revised language to the charter:

> Any proposals to use zoning laws and ordinances to regulate the location of sex work and/or sex work businesses must be consistent with zoning laws governing other businesses, and should only be enacted with the full participation of sex workers and clients.[25]

LICENSED BROTHELS: THE CASE OF NEVADA

The absence of a sex worker perspective in the implementation of regulatory policies is particularly striking in the only legalized brothel system in the United States in the state of Nevada. In 1971, the state legislature voted to legalize regulated prostitution within licensed brothels.[26] Only smaller counties (with populations below 200,000) were allowed to license commercial sex facilities. Because Nevada's major cities (including Reno, Lake Tahoe, and Las Vegas) are located in densely populated counties, they remain ineligible for licensed prostitution. The apparent objective was to separate "sin industries" by concentrating gambling in the large cities, and allowing rural counties to profit from a regulated sex trade. One Nevada observer notes "You can't be so vulgar that you offend middle-class America, which fills your hotels. It [legal prostitution] must not become so open, so raw, that it hurts the real business, which is gambling."[27]

Policies intended to restrict the sex business to smaller counties have not eliminated prostitution in the large tourist centers. The result is that illegal prostitutes continue to far outnumber those working legally in the state's licensed brothels.[28] Thus, while Nevada has legalized some forms of prostitution, it continues to criminalize most of its practitioners. Indeed, because the state has given brothel owners an outright monopoly on legalized sexual commerce, all independent prostitution is a criminal offense. The effect is that no woman can work legally without agreeing to share her income with a state-licensed "pimp." One former brothel worker, Laura

Anderson, argues that the system results in mandatory exploitation:
> Prostitutes are giving up too much autonomy, control, and choice over their work and lives. Because prostitutes are not allowed to work independently, or outside the brothel system, Nevada has essentially institutionalized third-party management with no other options.[29]

Under the Nevada system, prostitutes employed by one of the states' thirty-two licensed brothels do not even enjoy the status and rights of a worker; instead they are defined as "independent contractors" with no claim to health benefits, vacation pay, or retirement benefits. Brothel prostitutes are required to register with police and, once hired, they are required to live on the premises while working.[30] Confinement to the brothel serves two ends: first, it reassures local residents concerned about the impact of the presence of prostitutes on their community by ensuring little or no contact with the women working in the trade; and, second, it facilitates surveillance of an ever-available workforce.

A standard shift in a Nevada brothel runs twelve to fourteen hours a day, seven days a week, for a twenty-one day stretch. One worker, "Lindsay," describes her work day: "My shift is from 3 p.m. to 3 a.m. I get up at 1 p.m. I get to sleep late, have two hours to bathe, shower, and get on the floor. Sundays through Thursdays, I work fourteen hours."[31] Her motivation, she says, is "solely financial." While women do manage to earn substantial incomes working long shifts in the Nevada brothels, fifty percent of every transaction goes to brothel management. Minimum fees for sexual services are between $20 and $30 dollars in Northern Nevada;[32] workers' incomes are often further reduced through brothel fees for room, board, and supplies (including condoms), as well as through mandatory tipping to house employees.[33] One of the most serious indications of workers' lack of independence is the fact that if a prostitute decides to refuse a customer, "Management must be provided with what it deems an acceptable reason."[34]

The only clear benefit of the brothel system to those "employed" within it may be its legalized status. Other parties, including owners, clients, and local municipalities, enjoy far more substantial advantages from the legal monopoly held by licensed third parties on the sale of women's sexual services. Counties in which the licensed brothels are located, for example, have experienced remarkable financial benefits from the trade. The Chicken Ranch brothel, located just across the county line from Las Vegas, contributes both substantial taxes to the county in which it is located as well as thousands of dollars a year in "charitable contributions" toward such municipal services as parks and recreation, the fire department, and senior citizen's programs.[35] In another municipality, the money made from licensing brothels generates the county's entire operating fund, while in a third, brothel licensing fees support the county hospital.[36]

The president of the Nevada Brothel Association argues that brothels not only make good neighbors but good sense, offering the only real protection available against the dangers of unregulated sex: "Do we want [prostitution] with no protection, no organization, no medical attention? Or do we want to turn the coin and have it legal, controlled for safe sex, and minimized for risks?"[37] This is protection and control from the perspective of the community, the owner, and the client but, once again, not from that of the worker.

▼ ▼ ▼

Trojan Whores:
Regulation and Self-Organization in the AIDS Epidemic

> At the 1991 annual conference of the National Organization
> of Women in New York, an American medical doctor asks me
> about "the safety of prostitution in the Netherlands." I start to
> tell him about some of the benefits of decriminalization: police
> become a potential resource rather than a risk for the women,
> women are increasingly freed of the need for a pimp.... He
> interrupts me: "No, no, I mean are there regular and manda-
> tory medical controls for STDs?" This is "safety" as seen from
> the perspective of a (potential) client.

Prostitution historically has been linked to the contamination of "public health" by sexually transmitted diseases. Policies developed to respond to this perceived threat have entailed opposing efforts to regulate prostitutes (through mandatory health testing) or to abolish prostitution (through prohibition). In the late nineteenth century, policy makers concerned with the spread of syphilis succeeded in passing legislation in many countries requiring the licensing and mandatory testing of prostitutes.[38] Their efforts were presented as a pragmatic attempt to protect the public health in the face of the enduring social problem of prostitution. Through the choice of mandatory testing of prostitutes but not clients, the policy implicitly excluded sex workers from the "public" whose health was to be protected.

British and American social purity feminists of the time observed that this policy relegated an entire class of women to the status of expendable resource. Instead of institutionalization of prostitution through regulation, they advocated the abolition of prostitution through prohibition. Within a few years of the passage of the regula-tory measures, abolitionist activists had succeeded in forcing the repeal of such policies in Britain and the United States.[39] Prohibition quickly replaced regulation.

As with late nineteenth and early twentieth century policies designed to curtail the spread of syphilis, current responses to the AIDS epidemic have focused on the presumed role of the prostitute as infectious agent. Little attention has been paid to the fact that before sex workers can transmit disease, they must first themselves have been infected. The lack of interest in the "contamination" *of* prostitutes—rather than *by* them—exposes the belief that prostitutes (like homosexuals) are always already "sick"; their eventual literal infection by a sexually transmitted disease does not represent a significant change of status. The message appears to be that for the "whore" who has abandoned proper womanhood through participation in money-driven promiscuity, just as for the "pervert" who has relinquished his manhood through homosexuality, disease and death are the natural, the expected, and the sanctioned punishment.

One particularly explicit statement of this belief was made in 1988 by a Texas judge. In ruling on a murder case, the judge said he "gave an 18-year-old murderer a more lenient sentence than prosecutors had sought because the two victims were homosexual.... 'I'd put prostitutes and gays at about the same level,' he said, 'and I'd be hard put to give somebody life for killing a prostitute.'"[40] The assumption is not only that such groups "deserve what they get," but that they have somehow themselves created the conditions for their abuse. Their very presence in the world poses a threat to which others simply respond.[41] HIV infection only makes the threat more literal. As AIDS educator Priscilla Alexander notes:

> The issue of "Blame the Prostitute" is the same all over the world.... The studies out of Africa are very misleading. In one study in Zaire, eighty-eight percent of prostitutes were positive on the AIDS antibody test and only twenty-eight percent of customers. In Kenya, fifty-four percent of prostitutes and nine percent of customers were positive. Everybody says this is proof that prostitutes are transmitting the disease and I say that this is proof that the customers are giving the disease to the prostitutes.[42]

Because prostitutes are understood to be a *source* of the epidemic, policies designed to curtail AIDS emphasize identifying and isolating commercial carriers of the virus. In such diverse countries as Austria, the Philippines, South Korea, Sweden, Thailand, and the United States, sex workers are routinely tested for HIV either as a condition of legal registration or, in those countries where their work is still criminalized, in connection with being arrested.[43] Despite the ineffectiveness of testing one part of the sexually active population while excluding their partners (workers but not clients) such strategies are seized upon by health officials as a high-profile intervention involving less political risk than explicit safe sex education and condom distribution. In Bombay, India, for example, when seventy percent of arrested prostitutes tested positive for HIV, the official response was a call for general and mandatory testing of all sex workers.[44] No comparable widespread outreach campaign was instituted to educate clients, leaving a new generation of sex workers at risk of infection. In a separate study of truck drivers in India, ninety-four percent reported that they visited sex workers regularly and eighty-four percent revealed that they had had a history of sexually transmitted disease. Still, over three-quarters had never used a condom. A majority of the men studied admitted a lack of knowledge about proper use of prophylactics and reported significant problems with the availability of condoms.[45] In this context, a policy of mandatory testing and licensing of sex workers simply sentences wave after wave of women to eventual HIV infection.

Mandatory testing policies actually can undercut sex workers' attempts at condom compliance by providing "supposed security for clients ... [making them] even less willing to use condoms because they assume the women are 'clean.'"[46] This poses a particularly serious risk to the health of sex workers, as HIV appears to be far more readily transmittable from an (infected) male to a female than vice versa.[47] Thus, where mandatory testing undermines sex workers' ability to demand condom use, it is the *women's* health that is most jeopardized. The message of mandatory testing is as clear as the strategy is faulty: clients' health is to be protected, while prostitutes' health is expendable.

PROSTITUTES RESPOND TO THE AIDS EPIDEMIC

Attempts to prevent the spread of sexually transmitted diseases to the "general public" traditionally have relied heavily on either regulation of the prostitute's body through mandatory testing or on strategies of prohibition and punishment intended to abolish the commercial sexual transaction entirely. In the contemporary period, however, there is a third and historically unique alternative response: peer education and outreach. The objective of self-organizing among prostitutes is to create conditions of greater sexual safety for themselves as well as their clients. Such sex-worker generated risk-reduction efforts consistently emphasize the need for enhanced worker authority in relationship to both clients and the state. Prostitutes' self-advocacy organizations point out that worker control over safer sex can be taken away by such things as coercive social conditions, illegal status, drug addiction, client resistance, or employer policies that do not allow women to exercise discretion in choosing (or refusing) clients, or engaging in (or refusing) specific sexual practices.

In a competitive market such as the sex trade, fear of client loss to colleagues who do not demand condom use is understandable. Successful AIDS outreach programs to sex workers have taken such concerns seriously. An AIDS prevention project in Calabar, Nigeria, reported that prostitutes initially "expressed serious concerns about potential loss of income if they rejected clients who refused to use a condom. As it was, they were earning relatively little money...."[48] But as the women organized, with help of peer educators, they found a way to protect both their income and their health:

> After some discussion, they decided, as a group, to raise their prices in order to make up for lost business, raising them again some months later. The project staff was able to convince the owners of the bars and hotels not to raise the room charges commensurately, thereby enabling the women to realize a greater share of the income from their work.[49]

In more affluent regions of the world, those sex workers who are most socially marginal—poor, minority, and illegal workers, drug prostitutes, and older women—may face similar pressures to practice unsafe sex. At a disadvantage in the competition for clients and facing greater threats to their daily survival, they may feel less able to demand compliance.

At the second International Whores Congress in 1986, one Swiss sex worker observed: "As a fifty-seven-year-old prostitute, and therefore a bit older than many of you, I cannot use condoms.... I could not make any money at all. So I very rarely use condoms."[50] When survival is threatened, problems of health and other more long-term concerns may be forced to the background and tip the scales toward unsafe sex. In New York City, for example:

> Many street sex workers in the South Bronx stroll to support a drug habit. To say that they are at risk for HIV may be correct. However, they have other, more immediately threatening occupational risks, from both the visible and unprotected nature of their employment and from poorly managed IV drug use in a city where there is minimal access to new needles.... With the constant threat of arrest, no housing and little income, AIDS just isn't the biggest problem on the block.[51]

As the situation in the South Bronx reveals, even in those parts of the world where condom use in sex work is common among sex workers, some prostitutes find it difficult to demand protection against HIV infection. Often this is the result of direct pressure by clients and employers. In Germany, for instance, client and brothel-owner resistance to condoms meant that, as late as 1986, condom use in that country's sex trade was reported to be the exception rather than the rule. At the second World Whores Congress, German sex workers complained:

> "Perhaps we stand alone here but there is hardly any work done with condoms in Germany. If you work with a condom in Germany you will make very little money in any part of the sex industry." Another speaker at the conference noted, "In sex clubs in Germany, you are not even *allowed* to work with condoms."[52]

As Hansje Verbeek of the Dutch Red Thread notes, "any prostitute will preferably work with a condom, but isn't [always] in a position to make her own decisions.... An adequate policy for fighting AIDS should therefore focus on customers and employers in the first place."[53]

There is evidence that such a comprehensive strategy targeting all parties in commercial sex is effective. Two years after the Whores Congress in which Priscilla Alexander discussed the alarming rates of HIV infection in Africa, a Kenyan researcher, Elizabeth Ngugi, reported that AIDS education campaigns were having a dramatic impact. While occasional condom use among prostitutes in one area of Nairobi had been only eight percent in January 1985, she reported

that less than a year later such occasional use had risen to ninety percent, and overall use had reached fifty percent.[54] Sex workers were
clearly eager to reduce their risk of infection if condoms could be
made available and client resistance could be tackled through educational campaigns.

The Kenyan campaign offers a useful contrast to official American
responses to prostitution in the age of AIDS. Throughout the 1980s
and early 1990s, American public health officials addressed the HIV
epidemic primarily by emphasizing abstinence outside of marriage
and monogamy within it, including explicit messages discouraging
participation in commercial sex. One pamphlet produced by the U.S.
Department of State, Office of Medical Services, for example, advised:
"Avoiding exposure to the virus is the best preventive measure ... Do
not have sex with multiple partners, or with persons who have had
multiple partners (e.g., prostitutes)."[55] In fact, however, the *number*
of sexual partners is relatively unimportant in the transmission of
HIV disease; far more significant is the *kind* of sex practiced, with
those activities involving the exchange of blood and semen (potentially containing the HIV virus) being the most dangerous.

Many of the most commonly engaged in commercial sexual practices do not involve high risk activity. Visual and verbal fantasy sex
(erotic dancing, peep shows, phone sex), designed for clients' mas-
turbatory pleasure, do not transmit disease. Even many acts involving
physical contact are not efficient in transmitting HIV: much of the
sex negotiated on the street, for instance, involves only hand and
blow jobs.[56] In the indoor sex trade, too, such safer sexual activities
as massage, hand release, pearl necklace, and fantasy stimulation are
common.[57] Furthermore, for higher-risk penetrative sex, condom
usage is routine in many sectors of the American commercial sex
trade. This combination of high rates of condom use and safer sexual
practices in the commercial sex trade have resulted in a low inci-
dence of HIV infection among women in prostitution in such
places as the United States, Western Europe, Australia, and
New Zealand.[58]

In fact, some sex worker rights organizations, such as the Dutch
Red Thread, argue that stigmatization, not disease, is the most critical

problem facing sex workers in the context of the HIV epidemic. The organization is committed to disrupting the image of prostitutes as "disease carriers" and resists the notion that HIV presents a particular problem for prostitutes as such. Hansje Verbeek of the Red Thread argues that "there is no need for special information for prostitutes, they do not need different information than other women."[59] "Special information" intended for prostitutes, she argues, really needs to get into the hands of all women regardless of their professional identities:

> All sorts of sexual techniques are described in brochures for prostitutes that are not mentioned in more general brochures as if these techniques do not occur in unpaid sex ... by considering prostitutes as an exception, they will be stigmatized. [60]

Similarly, Gloria Lockett, director of the California Prostitutes' Education Project, Cal-PEP, suggests:

> Career prostitutes know that they have to use condoms all the time, they know how to use their hand, they know how to use their mouth, instead of their vagina. They know all these tricks to make the guys think that they're not using condoms when they really are.... I mean the career prostitutes don't need us to tell them much. In fact, they can teach all of us a lot. Serious.[61]

Emphasizing the safe sex skills of professionals is a necessary corrective to the image of sex workers as "pools of contagion" and "reservoirs of infection."[62] Such a strategy, however, carries certain dangers; foremost among these is the risk that HIV-positive sex workers may become further marginalized in their professional communities. On a global scale, the danger exists that, in an attempt to uncouple AIDS and prostitution, areas with low HIV rates among prostitutes (such as the United States, Western Europe, Australia, and New Zealand) may be held up as the norm, while those with high infection rates (such as many African countries, Brazil, and Thailand) might be dismissed as unfortunate exceptions. One HIV-positive sex worker in New York warns:

> It's a mistake for the hookers' movement to play down the number of HIV-positive prostitutes, as if our lives

don't count.... I was infected, it seems, years ago, before
any of us knew how to prevent it.... I don't blame sex—
and money is free of AIDS.... I'm lucky to be a gay male,
for the gay movement has jelled around the issue of
AIDS.... But what do women pros have when the hookers' movement often denies that pros with AIDS are part
of our community? It's time to change that.[63]

Even sex workers who routinely make use of condoms during professional sex face some risk of HIV infection. This reality should not
be masked in the interest of uncoupling prostitution from the stigma
of disease. While latex barriers are extremely effective in reducing
sexually transmitted disease, condoms can, and infrequently do,
break. Such accidents are especially common among those new to the
trade and as yet unskilled in minimizing the danger through the use
of adequate lubrication to reduce the amount of friction.[64] One sex
worker who had a condom break during her first day behind the windows in Amsterdam described it as an unavoidable occupational risk:

That's the risk of this kind of work. It happens to every
prostitute sometime, I bet.... I noticed that the other
women all have ways to convince themselves that the
risks aren't really so high. Right after it happened ... [my
colleagues] started telling me "oh you don't have to
worry about that [AIDS]. That's not such a problem
here. You're not working on the streets or something."
Like if you work the streets you get AIDS but if you work
behind the window you don't. Right.[65]

Condoms used properly do substantially reduce health risks, though
they cannot eliminate them. In addition, they provide an enhanced
sense of emotional and professional distance. In her study of parlor
workers in New Zealand, for example, Karen Austen Woods found
that all of the workers endeavored to maintain a level of emotional distance through the use of condoms. One sex worker noted: "It's a job
and as far as I'm concerned when you use a condom, it's like a shield—
it distances you from the client ... it's a barrier against intimacy."[66]

This occupationally useful association of latex with a lack of intimacy, however, may present a danger off the job by discouraging condom use with intentionally intimate partners: "If I had to have sex

with [my partner] with a condom now ... I'd think of him as a client ... It just wouldn't be as good with a condom because I use condoms at work."[67] Sex without a latex barrier thus serves to distinguish between more and less significant sex: "There's a big difference between ... fucking someone and making love to someone. A real big difference. When you're fucking someone you use a condom. When you make love to someone you don't."[68] The result for sex workers is that prostitutes tend to contract venereal diseases more often in their private contacts than their work.[69] The disinclination to use condoms in the context of intentionally intimate sex is by no means unique to prostitutes. As one sex worker expressed it: "Well, it's just like any relationship, most people that are in relationships don't need condoms."[70] Or at least they think that they don't. AIDS is fast becoming one of the leading causes of death among young hetero-sexual women in the two countries with highest numbers of HIV cases, Brazil and the United States.[71]

But for women in the sex trades, the ability to demand safer sex with intimate partners may be further complicated by the social stigmatization of their sexual knowledge and expertise. One sex worker in Woods' study, for example, was only able to insist on con-dom use by acting "innocent":

> I don't like him knowing that I'm a working lady, so I make out that I'm dumb and don't know anything. I give it [the condom] to him to put it on. I don't want to put it on myself because for sure he's going to know, you know ... "she's real good at this ... "[72]

For some women, the fear of disclosure outweighs their concern over the risk of infection: "I thought I'd better keep quiet ... if I mention condoms, he'll think I'm dirty."[73]

Being found dirty or whorish by men is a serious threat. One sex worker in New Zealand described her (now ex-) husband's response to her request they use condoms:

> No way Jose. Arsehole. There was no use trying to per-suade him. As soon as you mentioned it, he'd get up in arms and belt me. Not only me, too, the kids as well ... it was more risk than not using them.[74]

In a study in the United States, many women seeking refuge in a battered women's shelter reported that regardless of whether they had ever engaged in commercial sex, their husbands or boyfriends frequently referred to them as "whores" as a part of, and justification for, their violence.[75] Priscilla Alexander, advisor to the World Health Organization on prostitution and AIDS, warns,

> Until a woman who suggests using a condom is not distrusted as a "whore," and a "whore" is not considered expendable, how can we hope to stop HIV and other STDs? ... The destigmatization of prostitutes, and those on the margins of sex work, is essential.[76]

Socially and legally sanctioned hostility toward prostitutes and whorish women makes the idea of "safe sex" something of a bitter joke. For women, safer sex campaigns will remain fatally inadequate unless they challenge the very unsafe conditions of women's lives. Karen Austen Woods concludes:

> Overcoming barriers to condom use requires more than just simply changing the existing laws which disadvantage women and/or stigmatize sex industry workers. It requires a fundamental change to the way existing social relations between men and women are organized: it entails challenging a system that fails to prevent repeated domestic violence against women and support their right to say no to sex, and which divides women into categories of "good" and "bad" depending on what they do for a living.[77]

STRATEGIC USE OF STIGMA

Paradoxically, the stigmatization of prostitutes in the AIDS epidemic has provided a possible legitimation strategy for some sex workers. In countries where civil and employment rights for sex workers attract little popular or state support, efforts to involve prostitutes in the protection of the "general population" against sexually transmitted diseases have often been enthusiastically promoted. In such a context, sex workers may accept the identity of disease carrier in order to gain a place at the policy table and to secure funding for their own outreach programs. In 1989, the San Francisco Chronicle reported that in the midst of the AIDS crisis, prostitution has experienced

> a remarkable turn-around, a group that has been traditionally shunned and stigmatized is now being enthusiastically embraced.... Even the government is getting into the act, with state agencies offering money.[78]

Prostitute-controlled organizations, however, tend to understand their mandate in much broader terms than the agencies funding them. In Thailand, for example, the prostitutes' organization EMPOWER has responded to the AIDS threat with strategies going well beyond narrowly defined safe sex education and the distribution of condoms. EMPOWER runs English-language classes to help workers better negotiate with clients, offers counseling services, runs workshops on women's rights and even provides professional information to women considering migrating to other countries about working conditions, laws, and support organizations for migrant prostitutes.[79]

Similarly, in Australia, prostitutes' rights activists made conscious use of government concerns about HIV to further their goal of organizing sex workers in New South Wales:

> [With] the government saying things like "Oh, these prostitutes have got AIDS and are now passing it on to the nice heterosexual community," we said, "Well, give us a million dollars and we'll stop it." They did not quite give us a million dollars but they gave us 120,000 dollars which is not a bad effort. What it enabled us to do, next to our basic lobbying for removing further laws on prostitution, is to reach every single parlor, or brothel if you like, in the metropolitan area of Sydney and in some major country areas of New South Wales.... [The managers of the parlors] aren't too sure if we aren't an arm of the government now that we've got money from the government so they are a bit unsure of us. We use all these sorts of things to get them on our side and it is working very well.[80]

Having gained access to the parlors, the prostitutes' rights organization, PROS, provided women workers with condoms, information about STDs, the law, and taxation. The AIDS epidemic was used also as an opportunity to push for greater decriminalization of the Australian sex trade; the AIDS Council of New South Wales called "on the police department to abandon the crackdown on brothels in the interests of controlling the AIDS epidemic in New South Wales."[81]

In Western Europe, TAMPEP, the Transnational AIDS/STD Prevention Project, received European Community funding in 1993 to do outreach work in three countries (the Netherlands, Italy, and Germany) specifically targeting migrant women sex workers from Latin America, Africa, South East Asia, and Eastern Europe. While TAMPEP organizers express genuine concern about migrant prostitutes' elevated risk of HIV infection, they also acknowledge that the epidemic has been useful in focusing attention and resources on an otherwise neglected population. TAMPEP coordinator Licia Brussa observes:

> We are an STD and AIDS prevention project, so in the first instance, a health outreach organization. But of course we are involved in helping the women sort out all kinds of work related problems.... Before the AIDS epidemic, getting subsidies to work with migrant prostitutes would have been unlikely. National governments had little interest in anything except deporting them if they could as illegals, and certainly not in improving their social conditions.[82]

TAMPEP has benefitted from the fact that even prior to the AIDS crisis, local prostitutes in the participating countries of Italy, Germany, and the Netherlands had already secured a measure of social and political legitimacy. The language of TAMPEP's outreach materials reflects this understanding of prostitution as employment and dangerous working conditions, not sex work itself, as the key problem:

> The goal of the project is to increase the effectiveness of AIDS and STD prevention among migrant prostitutes and to improve their professional skills in such areas as negotiation with clients.... TAMPEP is not intended to motivate prostitutes to stop working. The project respects the choices they are making. Prevention work in the area of STDs and AIDS aims at increased knowledge of the best means of working in prostitution safely and in good health.[83]

While foreign prostitutes in the Netherlands may secure some benefit from increased concerns about the role of prostitution in the AIDS epidemic, Dutch prostitutes who have already secured a measure of social legitimacy are not as eager to make strategic use of stigma. Initial efforts by the Red Thread to destigmatize prostitution occurred prior to concerns about HIV. Already in 1984, the organization received state funding to assist in promoting prostitutes' rights and in legitimating commercial sexual labor as "work." In the context of the AIDS epidemic, then, the Red Thread has repeatedly emphasized that their focus is on protecting sex workers from ill-advised state policies and new regulations rather than attempting to get them out of the trade or into latex. The Red Thread, however, does admit that sex-worker specific AIDS outreach can be coopted for broader purposes:

> A female fieldworker who is trusted by the prostitutes can inform them not only about AIDS and other STDs, but also about other things that are relevant such as working methods. She can urge the women to organize themselves, inform them about their rights and give them support.[84]

Such efforts to improve working conditions and to teach sex workers professional skills run counter to the popularly held idea that the ultimate goal of any prostitute outreach program should be short-term rescue work and long-term abolition. In the United States, where abolition sentiments are strong, AIDS outreach programs to prostitutes often cater to that bias in public descriptions of their work. For example, in an article on AIDS peer education programs for California prostitutes, the San Francisco Chronicle reports:

> Reformed Bay Area prostitutes, worried about problems such as AIDS and frustrated by a lack of public concern, are launching a unique volunteer campaign that includes sending ex-hookers back into red light districts to coax women out of the sex trade.[85]

One of the organizations discussed is the California Prostitutes' Education Project, Cal-PEP, which the article describes as "gently offering advice to sex workers who want to leave the industry." This characterization of Cal-PEP is challenged by Director Gloria Lockett who suggests, "It's their option if they want to stay on the streets," but, mindful of her audience, she hastens to add, "but we want sex workers to know that there is a way out and we can help them."[86] In other contexts, Lockett has vigorously defended prostitution as legitimate work,[87] but acknowledges the need to publicly describe the organization as a "way out" rather than a safe way to stay in:

> We have had some funders who have said things like....
> "We're real leery of giving anything to a group of people that has the word 'prostitution' in their name." That's one of the reasons why we've got a couple of different names now. For one grant, we wrote it under the name "California *Prevention* Education Project" because when some people heard the word "prostitution" they just backed off.[88]

Like so many other prostitute-controlled outreach programs, Cal-PEP has made use of concerns about AIDS in order to focus attention and resources on the problems of marginal populations such as African American prostitutes, drug addicts, and street people. Gloria Lockett explains:

> We've become this outreach program with a reputation of going in places other people may call risky, and dealing with all kinds of people that are on the streets.... For years its always been the white people coming in researching us, instead of us researching each other.... There's a tremendous feeling about being able to help my people not only by helping them from AIDS and STDs, but also by educating them to be researchers.[89]

Still, for sex workers, "legitimation through disaster"[90] in the context of the AIDS epidemic offers only a provisional and fragile legitimacy.[91] Gloria Lockett wearily notes:

> The fact is, we are ex-prostitutes.... Somebody made a statement not too long ago calling us "Cal-WHORES" instead of Cal-PEP. It gives me headaches to make sure that I do things right all the time because of my background. I know people are watching me. I know people want us to mess up ... either for being Black or for being a prostitute or for being a woman, or for all three of those.[92]

Lockett's concern is not exaggerated; just a few months after making that statement, Cal-PEP was the subject of a front-page *San Francisco Examiner* story discrediting the organization because of the directors' "sordid pasts." In the article, "Ex-felon directs safe sex project; group aimed at prostitutes involves taxpayers' dollars,"[93] Lockett once again found herself in the position of defending the legitimacy of "former prostitutes" being funded to do even peer outreach: "We come from that life. We make no apologies ... That's one of the reasons why Cal-PEP works." The value of peer education in the context of the AIDS epidemic was not adequate to satisfy critics. The paper reported that an official of Alameda County which "provides taxpayer monies to Cal-PEP vowed an investigation saying he was never advised of the past associations of Cal-PEP officials. 'Even taking into account the forgiveness of people who have been on the street ... this would raise eyebrows.'"[94] Cal-PEP's discrediting experience suggests that in the absence of widespread and effective campaigns to decriminalize and destigmatize professional sex, the subversive use of the identity of "disease carrier" offers only very tenuous legitimacy to sex workers and their representatives.

▼

Chapter 7
Sex Worker
Self-Advocacy

Marlene Willoughby   © Annie Sprinkle

The first autonomous prostitutes' self-advocacy organization, COYOTE, was founded in 1973 by an American former sex worker, Margo St. James. During the following decade, as similar groups formed in many other countries, sex workers began organizing internationally.[1] By the mid-1980s, two World Whores' Congresses had taken place in Europe (one in Amsterdam and one at the European Parliament in Brussels) under the auspices of the International Committee for Prostitutes' Rights (ICPR). Organizers explicitly prioritized strategies of self-representation: "The first priority of the International Committee for Prostitutes' Rights is giving voice to whores."[2]

The "Real Whore" and the Authority to Speak

Self-advocacy efforts by sex workers have been complicated by challenges common to all forms of organizing rooted in identity politics. Most significantly, attempts at self-representation have exposed conflicts over who has the authority to speak for and about the prostitute. Margo St. James of COYOTE, for example, notes:

> Being a spokeswoman for an invisible constituency, which must remain invisible, has its disadvantages. The media are always insisting on a "real" prostitute to interview, and often I am told, "You're atypical, you're not a real whore."[3]

Sex worker Jo Doezema confirms this problem:

> I sometimes wonder about the idea that came out of the early prostitutes' rights movement that if prostitutes just publicly told our life stories it would change peoples' attitudes. I've found that people have an almost inexhaustible capacity for making exceptions to a rule they believe in. When I've given talks, I've noticed that people's basic ideas about prostitution remain unchallenged. Instead they just think, "This is a prostitute who doesn't conform to my idea of prostitution therefore she is different." ... Everybody who doesn't conform has to be an exception.[4]

Conflicts over the identity of the "real whore" are waged not only between the public and the prostitute, but among prostitutes themselves. Jo Doezema observes:

> Somebody who's been working behind the window for ten years, that's a real whore; somebody who has been working in a club for three months is not a real whore. For somebody who has worked in a club for ten years, somebody who's addicted to drugs and only works on the street when she needs a fix isn't a real whore. ... It has become a bit of a monster because people are using this whore identity against each other: "I'm a Real Whore, and I don't agree with what you are saying, so you're not." It's the one argument that can discredit any whores' rights activist ... [5]

The question of whether the reality of the street is more real than that played out indoors, or whether a "temp" can be as real as a "pro," is, as Doezema suggests, never an innocent one. The choice of one representation over another is always strategic. Attempts to challenge the stereotype of the multiply marginalized sex worker (as poverty stricken, drug addicted, physically abused, and working the streets), for example, has inspired some groups to propose in its place a desexualized, "functional" and middle-class image of the real prostitute.

Valerie Jenness suggests that this proposal is a part of "normalizing" prostitution: "To the degree that prostitutes are displayed to the public as 'normal,' the stigma surrounding prostitution can be diminished ... "[6] Thus, sex workers who most closely resemble the non-prostitute "norm" are presented as the public face of prostitution. Working-class street prostitutes then become an "image problem" for those intent on improving the status of their profession.[7]

One British escort worker, Barbara, for example objects to the depiction of sex workers as "women who stand on street corners, who wear microscopic miniskirts, who are foul-mouthed junkies, who are violent, with severe psychiatric disorders, and who were abused as kids. Why are we not portrayed as completely normal people?"[8] Similarly, a German sex worker, Jasmin, rejects the image of the prostitute as "a woman with a wig, lots of makeup, high heels, short skirt, and fishnet pantyhose ... I would never wear clothes like that. Never, ever at all!"9 These middle-class prostitutes' professed identification with "straight" society over street society is intended to challenge stereotypes of prostitutes. Unfortunately, one consequence may be to reinforce the stigmatization of more socially marginal sex workers. The street whore becomes an embarrassing stereotype to be rejected in favor of a more sanitized version of the professional prostitute as "normal" woman.

A reflection of this ongoing conflict over identity and representation can be seen in competing statistical claims about the composition of the sex trade. Because of methodological problems in studying a largely underground, secretive, and illegal practice such as prostitution, studies of commercial sex frequently have relied on "captive populations" such as prisoners, clinic patients, and participants in drug rehabilitation programs.[10] The greater visibility of street prostitution over the indoor trade also has tended to attract the attention of researchers and law enforcement officials. For this reason, street prostitutes tend to be over-represented in both arrest rates and in scientific studies.[11] As one researcher notes,

> Those studies tell something about prisoners, IV-drug users, patients and runaway children (perhaps also about the role of commercial sex in their lives), but do not provide a profile of "The Prostitute."[12]

In fact, the proportion of street prostitutes varies enormously from country to country, and even within different areas of the same country. In Italy, Spain, and Brazil, street prostitution may comprise the bulk of the sex trade.[13] But in many countries the indoor trade is the dominant—if hidden—form of sexual commerce. For example, in Amsterdam, where indoor prostitution is informally decriminalized, police place the number of prostitutes working in that city's sixty clubs and behind the approximately 340 prostitution windows at about 10,000; according to police estimates, street prostitutes only number about 500 to 1,000.[14] Even assuming that police may underestimate the numbers of women working in the illegal sector, Amsterdam street prostitution probably represents no more than ten percent of the trade.[15]

Making accurate assessments of both indoor and street prostitution in American cities is particularly complicated because all forms of prostitution are illegal in the U.S. The most cited figure for street prostitution in urban areas of the United States is between ten percent and twenty percent.[16] Critics of prostitution, however, often charge that these statistics grossly misrepresent reality by intentionally de-emphasizing the experience of the most marginalized prostitutes. University of Washington researcher Debra Boyle, for example, asserts that "for every woman who chooses to work as a high-priced call girl ... there are 1,000 on the street who are enslaved or entrapped, often with only a seventh-grade education."[17] The comparison being drawn is not simply between the indoor and street trade, but between ideal types of prostitution. The indoor trade comes to stand for "high-priced call girls" who have "chosen to work," while the street trade is characterized by those who are "enslaved or entrapped." What is at stake in these warring statistical claims is the very characterization of commercial sex itself.

Self-representation and self-advocacy by prostitutes is further complicated by the fact that many women performing erotic labor do not identify as sexual professionals. Prostitution is often considered to be a temporary activity rather than an identity. Licia Brussa suggests that this is certainly true for most migrant prostitutes whose identity is often more closely tied to questions of nationality, legal status, or family role than profession:

> Migrant prostitutes see working here as a very temporary solution, it's not their identity. But if it becomes a longer stay, more than a couple of years, then things really start to get difficult. Either they have to be prepared to go back without the money they intended to earn or, if they decide to stay, they have to become more professional in their approach to the work.[18]

Within the trade, those who fail to work "professionally" represent a threat; it is feared that they will work under the prevailing wage or perform practices (such as working without a condom) other sex workers refuse. The resulting competition and prejudice can seriously undermine solidarity within the workforce. Furthermore, the unequal vulnerability of those differently positioned in the trade (i.e., documented/undocumented; legal/illegal; indoor/street work) tends to result in the most outspoken voices within the self-advocacy movement belonging to those who are most secure. In the Netherlands, for example, prostitutes with Dutch citizenship or legal residency dominate leadership positions in the prostitutes' rights movement despite the fact that undocumented foreign workers comprise the majority of the commercial sex workforce in many large cities. Similarly, in the United States, leadership positions are most often occupied by those with the most protected status such as "former" prostitute or prostitute "advocate." COYOTE, for example, has been consistently led by former (or non-) prostitutes, with one important exception: during the early 1990s, the organization was in the hands of an active sex worker. One consequence of that shift in leadership was that COYOTE temporarily became a more service-directed and less publicly political organization. One COYOTE member remarks:

> Unlike Margo, [the new director] didn't want to get too personally involved with politics because of the risks.[19]

The new director understood the objectives of the organization less in terms of politics than as service to those, like herself, engaged in a criminalized profession:

> I don't really see myself trying to build a movement. I'm just trying to get sex workers together. Besides, I think it's more accurate to talk about a community of sex workers than a "movement." A movement has to be public and most prostitutes aren't interested in that. [20]

Peer Education

Because of the risks facing prostitutes engaged in high-profile political work, many sex-worker self-advocacy organizations focus their efforts on community building and education within the ranks. These efforts at peer education and outreach not only challenge the atomized and independent nature of most sex work but also offer at least a partial solution to the problem of workers entering the trade with little or no training. In New York City, the prostitutes' rights group PONY offers a broad range of professional skills building workshops for sex workers including:

> seminars on relevant laws and taxes, on health and safety, and on computer and entrepreneurial skills ... job placement for those ready to make a transition out of the industry ... [and] classes on suing clients who write bad checks, finding a good doctor, choosing a bail bondsman and keeping him on retainer, and determining if a potential client poses a risk.[21]

But in abolitionist countries like the United States, even such peer education efforts expose organizers to legal risks: sharing of information and resources between prostitutes is technically a criminal offense of conspiracy and pandering. For this reason, outreach must remain relatively inconspicuous and underground.

In countries where prostitution has been decriminalized, such as the Netherlands, sex workers are able to more publicly organize and educate those in the trade. The Red Thread, for instance, has a "drop in" afternoon every Thursday for colleagues to share information about work, taxes, insurance, and other matters. The organization also has a reference file for use by prostitutes with information on different job locations and working conditions. For example, the file identifies which clubs require drinking on the job, what each employer's cut of the prostitute's income will be, the presence or absence of a house doctor, penalties and fines, working hours, drug use, if any, and condom policies. The Red Thread explains the function of the file as "a way we can warn each other about disreputable businesses and recommend others."[22]

In addition to these peer-based information sharing strategies, there are also a number of privately run training programs offered in the Netherlands for those interested in working in prostitution. The first of these programs was established in 1994 by a sex worker/brothel owner, Petra, in the city of Rotterdam. The course was marked by controversy because it was financed by the Dutch association of brothel owners, the Vereniging van Exploitanten van Relaxbedrijven (VER).[23] The four-day course covered subjects such as health, safe sex techniques, and grooming tips ("don't use too much perfume or lipstick in order to avoid leaving unwanted traces on the client"). Despite the organizers' insistence that the program is intended to assist women working in the trade, critics argue that a course underwritten by management is more likely to emphasize improving service for clients than empowering workers. Petra's description of her course indicates that such concerns may be legitimate: "The essential feature of the training is to teach girls to stay themselves and maintain their self-respect. Then the client will feel much better."[24]

Educating the Public

Educational efforts by sex workers often extend beyond the workforce to include outreach to clients, police, and the general public. Such efforts are essential in destigmatizing prostitution and creating a climate of respect for workers. The San Francisco-based publication, *Whorezine*, for example, periodically runs a feature, "johnzine," on proper behavior for potential clients. Information provided includes both practical and attitudinal tips:

> Prostitutes are people. Treat them with the same respect you'd want back plus some. Take a good shower, and wash everywhere ... Try not to attract too much attention to yourself and beware of undercover cops posing as hookers ... Leave your checkbook at home. Pay in cash. Don't try to bargain whores down. They're not all rolling in the dough and they have just as many, if not more, expenses than you. For most of them, this is their living. On the other hand don't try and bribe someone into doing something they don't want to do, especially sex without condoms ... Don't crank call. A hang-up is a hang-up whether you're nervous or being an asshole . ... It's an adventure; keep an open mind. Don't look for only the "perfect one." ... If the person isn't quite what you expected, have an excuse ready ... and give them money for their time ... Tips are appreciated.[25]

With the advent of feminist sex radicalism of the 1980s and 1990s, a female market for sexual services and erotic performances has developed in many large cities including Amsterdam and San Francisco. Workers performing erotic labor for women have discovered that their clients and audience members require education on commercial sexual etiquette. Lesbian sexual performer Julia Queery, for example, has found it necessary to develop specific guidelines for audiences to follow when viewing sexually explicit live performance:

> Part of what the audience had to agree to was to honor the performers. I felt like we had been punished after the first show, because people got turned on and they didn't want to have to take responsibility for that, so they blamed us.... Some of us have been talking about going around the country teaching women how to produce sexual performances in a way that both keeps them safe from their audience and their audiences feeling safer, too.[26]

In 1994, the Dutch lesbian sex magazine *Wildside* published a guide featuring instruction from three professionals on proper "jane" behavior: "First take a shower, put on beautiful lingerie, or go with a girlfriend. You are giving yourself a gift, make a nice adventure of it with the prostitute you encounter."[27] The magazine explains the "rules of the game" as follows:

> When you make contact with a prostitute, it's important to make clear agreements. That means that you must know what you want and how you want it.... You should be as honest as possible. You certainly can say that it's your first time, that you don't know what you're doing, that you are terribly nervous and need some suggestions from her.... She'll let you know if she agrees to your desires. Be sure that you know how much things are going to cost beforehand. If something costs fl. 50, and you pay with a bill of a hundred, it's not out of place to ask for the other fifty back. Business is business.[28]

Wildside also assures its readers that it is possible to be a good client: "Despite the fact that for many women, it might sound paradoxical, it is very possible to be a civilized client. It helps to introduce yourself just like you would to anyone else, to keep to what has been agreed to, and to show appreciation for each other."[29]

While in Amsterdam, an American guest asks me if I know men working in the sex trade in that city. "Not many," I confess, "women are already a big enough topic for me." "Oh, well," she sighs. Apparently it's not the comprehensiveness of my research that concerns her; her interest is more personal. "Not that I'd have to pay for it, of course. I mean women don't have to pay for it. But still, well, you know … " Later, as if in an unrelated story, she tells me that she gets a massage every week. She can't imagine doing without it. Her life is stressful: her marriage just ended and her "ex" immediately remarried after the divorce; her daughter is pregnant and dropping out of high school; her business is expanding and full of risk. Being regularly touched helps her survive it all.

Her massage therapist recently advised her to just leave it all behind for a bit. "He was working on the knots in my back and neck when he told me to take a vacation in the tropics, swim in warm water, relax, do nothing, eat great food, have lots of sex. It sounded great, so I asked him to join me." In exchange for his airfare and lodging he was to provide ninety-minute massages, three times a day. "I made clear before we left that sex would only happen if we both wanted it. Well, I did. He didn't. He didn't even like lying next to me while I masturbated."

Her story made me acutely uncomfortable. I was impressed that she had actually attempted to do for herself what "women don't have to do": pay for sex. But I was struck by what a demanding client she was: for a few hundred dollars in airfare and accommodations, she had anticipated a five-day-long trick with a companion who would provide four and a half hours a day of professional massage, and night service, too. Transforming the meaning and experience of prostitution clearly will involve more than just a gender reversal of roles. It also will require a re-education of clients on the proper value of erotic labor.

Changing the Subject

Self-advocacy efforts by sex workers have included not only peer and client education campaigns, but also have involved symbolic interventions designed to "change the subject" of commercial sex, by turning the inquiring eye typically directed at sex workers back at the public and the sex industry itself. In 1990, for example, the

Prostitutes of New York, in collaboration with the AIDS activist arts collective, Gran Fury, produced an installation in the window of the New Museum of Contemporary Art. The piece, "Love for Sale: Free Condoms Inside," included a giant "peep hole" in the shape of an eye which "both revealed sex and served to reverse the gaze, inviting the passerby to imagine, "How does a sex worker look at the world? What does a sex worker see?"[30] The installation included messages such as, "Stop the cops' routine confiscation of condoms" and "Decriminalize desire" intended to show "sex workers speaking from a position of authority to all who passed by about how to prevent AIDS."[31]

Similarly, at the 1991 NOW National Conference in New York, sex workers rented display space in an area set aside for political commerce. A sign on the Union Labia table invited browsers to help themselves to free condoms "courtesy of New York prostitutes." The table quickly became an impromptu advice booth for NOW participants who brought their questions regarding safer sex to the "pros" staffing the table: "I'm going to have sex with a new man tonight. Do you think I need to use a condom for oral sex?" "Have you noticed whether nonoxinal-9 numbs the vulva and clit like it does the tongue?"[32] By offering advice to (other) feminists, sex workers challenged the underlying expectation of the conference that it was the prostitute who inevitably required the assistance of the feminist.

Many women working in the sex trades (including Annie Sprinkle, Candida Royalle, and Laddawan Passar) have turned the gaze back on the public through the lens of a camera. One California sex worker, Alena Smith, produced a photo exhibition of clients' genitals:

> In 1986, a local feminist inspired me by a comment she made about pornography. She said something like "I wonder how guys would like it, having their genitals photographed for public display by a woman." I told her I'd help her find out; I'd screen the guys for her, set them up and she could take the photos. She decided not to pursue it but about a year later I did it myself. I found most of my models by answering "men wanting to meet women" ads.... [I explained] I wanted models from the waist down, no payment except sexual gratification. Every single one of the men who ran an ad responded. [33]

Each photo in the "Subjects at Hand" exhibition was accompanied by a brief description of the model and the encounter:

> Married. In his 40s. Told me of his actual exhibitionist fetish. Likes the idea of exposing himself to adult women.

> Got it up, but couldn't get off. Obviously not used to having to have an orgasm with a strange woman and in daylight. I sympathized with him.

> Older fellow. Hadn't had sex for more than a year. Very sensitive to the touch. He whipped it out and then tucked it quickly away and left.

The photos of mostly flaccid cocks, which had been scheduled for a one night private showing at the local YWCA, were ultimately banned. The executive director of the facility informed Smith that her show was "pornographic which is abusive to both women and men and is against the express purpose of the YWCA."[34]

Changing the Meaning

Sex worker self-advocacy strategies are directed not only at transforming the social *conditions* under which their work takes place but also at improving the *status* of those performing erotic labor through a transformation in the *cultural meanings* attached to prostitution. One such strategy involves redefining the commercial sexual encounter as an explicit act of submission on the part of the client who pays for professional domination and discipline not just "sex." Lupe, a sex worker who moved from stripping into professional domination work, notes:

> Lots of strippers fantasized about becoming a pro-dom, having this mysterious lifestyle, handling all these implements of torture, having men groveling at your feet and calling you "mistress." Being a regular prostitute had no mystique associated with it at all. It was like you got dressed up and fucked a guy. Big deal.[35]

In practice, however, both pro-dom work and "straight" prostitution involve far more complicated power dynamics between client and worker than their respective images suggest. Lupe explains:

> I notice that professional domination work is very much about bottoming from the top. The client is paying you

to amuse him. He's really running the show. Supposedly as a pro-dom I get to do whatever I want to him, but in fact, I have to know exactly what he likes and doesn't, and if his dick isn't hard, I have to find something that will make it hard. They're not true submissives in the sense that they're not willing to hand over their power and get done.[36]

Lupe argues that in "straight" prostitution, on the other hand, roles may be reversed with the sex worker pretending to "hand over power and get done" while in fact maintaining control:

With [non s/m] prostitution, I get to top from the bottom. I mean he may be fucking me, but I am absolutely running the fuck. It's an intricate dance, but I think it's one I play very well. I let the guy think he's in control. But I am.[37]

Redefining prostitution as "professional domination" works to change the meaning of commercial sex by securing a sex worker's authority through the explicit power play and "perversion" of the encounter. More typical of strategies of redefinition, however, are efforts to recreate sex work as a "wholesome" and "normal" service. One such attempt involves licensing sex workers as credentialed "sex therapists" or "surrogates." As licensed sex therapists, prostitutes presumably would have access to some of the authority and social status associated with those in the therapeutic arts. This strategy of professionalization is particularly popular among researchers and commentators outside of the trade who are themselves members of the professional caste. Feminist philosopher Laurie Shrage, for example, suggests that by "redefining the 'prostitute' as an erotic artist or therapist, we hope to alter the kinds of qualities people seek and see in her, and to socially define her as a person that one can say hello to on the streets."[38] Similarly, feminist sociologist Lynn Chancer proposes that "one goal would be for prostitution to become a kind of sex therapy, professionalized and no longer stigmatized."[39] Underlying these proposals is the assumption that "professionalizing" the trade is a necessary step toward its legitimation. By taking prostitution off the streets and out of the hands of "unskilled labor," it presumably could be repositioned as a middle-class, professional activity, and thereby achieve social respectability.

Many of the problems with re-organizing prostitution as a form of "sex therapy" resemble those associated with all forms of professionalization through licensing. Not only would such a strategy fail to address the stigmatization of those unable or unwilling to be "credentialed," it inadvertently reinforces class prejudice by assuming that professionals alone deserve social courtesy and respect. Dutch prostitute and activist Margot Alvarez notes that in the Netherlands, the one official organization which matches "sex providers" with institutionalized individuals prefers to work with former medical personnel than with "real whores":

> There's actually an organization that serves as a sexual go-between for people with disabilities. I worked with them for awhile, but I finally left in a fury. They really have something against whores. They'd much rather work with ex-nurses; that's considered more appropriate. I got the feeling that I was tolerated because I knew how to "behave." But they didn't want too many women like me around.[40]

In addition, redefining prostitution as sex therapy serves to further pathologize non-marital, non-monogamous sexuality by placing it under the control of medical personnel. One American prostitute notes that this poses potential problems not only for the client who then becomes a "patient" but for the worker as well:

> I've been considering going to this school in Los Angeles to become a "sex surrogate" so I can do therapy legally. The thing is, it costs a lot of money, and then you're dependent on medical referrals for your client base.[41]

While sex therapy reconfigures commercial sex as a therapeutic art, another strategy of redefinition, "sacred prostitution," seeks to establish sex work as a spiritual practice. Here, exemplary "ancestors" are invoked to create a kinship between contemporary sex workers and such figures as Mary Magdalene, the ancient Greek hetairai, or temple prostitutes. The Swiss organization of sex workers, Aspasia, for example, was named after an honored Greek concubine from the time of Socrates.[42] Greek hetairai such as Aspasia, as well as the mythic figure of the sacred prostitute, are strategically selected to challenge the stigma of the harlot. Regardless of whether these stories are historically accurate or whether contemporary prostitution in any way resembles the practice of the so-called "temple whore," the recovered memory is proving useful for some sex workers in their attempt to reconstruct a destigmatized professional identity. Theodora, a sex professional with over twenty years of experience in the trade, notes:

> It's interesting to me to be living in a time when goddess imagery is coming back. I hope that we can use this as women to get in touch with images of ourselves as sexually powerful and compassionate beings. I feel like that is the image I work with; I'm embodying the goddess, embodying this incredibly healing force in the universe. That allows me to experience prostitution as anything but soul-destroying; in fact, I see it as the very stuff of the soul.... I would never suggest that that's everyone's experience. I would never deny that there are women in this business suffering. But what I want to offer is an image of what this business could look like.[43]

Cosi Fabian, a writer on and practitioner of "sacred prostitution," acknowledges that claiming kinship with the sacred prostitute is an act of creative interpretation and invention, but she argues, "when we create our own interpretations, we make the ceremony that more real, we make the worship our own."[44]

But just as the "sex therapy" model requires that commercial sex be "medicalized" in order to be destigmatized, "sacred prostitution" requires that it be "sanctified" to be found acceptable. Commercial sex that is strictly "recreational" has no place in either of these two schemes. Further, "sacred sex" suggests a level of involvement by the sex worker that may be inappropriate for some prostitutes or in some contexts. Sex worker and performance artist Annie Sprinkle, for example, insists on the importance of both forms of sexuality, the sacred and the profane. While her performance art is infused with a sense of sacred sexuality, the prostitution she engages in is

> the most basic, average Joe-Shmo tricks in the world. There is nothing spiritual or tantric about these guys.... I fuck them, and I spank them, and I call them a few names. And I feel great afterwards.... Because most of

> the time, I'm upstairs doing all this mental and creative work, being an artist who explores the outer edges of sexuality. That's a lot harder than turning these totally predictable tricks....So I like my fantasy of being both this down-and-dirty whore who is also an enlightened being who can heal people with her touch. Because being that down-and-dirty whore is sometimes very grounding.[45]

As Sprinkle suggests, there are multiple identities to be assumed by those performing erotic labor. Which identity will be most available and most appropriate for a worker in any given context depends more on strategic need and worker control than on uncovering the one "true" meaning of prostitution or the only "true" identity of the prostitute.

▼ ▼ ▼

Marianne, *staff worker at the Red Thread*
Amsterdam, 1994

I have very mixed feelings about prostitution. I work for the Red Thread and try to make sure that prostitution is treated with the same respect as any other kind of profession. I certainly do believe that everyone has the right to work as a whore. But I also know from my own experience that sometimes really awful things happen. I feel like, since I started working at the Red Thread about four months ago, I've been in a real consciousness-raising process. I didn't used to tell anyone I was a whore and, if they found out, I was ashamed to death. Now its like, "So what if I am a whore? What are you going do about it?" That change happened really fast, but in other ways I feel like I'm still struggling. For example, I still have a really bad attitude about clients.

I've always said that there are "men" and then there are "clients." Clients are the slimy guys, and I can pick them out in a minute. They compliment you up one side and down the other, when in fact all they really want from you is sex. And of course they assume that you really want them. That's real client behavior. Sometimes at the office, somebody will say, "He's a real client," and then we all know immediately what's up. They're slimy and pathetic all at once. The pathetic part is that they really need you and you don't need them at all. Some of them really have problems making social contact and they imagine that you really need them to take care of you. There's this one guy I know who goes directly from his work to the district to wait for a street whore who will talk to him. Then he offers her everything from a place to live, to food and methadone—she doesn't even have to fuck him. He just wants the company. He's so socially inept that he can't make contact with regular girls; they're scary to him. But heroin whores are safe. I sure made use of him; and I remember thinking that he was really stupid to let me do it. That's one of the sad thing about prostitution: it wasn't just that the clients didn't respect me, lots of times I didn't have any respect for them either.

Not that there weren't some nice clients, too, of course. But in my experience, they were in a minority. That might have had to do with the fact that I was a heroin whore. When you're working on the streets, you get men who want a quick fuck usually as cheap as possible. Fl. 50 was standard, and I never worked below the price. But somehow they always made you feel cheap. Especially after they came, then you were just another dirty heroin whore. You had seen them in a moment of vulnerability so it was like afterward they had to put you in your place. Sometimes I have to remind myself that there were some really good clients, too. Men who were respectful, who knew what they wanted and were willing to pay for it. The problem is, that the easy ones are also the easiest to forget. It's the really creepy guys that stick with you. Like one of my last clients who tried to convince me to work without a rubber. I told him no, but he kept insisting: "Come on, I'll give you a hundred guilders. It's better that way." I insisted on the condom, and after it was over he had to make me feel bad: "So how come if you know so much about medicine you're dumb enough to shoot heroin?" It was so typical, after he'd fucked me he needed to tell me that I was just a stupid heroin whore.

For a lot of them that's all I was, a dirty junkie whore. You have to remember that I was completely dependent on prostitution for money to buy drugs. That's a hard combination; in fact, it's almost impossible for me to separate out the two. But, you know, I hate it when people say, "Prostitution destroys women." Look at me; I wasn't destroyed. And it wasn't all bad. It might be hard to understand after I've told you that I had some bad experiences, but those were also really exciting times. Working and using wasn't always fun but it was never boring. And you can't say that about a lot of people's lives.

I think I developed a real feel for people by doing that work. Within an hour of meeting someone, I can sense who they are and who they want me to be if I want a specific outcome. I've become an excellent judge of character; I can figure out really fast if someone is trustworthy or dishonest. It's a survival skill in the trade; in the first moments of negotiating with a client, I had to decide whether to get into his car. And if I had a feeling that I shouldn't, then I just wouldn't. It takes a lot to spook me now. I'm not afraid of being on the streets of the city at night, I'd hitchhike almost anywhere, and I can talk to anyone. Prostitution taught me that, and those are no small accomplishments for a woman.

I'm not saying everyone should do prostitution, but I really agree with the Red Thread that we have to be able to decide that for ourselves. I can't portray it all in glowing terms; that would be dishonest. But I also know that the Red Thread is doing something really important by putting out the message that there is nothing wrong with being a whore. Maybe if people just understood that we are workers who pay our taxes just like anybody else, they'd stop treating us with such disrespect. That's one of the reasons I go talk to the new cadets at the police academy. I think if they hear my story and have a face and a name to attach to it, they might start to see whores differently. Last time I went, I ended my talk by asking the cadets how they would feel if someone they knew told them that she was a whore. One of the students said something like, "After hearing you talk, I'd feel honored if someone told me that. It would be a way to say that I was important to them, because it's clear you could get really negative reactions." Imagine how different it would be to come across a cop like that at work.

The older cops working in the Red Light district now are awful. Last spring we were invited to a meeting with the DCP team [police team responsible for controlling prostitution and registering prostitutes in Amsterdam's Red Light district] and it was impossible to get them to take us seriously. It was unbelievable watching them act like a bunch of macho teenagers, making jokes and practically slapping us on the back. They didn't hear a thing we were trying to say. They kept telling us that prostitutes shouldn't worry about being registered, but we've had lots of reports that suggest otherwise. One woman we know registered and then when she tried to buy some land in another country she wasn't able to because of her history in prostitution. And we've heard stories of women who've been unable to get loans to start businesses because they're registered as prostitutes. But the cops just ignored our concerns and then treated us with this disgusting familiarity. I keep hoping that the new generation coming out of the academy will be different. At least they will have met me and know that whores aren't stupid; we really are the authorities on our own lives.

▼

Margot Alvarez, *Director of the Red Thread*
Amsterdam, 1994

My parents were active communists and immigrants, so I learned early in life to stand up for myself and my beliefs. My father was a union activist for forty years and my mother was a powerful figure in her own right. She got divorced in a time when that was wrong, wrong, wrong for a woman to do. With role models like that, I always felt encouraged to be unconventional.

I started working behind the windows when I was twenty-one. For the first five or six years, I worked full time. During that period, I was involved in a difficult relationship that gradually became more and more like a pimp/whore situation. I really learned a lot from that, like how never to allow it to happen again. I'm not afraid of much anymore, and it only cost me a broken nose. I finally left him when I was twenty-six, but it meant leaving everything—and I do mean every-

Margot Alvarez © *Gon Buurman*

thing—behind. After five years working as a whore full time, six days a week, ten hours a day, I had earned a ton of money. I had a gorgeous house furnished in beautiful art deco and Chinese antiques. I thought I was being clever putting it all in his name: as a whore, that can sometimes be handy from a tax standpoint, because anything in your name can be seized. But in the long run, it worked against me because when I left him, I lost it all. Now it doesn't matter so much. I mean, my life is a lot more important than a nice Chinese cabinet.

After I left that relationship, I decided that I needed to get some distance from the work so I took a year off to decide what I wanted to do. Besides, I had worked really hard for years, and I needed a bit of a vacation. I went on welfare, moved to Amsterdam, and supplemented things by doing a little cleaning work. Basically I just enjoyed myself. Coincidentally, within months of my arrival in Amsterdam, the very first discussion group for prostitutes was organized. A social worker told me about it, so I decided to go. I didn't know anyone in town yet, and whores are always the most interesting women around. I thought I'd attend the group and maybe make some new friends. The strange thing was that, there I was feeling terrific and newly liberated while, unfortunately, a lot of the other women seemed really broken. Some of them had terrible histories of abuse and they hadn't processed any of it yet. It wasn't like all of the women's problems were a result of their work, though. One woman, for example, had been in a terrible accident which left her badly scarred. That meant that her livelihood had been taken away from her, and, of course, as a prostitute she didn't have any insurance. After fifteen years of earning a good income, suddenly she had nothing and no prospect of ever being able to go back to it.

The interesting thing about that group was that the more we talked about our experiences, the more we decided that the work itself was okay. The things that people had had problems with were at the margins of the profession, like drugs, or pimps, or bad working conditions. Plus a lot of women suffered from the pressure of trying to keep their work a secret. A big difference for me was that I had never led a double life. My parents always knew that I was a whore, and while they weren't thrilled about it, they accepted it. I wasn't willing to be secretive about my work because to be really secretive I would have had to work in a club, and I knew that the women in the clubs were exploited like mad. Working behind the window meant that you could be your own boss. Of course it also meant that everyone could see you. Since I didn't want to have to hide every time a friend or family member walked by, and I wasn't willing to travel to the other side of the country to earn a living, I just decided to come out and be over and done with the problem. I actually think it's kind of strange how upset parents can get if their daughter is involved with prostitution. People are always warning against the dangers of prostitution, but if you look at how much violence and even rape occurs in marriage it's surprising you never hear a mother say, "Honey, don't get married. It's far too dangerous."

In any case, I never really had a big problem with the stigma of being a whore. That was probably because I was earning so much money. If I went into an expensive store or restaurant, they bowed just as deeply for me as they did for the President. Money is power; I was only twenty-two or twenty-three but I could go into the most exclusive shops and buy whatever I wanted. I drove a Jaguar. Respect and courtesy can certainly be bought in this society. But just because I didn't have to worry constantly about emotional or material survival didn't mean I wasn't aware of problems with the way prostitution was organized. In fact, maybe I saw the problems a little quicker than some women in the trade because I had been raised in such a political family.

What's interesting, though, is that it really wasn't until the discussion group that I had talked about it much. When you're working, you just can't permit yourself to dwell on the problems; you've got to keep your spirits up, smile, earn money. But when I heard the other women's stories, they were so familiar to me. I had seen a lot of bruises, saw women using a lot of speed or coke to be able to work the whole night through because if they came home with less than fl. 500 they'd be beaten. Nowadays, a lot more women work independently. But back then, it was kind of unusual for a woman to work without a pimp. I think it was part of the whole idea that a woman needed a man, whores included. The women's liberation movement has really changed that perception, so now you see a lot more women living and working independently—again, whores included.

Being in that discussion group really renewed my interest in working as a whore. Besides, it was a fascinating time to be a whore in Amsterdam: the first World Whores Congress had just taken place, Margo St. James [of COYOTE] had come over, and the Red Thread was founded. I was really inspired but I wanted to do it differently than I had before. I didn't want to work as many hours; I was satisfied with just making enough to cover the basics. After a while, though, I decided I wanted to earn more—and that meant learning how to pimp myself. Once I figured that out, I started working really professionally two or three days a week. I wanted to work as little as possible and earn as much as possible in that time; a hundred guilders an hour was my goal. That meant really pushing myself: "Put that book down, open those curtains, make contact with that client!" It meant that I could earn my money quickly and spend the rest of the week doing what I wanted and found important: working for the Red Thread. For years, that was an ideal combination for me. Ten or twenty hours a week volunteering at the Red Thread, and then a few evenings in prostitution.

For the past few years, though, I've worked full time at the Red Thread and basically the only clients I work with anymore are institutionalized with disabilities. Sometimes the sex is minimal in these encounters—at least sex as conventionally understood. The spastic clients, for example, often use a lot of muscle relaxers which means that they can't get an erection. If I'm going out on a call like that, I always try to remember to phone in the morning and tell them not to take their medication until after I'm gone. But often penetration isn't the main focus anyway. What's more important is to be touched for once in a less impersonal manner. They're always being touched in functional ways by those who wash or dress them. But there's a real difference between a nurse whose covered in rubber up to her neck putting you under the shower, or me washing your back with my breasts covered in soap. I mean even if you can't fuck, there are plenty of other fun things to do.

One of the pleasures for me in working with people who are institutionalized, is that it's sort of naughty. I mean, sex in a brothel or behind the window is kind of legitimate, but in an institutional setting, where the staff does everything they can to create a sterile environment, sex feels wonderfully improper. They always try to bring me in the back door; I'm not supposed to be too obvious. It makes everything just a little sneaky. That appeals to me, I guess. I like to make a bit too much noise so that the neighbors are shocked. The clients tend to appreciate that, too, at least the men do. I have had a few women clients as well, but they are much more concerned about both privacy and atmosphere. That makes them more difficult; you have to invest a lot of time in creating a comfortable environment, like spending forty-five minutes drinking tea and getting to know each other before you can get down and have some uncomplicated sex. It's work-intensive for a whore. But once a woman has reached the point where she is aware of having sexual needs that aren't being met, she can be very assertive. One of my women clients, a lesbian paraplegic, always asked for a receipt for "sexual therapy" after our sessions. She just sent it off to her insurance company and apparently they always paid it. We both decided that they were probably afraid to ask any questions. Actually there's an organization in the Netherlands that serves as a sexual go-between for people with disabilities. I worked with them for awhile, but I finally left in a fury. They really have something against whores. They'd much rather work with ex-nurses; that's considered more "appropriate." I got the feeling I was tolerated because I knew how to "behave," but they didn't want too many women like me around. I thought that was outrageous.

You can imagine that, with attitudes like that, one of the most important functions of the Red Thread is to help whores realize that we do have important skills. Most whores are really good talkers; you have to be able to chat anybody up. But its common for women working in prostitution to be unaware that that's even a talent. It's not like you get any validation from the outside world. Even within the women's movement, whores aren't really accepted as full members. It's like our culture offends them. I recently participated in a special feminist training program in policy and management. At one point the other women were discussing whether or not they dressed up when they met with funders. I chimed in with, "Oh, I undress for my funders." And everyone just fell off their chairs. But, in fact, I think that we're actually talking about the same thing. I'm not saying every-one has to do it, but if you pull on a nice dress when you go visit your funders, who are you to judge me for taking off my dress in a comparable situation? Look, if I have to go to bed with the Minister of Justice to secure a better position for whores, I'd be crazy not to do it.

▼

Samantha, *Co-director of COYOTE*
San Francisco, CA, 1992

I worked in a whorehouse in California for a while. The best thing about it was having a group of people around all the time, so you get this incredible camaraderie going. The other nice thing about working together is that it affords some kind of protection. And it's the madame who's risking a felony charge. But I finally decided to go out on my own. You just make more money when you don't have to pay for the expenses of the house and the referrals. I missed the contact, though, so I started a support group. Our first rule was "No men, no madames." If you had other women working for you, you couldn't come to our meetings. We were pissed off about all the money madames were making off us. Besides, the madames sometimes get mad if they know the girls are talking to each other. It cuts them out of the referral fee. If I see a guy who then wants to see someone new, I personally have five different women he can call.

The support group served a couple of functions: we got to talk about the work, make referrals, and warn each other about bad clients. We called it the "union." We used union meetings to try to convince women to charge more money; if someone wasn't charging $200 an hour, we'd invite her to the meetings and assure her that she was good enough to ask for more. We also talked about how to take care of ourselves in the work. For instance, I won't work just before my period because I'm afraid I'll kill one of my clients. If they touch me wrong, they're dead. I probably gave up $600, this week because of that. But those are my boundaries. Other women would have decided to go ahead and work, make the $600, and then buy themselves a whole new outfit. Everybody has to find ways to take care of themselves and it's different for different people.

My attitude is you should get in, make the money, and get out. If it's not good for you, you shouldn't do it. I know that not everyone has that choice. But that's not a problem with prostitution, it's a problem with the welfare system. It doesn't teach people skills, and now you have a third generation of people with these checks coming in who have been brought up on welfare, and that means they don't develop the same work ethic as the rest of the population. I also understand that there aren't the opportunities; but a woman could see that she could make a certain amount of money doing sex work, learn to save it, and use it to go to school. I sometimes get calls from a lawyer who wants me to help some woman who's been arrested three or four times to get off the streets and away from her pimp. She may be fine with doing the prostitution, and wants help getting set up in a house, running an ad, that kind of thing. But I can't help her. It's illegal to give that kind of advice. If we could legalize prostitution, I could work with those women. Teach them how to save. Teach them some skills at the same time that they are making the money.

But right now, COYOTE works with really functional people. I mean it's pretty much just me and the support group at this point and, it's true, we are a fairly homogeneous group. But it's all I can do to answer the phones, be a media resource, and offer my home for meetings. After Margo [St. James] left, the organization kind of died. Priscilla Alexander did a lot of writing and political type stuff, but the people who needed to be served, the sex workers, sort of faded away. Gloria [Lockett] was kind of keeping the flame alive, but her real project is Cal-PEP. I think that's because COYOTE really has better served call girls. For me, I think of COYOTE's function as raising money and raising consciousness, which should benefit everybody.

I'm tired of getting shit for not being out there enough or political enough or whatever. Listen, I get twenty people together every month talking to each other, finally being in a place where they can say, "I'm a sex worker." I don't know how many times you have to be able to say that before you don't give a shit what other people think. It's really isolating if you work for yourself. You wait for the phone to ring, talk to some jerk, and hope he shows up. There is so much silence and secrecy involved that you need to talk to somebody. I don't really see myself trying to build a movement; I'm just trying to get sex workers together.

Besides, I think its more accurate to talk about a community of sex workers than a "movement." A movement has to be public and most prostitutes aren't interested in that. They don't see what they're doing as an identity; it's just a temporary job. You're not going to get them to attend a demonstration; most of them don't even want anybody to know what they're doing. And it's all really risky. Gloria [Lockett] and I spend half of our time talking about what we can and can't do publicly, and how to get around the law. When we have COYOTE steering committee meetings, we could all be charged with conspiracy.

Maybe I'm just burned out on politics. It's all work, no pay, lots of complaints, and hardly any appreciation. But having people talk to each other, that makes sense to me. I was happy just having those twenty women meet twice a month in my home. But I took on COYOTE because I know that there are a lot more than twenty women out there.

▼

Gloria Lockett, *Director of California Prostitutes'*
Education Project and Co-director of COYOTE
San Francisco, CA, 1993

When I first moved to the San Francisco Bay Area in 1964, there were all these beautiful women working the streets. I mean, they had fur coats, and knit suits, and expensive shoes, and their hair all done up really nice. I liked the way they carried themselves; they were polite and they smelled really good. I looked at them and thought, "I could do that." Things are a lot different now than what they used be, and I think it's because of drugs. I mean, heroin has always been around, but it used to be that even the heroin addicts had to carry themselves nice because they had to compete with the other women on the streets. The worst addiction most women had was alcohol and if you were going to get drunk, you waited until after you finished working that night. You wanted to be in control so you wouldn't be taken advantage of. But crack has made such a difference, it's not funny. With crack you just can't keep it together, so things have gotten really bad.

None of that has really changed the myth about golden California, though. Everybody comes to California to work because there's not supposed to be any rain or snow and you don't have to heat bricks to stay warm. I mean, nobody tells you that it's cold as hell in San Francisco and that you always have to wear a coat because of the wind and fog. Besides, the police here are crazy, especially when it comes to career prostitutes, and especially if you're Black. The wise ones just up and leave. It's just ridiculous how many women of color go to jail and not because we commit more crimes. We're just easier to arrest. That's a big problem I have with COYOTE: it's so white. Those call girls aren't the people going to jail so much and that means they don't always get it.

Gloria Lockett   © *Jill Posener*

The other day we were having a planning meeting for our annual COYOTE conference. I already thought it was a problem to call it a "conference" which can be intimidating to some people. Anyway, one of the other organizers wanted the meetings to start at nine o'clock in the morning "so that everybody could attend." I said, "I don't think so. When I was working on the streets, the only time I got up at nine was to go to court." It was ludicrous. Sometimes people just can't see beyond their own situation. I think one of the reasons why people assume that COYOTE is just for call girls is that they were the ones to first come out and talk about what they were doing. They weren't working the streets so they weren't being constantly harassed by the police. And they knew how to use the media. It would be great if everybody could come out of the closet, but the risks aren't the same for everybody. I know a lot of other Black women who would love to be part of COYOTE, but they're afraid to go public.

I first got involved with COYOTE because of a horrible prostitution case against me, my lover, who was Black, and another woman, who was Black. The whole thing was so racist and sexist that we really needed some support. There were about seventeen federal counts against us and a lot of those charges were for traveling across state lines to work. Any time a prostitute goes from California to Nevada, she's committing a federal crime. We didn't even know that. Not that you have much choice. If you're a career prostitute, especially if you work the streets, you have to move around to make money and to stay out of jail. If you're Black, it's even harder because the good money is in all these white areas like Las Vegas and San Diego. Las Vegas was the most racist place I ever worked in my life, but it was where the money was.

Anyway, after the arrests, I went to Margo [St. James] for help and she was fantastic. She went to court with me every day for six weeks and it really made a difference. I don't think until all of us start working together, we're going to be able to really change things. No single group by itself can make an impact. We need everybody: street prostitutes and call girls, lesbians and feminists, everybody. We've got to figure out how to support each other in this.[46]

▼

Chapter 8
Compromising Positions

> When I read some of the stuff written by so-called "feminist allies" it feels like they are fighting over our bodies. Some of them say they are "pro-prostitution," as if it could be that easy. Then there are the others who say that prostitution is evil because it contributes to violence against women.... It's like prostitutes are just these bodies who are somehow connected to something bad and evil or something good and on the cutting edge of revolution. They just turn us into symbols.[1]

There is no such thing as The Prostitute; there are only competing versions of prostitution. The Prostitute is an invention of policy makers, researchers, moral crusaders, and political activists. Even sex workers themselves contribute to the creation of a normative prostitute by excluding those from their ranks who are not "real" enough or "good" enough.

The Prostitute functions as a "magic sign" whose meaning always exceeds its definition.[2] The prostitute is a shape-shifter alternately embodying sex, crime, gender, violence, work. As Gail Pheterson notes, the "category of the 'prostitute' is based more upon symbolic and legal representations ... than upon a set of characteristics within a population of persons."[3] Just as anthropologists create their own savage,[4] so too do sociologists and social activists create their own prostitute. For this reason, the prostitute is simultaneously a worker, a victim, a collaborator, a renegade, and a police statistic. Each of these positions represents a strategic account constituted by and giving expression to a complex field of power and resistance. The resulting account reflects as much on the needs of the individual or social movement invoking her as the reality of the sex worker herself. As Jane Flax points out:

> [T]he construction and choice of one story over others is not governed by a relation to truth, but by less innocent factors. These ultimately include a will to power partially constituted by and expressing a desire *not* to hear certain other voices or stories.[5]

In my own attempt to write a story of sex work, I have been struck by the fact that there is no one overriding narrative spoken by prostitutes on prostitution. There are instead competing and sometimes conflicting stories, each with its own integrity. Accounts of sex work presented in these pages, as elsewhere, are often contradictory, without one being "true" and the other "false." Discussions of sex—commercial and otherwise—necessarily reveal both victimization and agency, exploitation and engaged complicity; in short, both the violence and wild defiance of sex.

Writing this book has convinced me that we need to develop the capacity to listen to these stories without reducing them to competitors for the status of Truth. We need to listen for meaning rather than just "fact," to ask why a story is told in this way, how the location of the speaker shapes the tale, how the position of the audience affects what is heard, and to carefully consider what is at stake politically, personally, and strategically in invoking this particular version at this moment in this context.

It is surely no coincidence, for example, that my study offers a less bleak vision of commercial sex than that which is presented by militant anti-prostitution activists such as Cecilie Hoigard and Liv Finstad. In many ways, we each found the story we had expected to, the story most suitable for our own political purposes. In part, this is a reflection of the very different voices we have enlisted to tell the tale. Hoigard and Finstad researched the most socially and economically marginal sector of the sex trade: street prostitution. In my study, street prostitutes only comprise about ten percent of those interviewed. While this representation reflects the ratio of the street to indoor trade in the two locations in which I conducted most of my research, it remains a concern that the voices of the most marginalized might be overwhelmed by those more favorably positioned. A necessary companion, if not corrective, to this study can be found in the works of researchers who have made the subject of street prostitutes the focal point of their analysis.[6] Once again: there is no one true story and we would all do well to honor what I have come to think of as "the wisdom of the other hand."

Prostitution is not a simple story. As Tracy Quan of the New York prostitutes' rights organization, PONY, admits: "to embrace the identity of 'prostitute' is to embrace a multitude of contradictions."[7] Elizabeth, an Oslo street prostitute, applauds an anti-prostitution account of her experiences in the trade but still cautions: "Everything is always double. At least for me, what you have written is true. Imagine being so divided that you almost write with two pens and speak with two tongues."[8]

For this reason, the subject of commercial sex allows for no final conclusions; instead there is an urgent need for productive conversations across locations within the trade and beyond it. The creation of a more complex feminist prostitution politics will require building bridges not digging deeper trenches and slinging more mud. Rather than concluding, then, with an assessment of which story is most adequate, or which position most "correct," I would like to suggest a "hybrid perspective" that draws on the strengths of the conflicting accounts:

- the Radical Feminist insistence that injustice must be challenged, not accommodated;
- and the Sex Radical insight that subversion is a creative ally to opposition;
- the Abolitionists' recognition that simply because something appears to have "always" existed, it is neither inevitable nor unchangeable;
- and the prostitutes' rights' reminder that transformation does not reduce to a politics of prohibition.

A feminist prostitution politics rooted in such a hybrid perspective might allow us to redirect our energies away from fighting one another to pursuing collectively the following shared goals:

- A fundamental redistribution of wealth and power between women and men, as well as among women and men. Gross economic disparity between classes, races, sexes, and nations produces conditions of economic coercion and desperation that undermine meaningful "choice." No woman should be forced to engage in prostitution—or any other form of productive or reproductive labor—against her will.
- An organized and empowered workforce. A feminist prostitution politics that honors labor would evalu-

ate policies on the basis of whether they serve the interests of workers rather than employers or clients. Prostitutes, as all others who labor for a living, should be guaranteed full workers' rights and benefits.

- A decriminalization of consensual sexual activity. The state should not be in the position of criminalizing adult sexual behavior whether in the context of loving relationships, recreational encounters, or commercial transactions. Instead, our collective resources should be devoted to teaching respect for sexual diversity and creating conditions under which consent can be made more meaningful.

To secure these ambitious objectives will require a broad-based feminist alliance. As Gloria Lockett insists:

> We need everybody: street prostitutes and call girls, lesbians and feminists, everybody. We've got to figure out a way to support each other in this.[9]

▼ ▼ ▼

Afterword
Researcher Goes Bad and Pays for It

After years of researching the subject of sex for money, I decided to finally have some. In 1994, I joined twenty women who each paid about $75 dollars for sexual instruction from two American pros: Annie Sprinkle, performance artist, sacred prostitute and "post-porn modernist," and her self-identified "West Coast consort," Vision, a "sensuous massage" practioner from California. Annie had offered me a substantial "student discount" to attend, so I took my courage—and my yoni—in hand and agreed to participate. It would be a first for us both since it was Annie's maiden voyage teaching "yoni massage."

Like all first times, this one was both highly memorable and more than a little awkward. I spent much of the week following the event making lists of the things I didn't much like. Women are so good at critiquing sex. But in the spirit of "sexpert" Susie Bright, who once showed two and a half hours of porn to a dazed university audience and then asked that we not only remember what we hated and found offensive, but also what got us off, I'll start by remembering the excellent company. It was thrilling to be surrounded by women who had the courage to attend an event like this. None of us quite knew what to expect, and most of us certainly weren't practiced at paying for sex. Yet despite our fears, twenty of us had found our way out of the safety of our homes and on to those meditation cushions. It was heady being with women willing to take that kind of sexual risk with a group of strangers. It was also enormously satisfying to hear a roomful of women, socialized to be caretakers and -givers, committing ourselves to increased pleasure in our lives. And perhaps best of all, unlike most of the sex parties I've been to, *everyone* who paid to attend got laid.

The event ran from 4:00 p.m. till 1:00 a.m. on a Friday night. At the appointed hour, I arrived at the door of the New Ancient Sex Academy (NASA) where I was ushered upstairs to change out of street clothes into a bathrobe. We had been instructed to bring robes, along with massage oil, lube, towels, sheets, and items to create our own "ritual altar." As each of us descended, we were greeted and smudged with smoking sage by Vision. Then we were ready to pass from the outer chamber (with its platters of dried nuts and fruit, wine glasses, and pitchers of water), to the inner one, the sacred space where "sex magic" would be performed.

Standing in the passage, at a fold in the curtain, was Annie Sprinkle, or Anya, as she called herself for the occasion. Dressed in a whore-meets-goddess sequined robe and underwear, she invited each of us to select a tarot card from her deck. "Harvest," I heard her explain to the woman in front of me. My card made Annie pause. "Why don't you take another one," she offered. Apparently my first card represented "oppression." This actually felt appropriate for a driven political activist like me. In fact, one of my secret hopes for the ritual was that it might provide a catharsis for some of my anger and grief over global and more personal pain. I wanted the ritual to touch the place where I carry the images of my friends Dwayne and Steve, so thin and uncomfortable, in their last days with AIDS. I hoped that by paying to be touched, I might be able to experience surrender over something less brutal than the daily assault of TV images from Bosnia and Rwanda. It seemed the cards were unexpectedly speaking to me, the Oppression Girl, who always welcomes the world's pain to take up residence in her soul.

One of the things I have long admired about Annie Sprinkle is her insistence that ecstasy is a potent force to release into a tormented world. Her flyer for the massage ritual claimed that "a focused, sexually awakened group of women is a divine and extremely powerful force that can not only inspire each women in the group, but has the potential to contribute to the well-being of all life on earth." By signing on, I was admitting to an embarrassed hope that she might be right. In any case, it seemed safe to assume that I could use a little additional attention to ecstasy in my life. Among the "ritual objects" I brought to decorate my altar was a photo of two hundred thousand of us marching in San Francisco in one of the massive "Stop the Gulf War Before It Starts" demonstrations. Behind my friend's head was a banner reading "War is Murder" and another that simply demanded "Peace." That demonstration was an important collective ritual response to the insanity of our times. I figured, "Why shouldn't 'sex magic' be?"

My "oppression" talisman in hand, I entered the room and nervously scanned the other women settling themselves in the circle. Most were what I think of as "my age"—meaning thirties and forties—though there were also a couple of twenty-somethings. And then there was "Jo." She was a good bit older than the rest of us, in her sixties for sure, and not a thing noticeably New Age about her. She was also a little more chatty and less respectful than the rest of us younger good girls trying so hard to behave.

Annie began the ritual by passing a yoni hand puppet around the circle. We were to introduce ourselves speaking through our cunts. The puppet was a big vulva made out of black velvet and pink and purple satin, with a proportionately huge and erect clit. As each speaker spread its generous lips by opening her hand in the glove, a well-defined g-spot was exposed. Some women were so nervous they could hardly speak, and two broke into tears. But Jo, who was sitting somewhere in the middle of the circle, said she wasn't nervous at all, just darn curious. She had been married for thirty years, neither she nor her husband had been much interested in sex, and then he had died. And that was that. Except that one day one of her girlfriends asked, "Jo, have you ever had an orgasm?" "Well, I thought about it, and decided that I don't think I ever have. So here I am and I'm just as curious as can be."

I studied each of the women, on the lookout for the other dykes. I imagined the crowd would be mixed since the event had been produced by New Age heterosexuals; still, I assumed most of us would be queer. The workshop leaflet had clearly stated: "Note: You don't have to be a lesbian or bisexual to enjoy or participate in this ritual, but it doesn't hurt!" During the introductions, I was surprised, then, by how many women identified as heterosexual. After the introductions, Vision led us in a guided meditation grounding ourselves through our feet, followed by ecstatic dancing to New Age music and drums. These weren't the kind of tunes that normally moved me, but

I was doing my best. If we were going to be "exploring each others' g-spots" in mere minutes I wanted to be warmed up and well on my way to abandon.

Finally, Vision and Annie demonstrated the "yoni massage" as we all huddled around them in a semi-circle on the floor. This part was fascinating, though not so much for the massage technique (I quickly discovered that "Taoist Erotic Yoni Massage" is really just a mouthful for "Intro to Lesbian Sex.") What was really interesting was watching these two sexually powerful women attempt to negotiate who was going to run the fuck. On the one hand, Annie was the undisputed mistress of the massage, but it was she who was on her back with Vision kneeling above demonstrating the moves. Annie managed to hold on to control by literally holding on to the sheet of paper outlining the step-by-step description of each maneuver. She would read the steps aloud and then Vision was supposed to perform each move on her. But Vision couldn't remember what all the names stood for—not surprising given the coy designations such as "mooshy push," "tour de france," and "light my fire." Annie, however, wouldn't relinquish the cheat sheet, so Vision had to keep asking for explanations, and the result was lots and lots of talking. The demonstration became very technical, and the erotic and mystical fled the room. The twenty women watching became increasingly panicked about "performing" on each other. They delayed the fateful moment by asking for individual moves to be explained over and over again. This was the moment when I began to strongly suspect that there might not be many queers in the room: "Wait a minute," I thought. "These women don't understand even the 'one finger slow poke'?"

The endless talking, the technical descriptions and the resulting anxiety quickly dissipated any ecstatic energy we might have been able to build to that point. Perhaps, I thought, if Vision would just silently "do" Annie, now that they'd talked us through it so completely, some of the erotic tension might reappear. But apparently our $75 didn't include sexual performance, only instruction. So instead of being an audience to ecstatic sex, we were told to have some.

The massage would be broken into three parts, each part performed with a different woman. This was intended to give each of us the experience of "sharing sexual energy with several people" rather than seeing sex as a connection to any one person in particular. A woman in the circle nervously asked what the proper response should be if approached by someone she didn't want to "receive" from. Annie's reply was surprising: she suggested that we pay attention to our resistance and learn from it. "But," insisted the woman, "couldn't you tell someone 'no'?" Annie calmly repeated that it would be good to try to work with each other and learn. After the initial shock, I decided I rather liked the answer in this context. What was to follow wasn't about choosing a sexual partner, it was about consenting to a collective, commercial, sexual experience. None of us was going to be left behind because she wasn't wanted, and each of us was to take responsibility for our own sexual self-exploration. The top (or in ritualese, "the giver") was only a helpmate.

Ten women finally agreed to "receive" during the first round and built their altars around the perimeter of the room. I briefly considered trying to get matched up with Jo, thinking that a Real Lesbian might increase her chances of coming, and what an honor to midwife an older woman's first orgasm. But in fact I offered to "give" to the first woman who would meet my eyes. She dedicated her ritual to her boyfriend who, she said, wasn't able to or interested in hearing what she wanted sexually. She then added a second dedication to her boss's wife who had asked that she return with a full report on everything that happened. My partner looked genuinely enthusiastic about that invitation to "share." When we had to switch partners after a ten-minute massage, I was relieved that she was sorry to see me go. Annie then instructed us to move one woman to the right in a clockwise direction. Shock passed through the room as we realized that we would have no further choice in sex partners: whoever lay just to the right would receive stage two of the massage, and the following woman would be the one whose g-spot we would be exploring.

My second partner was outspoken about what she liked and what she didn't. I actually found myself a little irritated by her constant coaching: "a little to the left," "softer," "no that area is not sensitive at all, are you sure that is even my clit there?" I silently huffed, "What do you mean am I sure that's a clit? I am an experienced and skilled lesbian top, goddammit." As Annie had suggested, the ritual was certainly self-revealing, and I wasn't sure I liked everything I had paid to learn.

Suddenly, it was time to switch again. If my ego had been bruised by my last partner, I wasn't reassured by the self-presentation of my final one. The centerpiece of her altar was a huge wooden phallus, well over a foot long. She was wearing *two* large wedding rings. And she had been hyperventilating so badly during the nonsexual portions of the massage that I worried she might pass out. Annie was squatting next to her encouraging her to breathe normally. My partner explained that her head felt light and her hands were tingling. I decided her freezing palms needed more urgent attention than her yoni, but after several minutes of hand massage, she instructed me to move down. There was no shortage of courage in that room. Despite her terror, she knew what she wanted and found the way to ask for it.

Too soon Vision told us we had twenty seconds left before the final move in the massage, "the Big Draw," which involved clenching all the muscles in the body, holding for five seconds and then releasing. The Big Draw offered a climax of sorts for those whose orgasm remained elusive. Afterwards, I looked around and counted six women in tears; at least they had experienced the catharsis I knew I was seeking. After we had all showered down with antiseptic soap (the safer sex precautions were impressive), we were told to switch roles.

As I built my altar, Annie quietly approached me. Would I mind, she asked in a whisper, if she positioned Jo three mats back so I would be her final partner for the night? I quickly agreed even though I knew that Jo hadn't quite gotten into the swing of things. She had kept up a loud and nervous chatter through the entire first round. My chances of getting off, of reaching my cathartic destination suddenly felt much more remote. And despite the fact that I was *paying* for this sex, both the good girl and the reluctant bottom in me appreciated the opportunity to once again put another's need ahead of my own. Besides, I was a scholarship student; I might not get off but at least I was only paying half price.

And Jo *was* one of the more interesting women in the room, if only she could get out of her head and into her—and my—body. But the ritual wasn't doing its magic on Jo; she just couldn't quite let go and get down and dirty or uplifted and ecstatic. On the other hand, nothing phased her either; she greeted every aspect of the evening with chipper curiosity. After we switched partners for the final time, Jo was the very last woman to begin the massage. She just couldn't quite get her gloves on all the way. To move things along, we finally settled on hands with ghostly tips flapping in the breeze. Then suddenly Jo found her rhythm. There wasn't enough time for much subtlety, much less catharsis, but she impressed me with both her strength and her sudden focus.

Once the room quieted, Annie and Vision asked us to form a final circle and share any thoughts. One woman spoke for us all when she confessed that she was proud that she had found the courage to participate at all. Another woman noted with surprise her own pleasure in sexually "giving" to another woman; many heads nodded. A number of the women expressed excitement over what they had learned about their bodies, eager to report back to husbands or boyfriends. And finally I asked if I was right in concluding that I was the *only* dyke in the room. Yes, I was right. Part of me was delighted at the thought of a roomful of straight women paying to have sex with each other. But some other part, who apparently fancies herself a border guard in the Queer Nation, silently grumbled about lesbian sex secrets being sold to girls outside the life.

After we once again showered and dressed in our street clothes we reassembled for a fantastic sensual food feast of vegetables, breads, fruits, chocolate sauce, and whipped cream. And at 1:00 A.M., I was back on the street faced with walking all the way across town (no more public transportation at that hour), carrying a bag full of altar items, two towels, a sheet, and a blanket. I felt like a bizarre combination of working girl and bag lady.

That night I drenched the sheets in sweat as I tried to work through the experience in my sleep. I had paid for the sex, and it was good as far as it went. But I strongly suspected that I would have liked the whole experience more if I had been paid for it.

▼ ▼ ▼

Notes

INTRODUCTION

1 "Chapkis, who admits to never prostituting herself, has become Santa Cruz's celebrity apologist for pornography, sadomasochism, prostitution and other patriarchal ideals. She does this successfully by waving flags of sexual freedom and choice." Simonton, 1992, p. 8.
2 Chapkis, 1986.
3 Simonton, 1992, p.8.
4 The precise comparison Vrangrijk members made to me while explaining their decision was that living with Jo Doezema would have been like living with a police officer or a soldier, two other professions they wouldn't have allowed into the house. For a more complete account see Chapkis, 1994.
5 D'Emilio and Freedman, 1988; de Grazia, 1992; Foucault, 1978; Jeffreys, 1985; Kendrick, 1987; Otis, 1985; Walkowitz, 1980; Weeks, 1981; and Wells, 1982.
6 Alexander and Delacoste, 1987; Assiter and Carol, 1993; Barrows, 1986; Barry, 1979; Califia, 1994; Collins, 1991; Donnerstein, 1987; Dworkin, 1988; Enloe, 1989; French, 1988; Griffin, 1981; Gubar and Hoffman, 1989; Groen, 1987; Jenness, 1993; Lederer, 1980; MacKinnon, 1987; Millet, 1971; Nestle, 1987; Pateman, 1988; Pheterson, 1989; Reti, 1983; Roberts, 1986; Segal and McIntosh, 1993; Sprinkle, 1991; Vance, 1984; Williams, 1989 .
7 All but two of the interviews were conducted by me. The remaining two were done by members of the Dutch Foundation Against Trafficking in Women in keeping with their policy of shielding clients from reporters and researchers.
8 McClintock (1993) p. 8-9.
9 Interview with Carol Queen. 1992. San Francisco.
10 Interview with Jo Doezema, 1993, Amsterdam.

CHAPTER 1 THE MEANING OF SEX

1 Jeffreys, 1985, p. 47.
2 Ibid, p. 32.
3 Ibid, p. 97.
4 See for example Ferguson, 1984 and Sawicki, 1988.
5 Seidman, 1992, p. 187.
6 Davis, 1990, p. 35.
7 Steinem, 1978, p. 54.
8 Elshtain, 1988, p. 53-5.
9 Morgan, 1977, p. 181. Several critics have called this "femininism": "The femininist view of sex is ... women have sex as an expression of intimacy, but orgasm is seen as a male goal"; Rubin, 1982, p. 215.
10 Interview with Ariane Amsberg, 1994, Amsterdam.
11 Barry, 1979, p. 270.
12 Ibid, p. 205.
13 Barry, 1995, plenary address at the Nordic Prostitution Conference, Helsinki, Finland, May 1995. Emphasis mine. Barry opened her remarks with a strongly worded denunciation of conference organizers' decision to include a condom in conference packets: "The packet of material I received this morning [had] a condom in it which I assume is either part of the approach to normalization of prostitution or is it indeed a suggestion to those of us who have received it that we should be using it that way? I find this not at all cute or funny, I find it not at all educational or productive. I find it insulting."

14 For a conference report, see Kulp and Mudd, 1987, p. 6-7.
15 Kulp and Mudd, 1987, p. 6. Emphasis mine.
16 Ibid, p. 7. Emphasis mine.
17 Ibid. Emphasis mine.
18 Pateman, 1988, p. 208.
19 Fraser, 1993, pp. 174, 176.
20 MacKinnon, 1987, p. 149.
21 Ibid, p. 148.
22 Davis, 1990, p. 26.
23 Southern Women's Writers' Collective, 1987, p. 3.
24 Ibid.
25 Ibid, p. 4.
26 Ibid.
27 Dworkin, 1987, p. 134-5. Emphasis mine.
28 Dworkin, 1979, p. 203.
29 MacKinnon, 1987, p. 59.
30 Barry, 1979, p. 218.
31 Barry, 1992.
32 Ibid.
33 MacKinnon notes that "Marxism teaches that exploitation and degradation somehow produce resistance and revolution. It's been hard to say why. What I've learned from women's experience with sexuality is that exploitation and degradation produce grateful complicity in exchange for survival," MacKinnon, 1987, p. 61.
34 Ibid, p. 148.
35 Seidman, 1992. p. 187-8.
36 Ibid.
37 Wells, 1994, p. 132.
38 Ibid.
39 Ibid, p. 58.
40 Other writers challenging so-called "victim feminism" include American feminists Katie Roiphe, 1993, and Naomi Wolf, 1993. In her version of "power feminism," Roiphe, for instance, scrutinizes rape and other crimes of male violence against women for evidence of women's own complicity. A similar strategy is at work in current attempts to redefine racism as a question of individual failure; see D'Souza, 1995.
41 hooks, 1994, p. 80.
42 Vance, 1984, p. 1.
43 Sheiner, 1994, p. 4. It is interesting to note that the author of the offending piece defends his work in a reply to Sheiner by arguing that she misinterpreted his intent: "I was trying to convey exactly the sense of revulsion at the use of Third World women [in sex tourism]. I agree completely with those who deplore it, and always have. The sexual image in this piece was intended to be grotesque."
44 Lilly, 1991, p. 1-3.
45 Sawicki, 1988, p. 185.
46 Bhaba, 1987.
47 Califia, 1980, p. 27.
48 Marlatt, 1991, p. 260.
49 de Lauretis, 1984, p. 5.
50 Warland, 1991, p. 263.
51 Shange, 1994, p. 34.
52 Ibid, p. 38-9.

53 Califia, 1980, p. 107.
54 McClintock, 1993, p. 102.
55 Ibid, p. 113.
56 Connell, 1995.
57 Taussig, 1987, p. 16.
58 Kaplan, 1994, p. 22. Kaplan's suggestion that whores and dykes create sexual anxiety in men seemed to be confirmed at the 1995 U.N. Women's Conference in Beijing. The question of prostitutes' and lesbian rights proved to be among the most controversial considered at the conference. One government representative from Bangladesh insisted that an acknowledgment of lesbian rights would "open the floodgates for all kinds of behavior we can't accept. It is not innocent behavior." A delegate from Belize compared homosexuality to "prostitution and strip-tease dancing." See Burdman, 1995, p. 1.
59 Califia, 1988, p. 20.
60 Ibid, p. 22.
61 Duggan, et al., 1985, p. 145.
62 Levine, 1992, p. 47. Levine is co-author with Robert Stoller of the book *Coming Attractions: The Making of an X-Rated Video*, 1993.
63 Interview with Carol Queen, 1992, San Francisco, CA.

CHAPTER 2 SEXUAL SLAVERY

1 Colonel Montgomery, Barlay, 1968, p. 7.
2 More effective demands might have focused on economic reforms that would have directly addressed conditions of urban poverty leading a desperate mother to sell her daughter into prostitution.
3 See Walkowitz, 1980, p. 247: "evidence of widespread involuntary prostitution of British girls at home or abroad is slim" Walkowitz further notes that the average age of entry into prostitution in Britain at that time was approximately sixteen.
4 D'Emilio and Freedman, 1988, p. 209.
5 Ibid, p. 214.
6 Ibid.
7 Steinberg, 1989, p. 33.
8 D'Emilio and Freedman, 1989, p. 209. This claim, interestingly enough, resembles one made in the late 20th century by anti-prostitution and anti-pornography activists who claim these forms of commercial sex are bringing vile sexual practices into the sanctity of the home and family. See Barry, 1979, p. 205.
9 Ibid.
10 Segal, 1990, p. 177.
11 Enloe, 1989, p. 21.
12 Ibid, p. 23.
13 Angela Davis reports that deceptive recruiting techniques and harsh working conditions were commonplace features of early industrial capitalism, and not restricted to the sex trade. For example, in the New England textile mills, which employed twice as many women as men, deceptive recruiting was the norm: "The pioneering 'mill girls' had been recruited from local farm families. The profit-seeking millowners represented life in the mills as an attractive and instructive prelude to married life.... [The mills] were portrayed as 'surrogate families' where the young farm women would be rigorously supervised by matrons in an atmosphere akin to the finishing school. But what was the reality of mill life? Incredibly long hours—twelve, fourteen or even sixteen hours daily; atrocious working conditions; inhumanly crowded living quarters." Davis, 1983, p. 54.

14 D'Emilio and Freedman, 1988, p. 203.

15 Collins, 1991, p. 71.

16 Ibid, p. 77.

17 Gillman, 1981, p. 229. See also Gould, 1981, p. 129, 181, 197.

18 Collins, 1990, p. 177.

19 Wolff, 1990, p. 48.

20 Mazumdar, 1989, p. 2-3.

21 Census data suggest that between four and five hundred Chinese women lived in varying degrees of sexual bondage in San Francisco from the 1860s through 1880s. See Wolff, 1990, p. 49.

22 Ibid, p. 48.

23 Pascoe, 1989, p. 47.

24 See for example statements by Colonel Montgomery, British Secretary of the Anti-Slavery Society, made in 1968 about European girls trafficked among "clients of one race or another before being passed on to brothels," cited in Barlay, 1968, p. 7.

25 Barry, 1979, p. 121.

26 Ibid, p. 39.

27 Note, however, the use of the "harem" as one of only two identified destinations for trafficked women in Barry's discussion.

28 Barry, 1979, p. 39-40.

29 Ibid, p. 41.

30 Ibid, p. 40.

31 Ibid, p. 83.

32 Lee, 1991, p. 85.

33 Ibid.

34 Interview with Licia Brussa, 1994, Amsterdam.

35 Using information supplied by field workers, health workers, and the police, the STV estimates that between 1,000 and 2,000 women are trafficked into the Netherlands each year out of a population of 13,000 to 15,000 migrant prostitutes in that country. See Stichting Tegen Vrouwenhandel, 1993.

36 Hoigard and Finstad, 1993, p.206.

37 See Finkelhor, 1983. See also *Ms. Magazine* special issue on domestic violence, October 1994.

38 Barry explains her decision in *Female Sexual Slavery* to restrict her sample to women who had left prostitution as follows: "interviewing those held in slavery is impossible. [So] I began to look for the women who have escaped.... I restricted my interviews with victims to those who had either escaped or left prostitution." Barry, 1979, p. 6-7. The result is that Barry is only confronted by accounts from women who responded to conditions of abuse by leaving, not by staying and fighting, organizing and transforming the conditions under which they labored, nor by leaving a coercive situation in the trade for one in which greater control was possible.

39 Kirshenbaum, 1991, p. 13.

40 Hoigard and Finstad, 1992, p. 183.

41 This matches popular belief that the rape of a prostitute is less traumatic than that of a woman outside the trade because a prostitute is used to the abuse. The State Supreme Court of Victoria, Australia, for instance, ruled in a rape case involving a sex worker that the crime was less serious because the victim was a prostitute. See Perry, 1993, p. 18.

42 Ibid.

43 Hoigard and Finstad, 1992, p. 180.

44 Interview with Carol Queen, 1992, San Francisco, CA.

45 Hoigard and Finstad, 1992, p. 180.
46 Interview with Jo Doezema, 1993, Amsterdam.
47 Genc, 1994.
48 Tchudomirova and Mardh, 1994.
49 Interview with Lisa Hofman, 1994, Utrecht, Netherlands.
50 United Nations Convention for the Suppression of the Traffic in Persons and of the Exploitation of the Prostitution of Others, U.N. Yearbook 1949, UNTS vol. 96, p. 271.
51 Ibid. Emphasis mine.
52 STV, 1991.
53 Ibid.
54 STV, 1993.
55 STV, 1992.
56 UNESCO and the Coalition Against Trafficking in Women, 1991, p.1-2.
57 Ibid, p.1.
58 Ibid, p. 2. It should be noted that the Coalition's position, too, is supported by a number of international organizations including UNESCO, the Belgian French Community, the International Federation for Human Rights, and the International Council of Women.
59 Kirshenbaum, 1991, p. 13.
60 Korvinus, 1993.
61 From an unpublished document circulated by the signatories in response to the Coalition's proposals to the United Nations, 1993.

CHAPTER 3 EMOTIONAL LABOR

1 Jenness, 1993.
2 James, et al., 1975, p. 4.
3 St. James and Alexander, 1977, p. 68.
4 Interview with Sheriff Al Noren, 1988, Santa Cruz, CA.
5 Clarke, 1993, p. 149.
6 Carole Pateman makes this argument in her condemnation of both prostitution and surrogacy. See Pateman, 1988.
7 See for example, Hoigard and Finstad, 1992.
8 Ibid, p. 180.
9 Tucker, 1978, p. 72.
10 Ibid, p. 74. Emphasis in original.
11 Pateman, 1988, p. 204.
12 Ibid, p. 207. Emphasis mine.
13 Ibid.
14 For overview essays on the field, see Scheff, 1983 and Thoits, 1989.
15 See Thoits, 1989, p. 324.
16 As Thomas Scheff points out, this is the substance of one of the ongoing arguments in the field between social constructionists who argue that emotion and emotional expression is "culturally specific" and essentialists or universalists who "see emotions as biological, genetically determined reactions that are universal in the human species," Scheff, 1983, p. 335.
17 Note how "coming out" stories in the gay community, for example, tend to be couched in a language of self-discovery, of a conversion experience away from a socially imposed sexuality toward a more "real" reflection of the sexual self.
18 Lorde, 1991, pp. 148-150.
19 Ibid, p. 152.

20 Hoigard and Finstad, 1992, p. 110.
21 Hochschild, 1983, p. x.
22 Ibid.
23 Ibid, p. 7, emphasis mine. A more subtle and complex version of this argument makes use not of the concept of an authentic self or "soul," but rather of psychoanalytic understandings of the unconscious. Hochschild moves clearly in this direction. There remains a risk however of endowing those emotions resident in the unconscious with greater "authenticity" than those generated by the conscious mind.
24 Hochschild, 1983, p. 204.
25 Ibid, p.33.
26 Interview with Annie Sprinkle, 1993, Amsterdam.
27 Hochschild, 1983, p. 17-18.
28 Ibid, p. 41.
29 Interview with Jo Doezema, 1993, Amsterdam.
30 Hochschild, 1983, p. 133.
31 Interview with Ans, 1993, Amsterdam.
32 Hochschild, 1983, p. 189.
33 Interview with Lupe, 1992, San Francisco, CA.
34 Hoigard and Finstad, 1992, p. 183.
35 Ibid, p. 187.
36 Interview with Carol Queen, 1992, San Francisco, CA.
37 Interview with Lupe, 1992, San Francisco, CA.
38 Vanwessenbeek, 1994.
39 Hochschild, 1983, p. 27. It is a useful exercise to replace the word "emotion" with the word "sex" in this passage by Hochschild (i.e., "if we conceive of sex not as a periodic abdication to biology but as something we do ..."). This exposes the positive sense of control and personal sexual agency involved in describing sex as an activity that one "does" rather than a simple "abdication" to the needs of the body.
40 See Hoigard and Finstad (1992) for a disturbing account of the sometimes traumatic consequences of sex work for those in the trade.
41 Hochschild, 1983, p. 187.
42 Interview with Cheyenne, 1993, Oakland, CA.
43 Hochschild, 1983, p. 12.
44 Ibid, p. 37.
45 Ibid.
46 Note though that child care, much like sex work, is often considered "natural" for women (i.e., not real work), and hence given less respect (and pay) than other professions.
47 Hochschild, 1983, p. 187.
48 Ibid, p. 109.
49 Interview with District Attorney Art Danner, 1988, Santa Cruz, CA. In this regard, see Emma Goldman's 1911 essay, "The Traffic in Women," in which she asks: "Why is the cadet [pimp] more criminal, or a greater menace to society, than the owners of department stores and factories, who grow fat on the sweat of their victims.... I make no plea for the cadet, but I fail to see why he should be mercilessly hounded, while the real perpetrators of all social iniquity enjoy immunity and respect." Goldman, 1972, p. 155-156.
50 Hochschild, 1983, p. 91.
51 Ibid, p. 103.
52 Ibid, p. 84.
53 Interview with Maryann, 1995, Santa Cruz, CA.

54 Interview with Terez, 1993, San Francisco, CA.

CHAPTER 4 LOCATING DIFFERENCE

1 Winegar, 1994, p. 2-E.
2 WHISPER, n.d. (a), p. 9.
3 Interview with Jo Doezema, 1993, Amsterdam.
4 Interview with Terez, 1993, San Francisco, CA.
5 Interview with Jo Doezema, 1993, Amsterdam.
6 Interview with Licia Brussa, 1994, Amsterdam.
7 Interview with Carol Queen, 1992, San Francisco, CA.
8 Interview with Terry, 1993, San Francisco, CA.
9 Interview with Licia Brussa, 1994, Amsterdam.
10 Interview with Carol Queen, 1992, San Francisco, CA.
11 Interview with Terry M., 1992, San Francisco, CA.
12 Interview with Samantha, 1992, San Francisco, CA.
13 Ibid.
14 See Lewis, 1959, p. 106-127.
15 Interview with Nina Hartley, 1992, Oakland, CA.
16 Interview with Jo Doezema, 1993, Amsterdam.
17 Visser, no date, p. 9.
18 Interview with Marianne, 1994, Amsterdam.
19 Interview with Jo Doezema, 1993, Amsterdam.
20 Interview with Dawn, 1995, Santa Cruz, CA.
21 Interview with Lupe, 1992, San Francisco, CA.
22 Interview with Jo Doezema, 1993, Amsterdam. In 1993, a report appeared in the Dutch press arguing that prostitutes belong to the class of the "super rich." According to a Dutch academic, prostitutes can amass tremendous fortunes: "A whore who works two hundred days a year, earning about fl. 1,000 a day—which is certainly on the conservative side—belongs to the top 1% of all income recipients." Doezema responded to the article: "Yeah, that's true. For the top 1% of all whores."
23 Interview with Terry M., 1992, San Francisco, CA.
24 Interview with Cheyenne, 1993, Oakland, CA.
25 Interview with Theodora, 1993, Santa Cruz, CA.
26 Interview with Terry M., 1992, San Francisco, CA.
27 Interview with Jane, 1992, San Francisco, CA.

CHAPTER 5 PROHIBITION

1 These should not be taken to be mutually exclusive categories: sex workers are also academics, activists, and public officials. What is significant, however, is that growing numbers of participants in these policy debates publicly *identify* as prostitutes.
2 The only exception is very limited and highly regulated brothel prostitution in a few counties in the state of Nevada.
3 Pearl, 1987, p. 769-880.
4 Ibid, p. 772. In order to fairly evaluate these comparisons, it is important to remember that American cities do not bear primary responsibility for education, welfare, or health. State and federal programs administer many of these services. Nonetheless, municipalities do provide crucial supplements to these programs.
5 Ibid, p. 779.
6 Ibid. Despite the fact that only a fraction of those arrested actually serve time,

prostitution offenses still account for a large portion of imprisoned women. Pearl reported that in California, convicted prostitutes accounted for at least thirty percent of the population in most women's jails. In some cities, such as New York, the figure exceeded fifty percent.

7   Ibid., p. 789.

8   Interview with Art Danner, 1988, Santa Cruz, CA.

9   Pearl, 1987, p. 769.

10 Ibid.

11 Ibid., p. 784-5.

12 Diana Prince reports that sex workers are murdered at a rate four times that of women in general and that murders occur most often among those working on the streets. Prince, 1986.

13 Goodson, 1994, p. 3-4.

14 National Organization for Women, California Chapter, 1994.

15 Hoigard and Finstad, 1992, p. 200.

16 Britain, too, has moved in this direction. In the mid-1980s, British laws were rewritten to allow for the prosecution of clients. Until that time, "punters" were not liable for arrest unless they made "improper advances" to girls younger than age 16. With the passage of the Kerb Crawler provisions to the Sexual Offenses Act in September of 1985, clients now face prosecution regardless of the age of the prostitute.

17 Cities with car seizure laws include Detroit, Michigan; Hartford, Connecticut; Chicago, Illinois; Washington D.C.; and Portland, Oregon.

18 *Congressional Quarterly Researcher*, 1993, p. 507.

19 Ibid., pp. 507, 522.

20 Ibid., p. 507.

21 Marinucci, 1995, p. C3.

22 Pheterson, 1993, p. 44.

23 Kadetsky, 1987, p. 7. Responding to the perception that the crackdown further endangered sex workers' safety, a coalition of some thirty prominent local feminists (including two Santa Cruz city council members, directors of the University of California's Women's Center and Women's Studies program, members of the local battered women's shelter, and the Women Against Rape collective) presented the Sheriff and District Attorney with a letter of protest: "Don't Turn Pros into Cons."

24 In 1911, an amendment to the penal code (250-bis) institutionalized the distinction between working as a prostitute, which is legal, and organizing or profiting from the prostitution of another, which is not.

25 Visser, n.d., p. 7.

26 Overman, 1982, p. 10.

27 Ibid.

28 van Royen, 1993, p. 1.

29 Beems, 1993, p. 15.

30 Verbeek, 1987, p. 1.

31 Ibid., p. 2.

32 Ibid.

33 Ibid.

34 Alting, 1993. Combined efforts by the Red Thread and the Dutch Foundation Against Trafficking in Women successfully defeated the proposed revisions in late 1993. New proposals are currently being developed.

35 Weitzer, 1991, p.29.

36 *Congressional Quarterly Researcher*, 1993, p. 1.

37 Note that this extreme hostility toward prostitution is a recent development. In 1985, a

nationwide U.S. Justice Department survey on public perceptions of the severity of various crimes found that of 204 offenses (from "planting a bomb under a public building" to "playing hooky from school"), "prostitution ranked 174 immediately followed by a "store owner knowingly puts 'large' eggs into containers marked 'extra large,'" Pearl, 1987, p. 788.

38 See Pheterson, 1986.
39 Winokur, 1992, p. 1.
40 Ibid, p. A-14.
41 Goldberg, 1991, p. c-5.
42 Watanabe, 1988, p. 1. Notably absent from McIlroy's list of those affected by "moral pollution" are (single) men.
43 Winokur, 1992, p. A14.
44 Ibid.
45 Ibid, p. A1.
46 Ibid.
47 Ibid. p. A14.
48 Ibid.
49 Ibid, p. A1.
50 Ibid, p. A14.
51 Ibid.
52 Ibid. In 1994, the newly appointed head of the San Francisco Vice Squad, Joe Dutto, proudly proclaimed that citywide solicitation arrests were at their "highest level ever." See Meir, 1995, p. 20.
53 Winokur, 1992, p. A-14.
54 Ibid.
55 Ibid, p. A15.
56 Ibid, p. A14.
57 Scott, 1992, p. 17.
58 Winokur, 1992, p. A14.
59 Ibid.
60 Hoenson, 1994.
61 About thirty percent of Red Light district residents expressed fear of being alone on the streets of their neighborhood at night, compared to an average of twenty-seven percent for the Amsterdam region as a whole. See Hoenson, 1994.
62 Ibid. It is also of note that residents of district two were more likely to report contact with their neighbors and to agree that "different ethnic groups get along well with each other here" (Seventy-nine percent in district two versus a regional average of sixty-eight percent). District two is racially mixed.
63 For twelve years, law enforcement in the California coastal community of Santa Cruz exercised discretion in choosing not to enforce anti-prostitution laws against county massage parlors. In late October 1987, however, the Sheriff's department shifted strategies and shut down all of the parlors using a "red-light abatement procedure."

CHAPTER 6 LEGALIZATION

1 The Red Thread, for example, reports that while window and street prostitution are the most visible forms of sex work in the Netherlands, "the majority of prostitution is practiced in private clubs, 'private houses,' and through escort agencies." See Verbeek, 1987, p. 9.
2 Visser. n.d., p. 13.
3 Ibid, p. 13-14.

4 Pheterson, 1989, p. 40-42.
5 Such policies have created problems for organizers of recent international conferences. Since both Japan and China have laws prohibiting prostitutes from obtaining visas to enter the country, protests have been organized by prostitutes' rights groups attending both the recent International AIDS Conference in Osaka in 1994 and the UN Conference on Women in Beijing in 1995.
6 Pheterson, 1989, p. 40-42.
7 Ibid, p. 105.
8 Ibid, p. 104-5.
9 Interview with Ron Beekmeijer, 1994, Amsterdam.
10 Ibid.
11 Ibid.
12 Verbeek, 1987, p. 3.
13 Ibid.
14 Beekmeijer estimates that seventy to eighty percent of the women working in Amsterdam's window prostitution trade are foreign, and that eighty percent of those are illegal.
15 Interview with Ron Beekmeijer, 1994, Amsterdam.
16 Verbeek, 1987, p. 4.
17 Shrage, 1994, p. 159.
18 Ibid.
19 Ibid, p. 160.
20 Verbeek, 1987, p. 4.
21 *Whorezine*, 1992, p. 8.
22 Jasmin, 1993, p. 35-6.
23 *Vluggertjes*, 1994, p. 21.
24 Pheterson, 1989, p. 40.
25 Alexander, 1995a.
26 Weitzer, 1991, p. 26. Currently eleven of Nevada's seventeen counties permit this form of commercial sex.
27 *Congressional Quarterly Researcher*, 1993, p. 516.
28 In Las Vegas, for example, police estimate that there are some two hundred street prostitutes working at any given time. In addition, even larger numbers of sex workers are employed on the main strip in the less visible indoor trade often under the management of agencies operating quasi-legally as "Entertainment Service Industries." See Becker and Levine, 1994, p. 33, 37.
29 Anderson, 1994, p. 40.
30 Ibid, p. 42.
31 Becker and Levine, 1994, p. 37.
32 Interview with Terry, 1995, San Francisco, CA.
33 See Becker and Levine, 1994, p. 39; and Anderson, 1994, p. 41.
34 Anderson, 1994, p. 41.
35 Becker and Levine, 1994, p. 38.
36 Ibid.
37 Ibid, p. 37.
38 See Walkowitz, 1980; and D'Emilio and Freedman, 1988.
39 Regulation of prostitution in Paris remained in effect until after World War II.
40 Belkin, 1988, p. 6.

41 In 1995, a Santa Cruz, California, public art project featuring a symbol of gay pride and survival, the pink triangle, was defaced with swastikas and slogans such as "Kill fags." The reaction of one appointee to the project's "sketch review committee" was telling: "I didn't want that panel to go up in the first place. I knew it would bring problems into the neighborhood." (public comment by the Santa Cruz City Arts Commission's "Art Wall Sketch Review Committee" member Christine Thorne. March 27, 1995). The public presentation of gay pride itself was understood by Thorne to be responsible for introducing problems into a previously untroubled community.

42 Pheterson, 1989, p.123-4.

43 In more than a dozen American states, including California, laws have been passed authorizing mandatory HIV testing of anyone convicted of soliciting, or engaging in, or agreeing to engage in prostitution regardless of the service offered or exchanged (i.e., even if the activity involves no risk of HIV transmission, for example hand jobs). A subsequent arrest following a positive HIV test is a felony charge. See *Coyote*, 1989, p. 1.

44 Alexander, 1995, p. 103.

45 Rao, 1994.

46 Pheterson, 1989, p. 133.

47 *Congressional Quarterly Researcher*, 1993, p. 510, reports that HIV is twenty times more transmittable from male to female. See also *Pony Xpress*, 1991, p. 6: "Prostitutes are in far greater danger of becoming infected than are their customers—who frequently try to persuade a prostitute to go without a condom by offering to pay more.... Since 1981, the percentage of [American] men who contracted AIDS through heterosexual sex has remained constant at two percent, while the percentage for women is twenty-eight percent."

48 Alexander, 1995, p. 110.

49 Ibid.

50 Pheterson, 1989, p. 118.

51 Synn, 1991, p. 38.

52 Pheterson, 1989, p. 116.

53 Verbeek, 1987, p. 6.

54 Pheterson, 1989, p. 138-9.

55 Alexander, 1988, p. 3.

56 Ibid.

57 "Pearl necklace" refers to the stimulation of the penis between a woman's breasts; Woods, 1993, p. 11. The phrase "fantasy stimulation" referring to such practices as cross-dressing, s/m, and other body and mind manipulations, I owe to discussions with sex worker Carol Leigh.

58 See Lambert, 1988, p. B10; and Cohen, 1989. Cohen, an epidemiologist, reports that a 1987 Center for Disease Control study of HIV infection among prostitutes in the United States, showed prostitutes in seven major U.S. cities with "strikingly low rates of HIV infection." The two areas with high levels of infection among prostitutes "reflected almost entirely the extent of drug use in each population and the extent of drug use related AIDS rates in those cities," CDC, 1987, pp. 158-61.

59 Verbeek, 1988.

60 Ibid.

61 Interview Gloria Lockett, 1993, Oakland, CA.

62 Terms discussed in *Coyote*, 1988, pg. 1.

63 Chakassi, 1990, p. 10.

64 See Woods, 1993, p. 11. Woods reports that "Most condom failure was attributed to human error—and part of learning how to use a condom entailed learning to minimize this risk by using adequate amounts of water-based lubricant and taking care not to accidentally tear a condom with teeth or fingernail."

65 Interview with Ans, 1994, Amsterdam.

66 Woods, 1993, p. 15.

67 Ibid, p. 31.

68 Ibid, p. 30.

69 Verbeek, 1988.

70 Woods, 1993, p.32.

71 In 1993, AIDS was the leading cause of death for women between the ages of twenty-five and thirty-five in Sao Paulo, Brazil; most were infected through heterosexual sex with boyfriends or husbands. See *Volkskrant*, 1995. A similarly high rate of HIV death among young women is reported in New York City; overall in the United States, AIDS is currently the fifth leading cause of premature death among women. See Reuters, 1993.

72 Woods, 1993, p. 22.

73 Ibid, p. 21.

74 Ibid, p. 23.

75 Gelfand, 1991.

76 Alexander, 1995, p. 115.

77 Woods, 1993, p. 38.

78 White, 1989, p. A8.

79 See Lee, 1991, p. 85; and Alexander, 1995.

80 Pheterson, 1989, p. 122.

81 PROS, 1989, p. 1. San Francisco Supervisor Hallinan established a taskforce in that city in 1993 to study possible decriminalization on similar grounds.

82 Interview with Licia Brussa, 1994, Amsterdam.

83 TAMPEP informational brochure, 1994, Amsterdam.

84 Verbeek, 1988, p. 5.

85 White, 1989, p. A8.

86 Ibid.

87 For example, see the interview with Lockett in Schneider and Stoller, 1995, p. 208-18.

88 Interview with Gloria Lockett, 1993. Oakland, CA.

89 Ibid.

90 The expression is Dennis Altman's, referring to the growing legitimacy of the gay community in the midst of the AIDS epidemic, quoted in Epstein, 1988, p. 49.

91 See Jenness, 1994, p. 107: "Establishing and securing legitimacy and institutional status for social movement organizations and their movements is always somewhat problematic. However, since legitimation is tied to social norms and values, it is especially problematic for organizations that have members and/or constituents whose status in society is socially defined as deviant. Deviants' organizations are necessarily embedded in layers of stigma, which compounds the challenge of acquiring organizational legitimacy."

92 Interview with Gloria Lockett, 1993, Oakland, CA.

93 Marinucci and Williams, 1993, pp. A1, A12.

94 Ibid, p. A 12.

CHAPTER 7 SELF-ADVOCACY

1 Self-advocacy groups include the French Collective of Prostitutes; the English Collective of Prostitutes; the Swiss Aspasia and the center for documentation on prostitution in Geneva; HYDRA and HWG of Germany; Comitao Per I Diritti Civili Delle Prostitute of

Italy; Canadian CORP; Austrian Association of Prostitutes; Group O of Sweden; the Red Thread in the Netherlands; SQWISI of Australia; the National Association of Prostitutes of Brazil; and the Encounter of Ecuadorian Women Sexual Workers.

2 Pheterson, 1989, p. 48.

3 Jenness, 1993, p. 116.

4 Interview with Jo Doezema, 1993, Amsterdam.

5 Ibid.

6 Jenness, 1993, p. 116.

7 A similar dynamic is at work when drag queens, leather folk, or butch lesbians become a public relations problem for assimilationist gays.

8 Barbara, 1993, p. 13.

9 Jasmin. 1993, p. 34.

10 For a review of methodological problems of prostitution studies see, Earls and David, 1989, pp. 5-28.

11 Pheterson, 1990, p. 398.

12 Ibid.

13 Ibid.

14 *Amersfoortse Courant*, 1994.

15 Those in the illegal sector have an obvious interest in escaping detection by the authorities.

16 See Alexander, 1987. This figure has attained the same mythical status as the often cited ten percent rate of homosexuality among the American population. While the figure is often cited, it is rarely footnoted to any concrete study. More common is to cite secondary sources which themselves offer no specific documentation. Also see Leigh, 1994. Leigh offers the observation that one reason for the confusion of conflicting statistics on street prostitution is that the ratios may be quite different for urban and more rural areas: "Whereas street prostitution accounts for between ten to twenty percent of prostitution in larger cities such as Los Angeles, San Francisco and New York, in smaller cities with limited indoor venues, street prostitution may account for fifty to seventy percent." Leigh, 1994, p. 17.

17 Ibid.

18 Interview with Licia Brussa, 1994, Amsterdam.

19 Interview with Terry, 1995, San Francisco, CA.

20 Interview with Samantha, 1992, San Francisco, CA.

21 Hamburg, 1994, p. A74.

22 *Vluggertjes*, 1994, p. 20.

23 It is interesting to note that as part of a campaign for greater legitimacy, the brothel owners' association changed its name in the mid 1990s, from "Vereniging van Exploitanten van Sexhuizen en Relaxbedrijven"—that is, "Association of Sex House and Relaxation Business Operators"—by eliminating explicit reference to "sex houses."

24 Koemans, 1994, p. 20. In 1995, a similar organization, the Prostitution Information Center (Prostitutie Informatie Centrum [PIC]) of Amsterdam also began offering a six-week training program on "Working in Prostitution."

25 John, J., 1993, p. 3-4.

26 Interview with Julia Queery, 1994, Eugene, OR.

27 Bout, 1994, p. 4-5.

28 Ibid, p. 6.

29 Ibid.

30 Tornado, 1991, p. 5.

31 Ibid.

32 It is telling that the Union Labia table provided the only formal opportunity for the discussion of sex during the entire conference outside of two workshops on the issue of pornography and violence.

33 Interview with Alena Smith, 1993, Santa Cruz, CA.

34 Jill Pasewalk, Executive Director of the Santa Cruz YWCA, May 27, 1987, correspondence to Alena Smith.

35 Interview with Lupe, 1992, San Francisco, CA.

36 Ibid.

37 Ibid.

38 Shrage, 1994, p. 86.

39 Chancer, 1993, p. 161.

40 Interview with Margot Alvarez, 1994, Amsterdam.

41 Interview with Terry, 1995, Santa Cruz, CA.

42 Aspasia was described by Plutarch as "a wise woman who had a great understanding of state and government," Wells, 1982, p. 7.

43 Interview with Theodora, 1993, Santa Cruz, CA.

44 *Whorezine*, 1993c, p. 23.

45 Interview with Annie Sprinkle, 1993, Amsterdam.

46 For a more extensive interview with Gloria Lockett on her work with the California Prostitutes' Education Project, see Schneider and Stoller, 1995, p. 208-18.

CHAPTER 8 COMPROMISING POSITIONS

1 Interview with Sandy, 1993, San Francisco, CA.

2 King, 1986, p. 65.

3 Pheterson, 1990, p. 398.

4 See Geertz, 1973, p. 347: "Every man has the right to create his own savages for his own purposes. Perhaps every man does. But to demonstrate that such a constructed savage corresponds to Australian Aborigines [for example] … is another matter altogether."

5 Flax, 1990, p. 195.

6 See especially Hoigard and Finstad, 1992 and Carmen and Moody, 1985.

7 Quan, 1991, p. 35.

8 Hoigard and Finstad, 1992, p. 113.

9 Interview with Gloria Lockett, 1993, San Francisco, CA.

Bibliography

Acker, Joan, Kate Berry, and Joke Esseveld. 1983. "Objectivity and Truth." *Women's Studies International Forum* 6 (4).

Alexander, Priscilla. 1987. "Prostitution: a difficult issue for feminists." Pp. 187-214 in *Sex Work: Writings by Women in the Sex Industry*, edited by Frederique Delacoste and Priscilla Alexander. Pittsburgh: Cleis Press.

――――. 1988. *Prostitutes Prevent AIDS: a manual for health educators*. San Francisco: Cal-PEP.

――――. 1995. "Sex Workers Fight Against AIDS: an international perspective." Pp. 103 & 110 in *Women Resisting AIDS*, edited by Beth Schneider and Nancy Stoller. Philadelphia: Temple University Press.

Alting, Sietske. 1993. Amsterdam: VPRO Radio, 6 June.

Alvarez, Margot. 1995. "Denktank." *Vluggertjes* 1:8. Amsterdam: The Red Thread.

Anderson, Laura. 1994. "Working the Nevada Brothels." *Gauntlet* 1: 40 & 42.

Assiter, Alison, and Carol Avedon, eds. 1993. *Bad Girls & Dirty Pictures: The Challenge to Reclaim Feminism*. London: Pluto Press.

Barbara. 1993. "It's a Business Doing Pleasure with You." *Social Text* 37, Winter:13.

Barlay, Stephen. 1968. *Sex Slavery: a documentary report*. London: Heiniman. P. 7.

Barrington, Judith, ed. 1995. *Intimate Wilderness*. Portland: Eighth Mountain Press.

Barrows, Sydney Biddle, with William Novak. 1986. *The Mayflower Madam*. New York: Ivy Books.

Barry, Kathleen. 1979. *Female Sexual Slavery*. New York: Avon Books.

――――. 1992. "Trafficking in Women: serving masculine systems." speech given at the National Organization for Women conference, Chicago.

Beems, Damaris. 1993. "Prostituee de dupe van bordel verbod." *de Volkskrant*. November 11: 15.

Belkin, Lisa. 1988. "Texas Judge Eases Sentence for Killer of Two Homosexuals." *New York Times* 17 December:6.

Bell, Laurie, ed. 1987. *Good Girls, Bad Girls: Feminists and Sex Trade Workers Face to Face*. Toronto: Seal Press.

Bout, Jet. 1984. "Lesbisch Hoerenlopen." *Wildside Magazine* 5 (2): 4-6.

Bunch, Charlotte. 1985. Interview on "Trafficking in Women," special report on Pacifica Radio. Berkeley: KPFA.

Burana, Lily. 1992. "Interview with Ira Levine." *Taste of Latex* 8.

Burdman, Pamela. 1995. "Women's Forum Stumbles Over Lesbian Issue." *San Francisco Chronicle* 15 September, p. 1.

Bursten, Varda, ed. 1985. *Women Against Censorship*. Vancouver: Douglas and McIntyre.

Califia, Pat. 1980. *Sapphistry: The Book of Lesbian Sexuality*. Tallahassee: Naiad Press.

――――. 1988. *Macho Sluts*. Boston: Alyson Publications.

――――. 1994. *Public Sex*. Pittsburgh: Cleis Press.

Carmen, Arlene, and Howard Moody. 1985. *Working Women: The Subterranean World of Street Prostitution*. New York: Harper & Row.

The Centers for Disease Control. 1987. "Antibody to HIV in Female Prostitutes." *Morbidity and Mortality Weekly Report*. 27 March:158-161.

Chakassi, Robert. 1990. *Pony XPress* 1 (1):10.

Chancer, Lynn. 1993. "Prostitution, Feminist Theory, and Ambivalence." *Social Text*, winter: 161-165.

Chapkis, Wendy. 1986. *Beauty Secrets: Women and the Politics of Appearance*. Boston: South End Press.

————. 1994. "Prostitution Politics Amsterdam Style." *Trash in the Streets.* Amsterdam, June 15: 5

Clarke, D.A. 1993. "Consuming Passions." in *Unleashing Feminism,* edited by Irene Reti. Santa Cruz: HerBooks.

Cohen, Judith. 1989. "Update on HIV infection and prostitute women." in *A Vindication of the Rights of Whores,* edited by Gail Pheterson. Seattle: Seal Press.

Collins, Patricia Hill. 1991. *Black Feminist Thought.* New York: Routledge.

Congressional Quarterly Researcher 3 (22):510

Connell, Robert. 1995. "Democracies of Pleasure: thoughts on the goals of radical sexual politics." in *Social Postmodernism,* edited by Steven Seidman and Linda Nicholson. Cambridge: Cambridge University Press.

COYOTE. 1988. *Coyote Howls* 1.

————. 1989. *Coyote Howls* 9 January:1.

————. 1992. pamphlet. San Francisco.

Davis, Angela.1978. "Rape, Racism and the Capitalist Setting." *Black Scholar* 9 (7): 28.

————. 1983. *Women, Race and Class.* New York: Vintage/Random House.

Davis, Karen. 1990. "I Love Myself When I am Laughing: a new paradigm for sex." paper presented at the Queer Theory Conference. University of California at Santa Cruz, 11 February 1990.

de Graaf Foundation. 1994. "Prostitution in the Netherlands: The Current State of Affairs." photocopied pamphlet.

de Grazia, Edward. 1992. *Girls Lean Back Everywhere: The Law of Obscenity and the Assault on Genius.* New York: Random House.

De Lauretis, Teresa. 1984. *Alice Doesn't.* Bloomington: Indiana University Press.

D'Emilio, John and Estelle Freedman. 1988. *Intimate Matters: A History of Sexuality in America.* New York: Harper and Row.

Diamond, Irene and Lee Quinby, eds. 1988. *Feminism and Foucault.* Boston: Northeastern University Press.

Donnerstein, Edward, Daniel Linz, and Steven Penrod. 1987. *The Question of Pornography: Research Findings and Policy Implications.* New York: Free Press.

Dorsman, Willy, ed. *Vrouwenhandel.* Amsterdam: Anne Vondeling Stichting, Amsterdam.

D'Souza, Denise. 1995. *The End of Racism.* New York: Free Press.

Duggan, Lisa, Nan Hunter, and Carole Vance. 1985. "False Promises" in *Women Against Censorship,* edited by Varda Burstyn. Vancouver: Douglas and McIntyre.

Dworkin, Andrea 1987. *Intercourse.* New York: Free Press.

————. 1988. *Letters From a War Zone.* New York: E.P. Dutton.

Earls, C,M, and H. David. 1989. "Male and Female Prostitution: a review." *Annals of Sex Research* 2:5-28.

Edwards, Susan. 1987. "Prostitutes: victims of law, social policy and organized crime." in *Gender, Crime and Justice,* edited by Pat Carlen and Anne Worrall. Milton Keynes, England: Open University Press.

Elshtain, Jean Bethke. 1988. "Why We Need Limits." in *Utne Reader* September/October, pp. 53-55.

Enloe, Cynthia. 1989. *Bananas, Beaches and Bases: Making Feminist Sense of International Politics.* Berkeley: University of California Press.

Epstein, Steven. 1988. "Nature vs. Nurture and the Politics of AIDS Organizing." *Outlook,* Fall:49.

Ferguson, Ann. 1984. "Sex War." *Signs* 10:1, pp. 106-112.

Finkelhor, David. 1983. *The Dark Side of Families.* Beverly Hills: Sage Publications.

"First National Encounter of Sex Workers." 1993, photocopied report. Machala, Ecuador. 28 June 19:3.

Flax, Jane. 1990. *Thinking Fragments: Psychoanalysis, Feminism & Postmodernism in the Contemporary West.* Berkeley: University of California Press.

Foucault, Michel. 1978. *History of Sexuality.* New York: Vintage.

Fraser, Nancy. 1993. "Beyond the Master/Subject Model." *Social Text* 37:174 & 176.

French, Dolores, with Linda Lee. 1988. *Working: My Life as a Prostitute.* New York: E.P. Dutton.

Geertz, Clifford. 1973. *The Interpretation of Cultures.* New York: Basic Books.

Genc, Mehmet. 1994. "The Socioeconomic Background of the East European Women Selling Sex in Istanbul." paper presented at the Second European Meeting on Migratory Prostitution. Istanbul, Turkey. 29 March.

Gelfand, Jane. 1991. "Being Called a Whore." unpublished senior thesis for Community Studies and Women's Studies. University of California at Santa Cruz.

Gillman, Sander. 1981. "Black Bodies, White Bodies." *Critical Inquiry* 12 (1).

Giobbe, Evelina. 1991. "The VOX Fights." *VOX Magazine.* 1(1).

Goffman, Erving. 1959. *The Presentation of Self in Everyday Life.* Middlesex, England: Pelican Books.

————. 1963. *Stigma: Notes on the Management of Spoiled Identity.* New Jersey: Pelican.

Goldberg, Leslie. 1991. "Walking Away From the Wild Side." *The San Francisco Examiner* 10 November:C-5.

Goldman, Emma. 1972. "The Traffic in Women." Pp. 155-156 in *Red Emma Speaks,* edited by Alix Kates Schulman. New York: Vintage Houe.

Goodson, Terry. 1994. "Report from the California NOW Prostitution Committee to State Board Delegates." unpublished document. 19 August:3-4.

Gould, Stephen J. 1981. *The Mismeasure of Man.* New York: Norton.

Griffin, Susan. 1981. *Pornography and Silence: Culture's Revenge Against Nature.* New York: Harper & Row.

Groen, Martine. 1987. *Hoerenboek.* Amsterdam: Feministische Uitgeverij Sara.

Gubar, Susan, and Joan Hoffman, eds. 1989. *For Adult Users Only: The Dilemma of Violent Pornography.* Bloomington: Indiana University Press.

Hamburg, Jill. 1994. "Streetwise Group Champions Workers in the Sex Trades." *New York Newsday* 15 May:A-4.

Hansen, Bob. 1994. "Your Tax Dollars at Work." *Santa Cruz Metro.* 11-17 August:22-24.

Haraway, Donna. 1989. *Primate Visions.* New York: Routledge.

Hekman, Susan. 1987. in *From Monism to Pluralism.* Boston: Haworth Press.

Hochschild, Arlie Russell. 1983. *The Managed Heart.* Berkeley: University of California Press.

Hoenson, Lodewijk. 1994. "Bevolkingsonderzoek in Wijkteamgebieden: algemene rap-portage." Bureau Onderzoek en Statistiek, Politie Amsterdam.

Hoigard, Cecilie, and Liv Finstad. 1992. *Backstreets: Prostitution, Money and Love.* University Park: Pennsylvania University Press.

hooks, bell. 1994. *Outlaw Culture.* New York: Routledge.

ICPR World Charter. 1983. *Social Text* 37: 185

Isis, women's world. 1990-1991. special issue on "Poverty and Prostitution." 24

James, Jennifer, Jean Withers, Marilyn Heft, and Sara Theiss. 1975. *The Politics of Prostitution.* Seattle: Social Research Associates.

Jasmin. 1993. "Prostitution is Work." *Social Text* 37, Winter: 34

Jeffreys, Sheila. 1985. *The Spinster and Her Enemies: Feminism and Sexuality, 1880-1930.* London: Pandora.

Jenness, Valerie. 1993. *Making it Work.* New York: Walter de Gruyter.

———. n.d. "From Sex as Sin to Sex as Work." unpublished paper, Department of Sociology, University of California at Santa Barbara.

John, J. 1993. "What They Don't Teach in School." *Whorezine*. April:3-4.

Kadetsky, Elizabeth. 1987. "Sex Workers Rub Noren the Wrong Way." *Santa Cruz Sun*. 5 November: 7.

Kendrick, Walter. 1987. *The Secret Museum: Pornography in Modern Culture*. New York: Viking.

King, Katie. 1986. "The Situation of Lesbianism as Feminism's Magic Sign." *Communication* 9:65.

Kirshenbaum, Gayle. 1991. "A Potential Landmark for Female Human Rights." *Ms. Magazine* September/October:13.

Klein, Renate Duelli. 1983. "How Do We Do What We Want To Do?" in *Theories of Women's Studies*, edited by Bowles and Klein. Boston: Routledge

Koemans, Monique. 1994. "Prostituee leert niet meer van 'madame'." reprinted in *Vluggerties*. 1: 20.

Korvinus, Berthy. 1993. National Council of Churches of the Netherlands. unpublished letter to the STV.

Kruijt, Michiel. 1994. "Escort van zes vrouwen." *Volkskrant* 5 March:17.

Kulp, Denise, and Karen Mudd. 1987. "The Sexual Liberals and the Attack on Feminism." *Off Our Backs* 17 (5).

Lambert, Bruce. 1988. "AIDS in Prostitutes Not as Prevalent as Believed." *New York Times*. 20 September, B10.

Lederer, Laura, ed. 1980. *Take Back the Night: Women on Pornography*. Toronto: Bantam Books.

Lee, Wendy. 1991. "Prostitution and Tourism in South East Asia." P. 85 in *Working Women: International Perspectives on Labour and Gender Ideology*, edited by N. Redclift and M. Sinclair. New York: Routledge.

Leigh, Carol. 1994. "Prostitution in the United States: the Statistics." *The Gauntlet* 1:17 & 70.

Lewis, Oscar. 1959. *Five Families*. New York: Basic Books.

Liberman, Ellen. 1992. "Prostitutes' Johns May Get TV Role." *Boston Globe* 20 December: 66.

Lilly, Bobby. 1991. "Musings on the Patriarchy and Other Thoughts." in *CAL-PEP News* 5:10, 12 June, pp. 1-2.

Lorde, Audre. 1991. Pp. 148-150 in *Intimate Wilderness*, edited by Judith Barrington. Portland: Eighth Mountain Press.

MacKinnon, Catharine.1979. *Sexual Harassment of Working Women*. New Haven: Yale.

———. 1987. *Feminism Unmodified: Discourses on Life and Law*. Cambridge: Harvard University Press.

Manning, Caitlin, and Glen Foster. 1988. *Stripped Bare: a look at erotic dancers*. Video Cassette. San Francisco: Foster/Manning Productions.

Marinucci, Carla. 1995. "Schools for Johns." *San Francisco Examiner* 16 April: Metro Section C3.

Marinucci, Carla and Lance Williams. 1993. "Ex-felon directs safe-sex project." *San Francisco Examiner* August 15:1 & A12.

Marlatt, Daphne. 1991. "Musing with Mothertongue." in *Intimate Wilderness*, edited by Judith Barrington. Portland: Eighth Mountain Press.

Mazumdar, Sucheta. 1989. "A Women-Centered Perspective on Asian American History." Pp. 2-3 in *Making Waves*, edited by Keysaya Noda. Boston: Beacon Press.

McClintock, Anne. 1993. "Maid to Order." *Social Text* 37:103-4.

––––––. 1993. Introduction to Special Section on the Sex Trade. *Social Text* 37:5-9.

Meir, Andrew. 1995. "Innocent Lost." *San Francisco Examiner Magazine* 8 January:20.

Mies, Maria. 1983. "Towards a Methodology for Feminist Research." in *Theories of Women's Studies*, edited by Bowles and Klein. Boston: Routledge.

Millet, Kate. 1971. *The Prostitution Papers: A Candid Dialogue.* New York: Avon.

Morgan, Robin. 1977. *Going Too Far.* New York: Random House.

Nestle, Joan. 1987. *A Restricted Country.* Ithaca: Firebrand Books.

New York Times News Service. 1992. "Neighbors Curb Prostitution." *Santa Cruz Sentinel* 20 April. P. 2.

Ngugi, Elizabeth. 1989. "Update on HIV." in *A Vindication of the Rights of Whores*, edited by Gail Pheterson. Seattle: Seal Press.

Oakley, Ann. 1981. "Interviewing Women." in *Doing Feminist Research*, edited by Helen Roberts. London: Routledge and Kegan Paul.

Otis, Leah. L. 1985. *Prostitution in Medieval Society: The History of an Urban Institution in Languedoc.* Chicago: The University of Chicago Press.

Overman, Luc. 1982. *Prostitutie in woonburten.* Amsterdam: Mr. de Graaf Stichting.

Pascoe, Peggy. 1989. "Gender Systems in Conflict: Marriages of Mission Educated Chinese Women." *Journal of Social History* 22 (4).

Pateman, Carole. 1980. "Women and Consent." *Political Theory* 8 (2):150.

––––––. 1988. *The Sexual Contract.* Stanford: Stanford University Press.

Pearl, Julie. 1987. "The Highest Paying Customers: America's Cities and the Costs of Prostitution Control." *Hastings Law Journal* 38 (4):769-880.

Perry, Michael. 1993. "Aussie Prostitute Rape Furor." *San Francisco Chronicle* 5 October.

Pheterson, Gail. 1986. *Vrouweneer en Mannenadel: over het stigma hoer.* The Hague: Ministerie van Sociale Zaken en Werkgelegenheid.

––––––. 1989. *A Vindication of the Rights of Whores*, ed. Seattle: Seal Press.

––––––. 1990. "The Category of 'Prostitute' in Scientific Inquiry." *The Journal of Sex Research* 27(23):398.

––––––. 1992. "Street Kids." paper presented at the Colloque International sur les jeunes de la rue et leur avenir dans la societe, Montreal. 24-26 April:5.

––––––. 1993. "The Whore Stigma." *Social Text* 37, Winter:44.

Pony XPress 2. 1991. Summer: 6.

Prince, Diana. 1986. "A Psychological Profile of Prostitutes in California and Nevada." Doctoral dissertation. United States International University.

PROS: the newsletter of the Australian Prostitutes' Rights Organization. 1989. June.

Quan, Tracy. 1991. "The VOX Fights." *VOX Magazine* 1 (1).

Rao, Asha. 1994. "A Study on Sexual Behavior Patterns of Truck Drivers and Helpers." paper presented at the Second European Meeting on Migratory Prostitution. 29 March. Istanbul, Turkey.

Reinharz, Shulamit. 1983. "Experiential Analysis." in *Theories of Women's Studies*, edited by Bowles and Klein. Boston: Routledge.

Reti, Irene, ed. 1993. *Unleashing Feminism.* Santa Cruz: HerBooks.

Roberts, Nickie. 1986. *The Front Line: Women in the Sex Industry Speak.* London: Grafton.

Roiphe, Katie. 1993. *The Morning After.* Boston: Little, Brown, and Co.

Rubin, Gayle. 1982. "The Leather Menace." in *Coming to Power.* Samois, Boston: Alyson Publications. P. 215.

Sawicki, Jana. 1988. "Identity Politics and Sexual Freedom." in *Feminism and Foucault*, edited by Irene Diamond and Lee Quinby. Boston: Northeastern Press.

Scheff, Thomas. 1983. "Toward Integration in the Social Psychology of Emotions." *Annual Sociological Review* 9:333-354.

Segal, Lynne. 1990. *Slow Motion: Changing Masculinities, Changing Men.* New Jersey: Rutgers University Press.

Segal, Lynne and Mary McIntosh, eds. 1993. *Sex Exposed: Sexuality and the Pornography Debates.* New Jersey: Rutgers University Press.

Seidman, Steven. 1992. *Embattled Eros.* New York: Routledge.

Shange, Ntozake. 1994. "Where Do We Stand On Pornography: Roundtable Discussion." *Ms. Magazine* 4:4 January/February, p. 34.

Sheiner, Marcy. 1994. Letter to the Editor. *Future Sex* 2, p. 4

Shrage, Laurie. 1994. *Moral Dilemmas of Feminism.* New York: Routledge.

Simmons, Marlisse. 1993. "East Europeans Duped into West's Sex Trade." *New York Times* 9 June:1.

Simonton, Ann. 1992. "Turning Pros into Cons." *Media Watch Newsletter.* Summer: 8.

Southern Women's Writers' Collective. 1987. "Sex Resistance in Heterosexual Arrangements." photocopied pamphlet.

Sprinkle, Annie. 1991. *Post Porn Modernist.* Amsterdam: Torch Books.

Stacey, Judith. 1988. "Can There be a Feminist Ethnography?" *Women's Studies International Forum* 2 (1).

Steinberg, Stephen. 1989. *The Ethnic Myth.* Boston: Beacon Press.

Steinem, Gloria. 1978. "Erotica and Pornography: A Clear and Present Difference." *Ms. Magazine,* November, p. 54.

Stichting Tegen Vrouwenhandel. 1993. "Advocacy: Foundation Against Trafficking in Women, the Netherlands." June. Utrecht: Stichting Tegen Vrouwenhandel.

———. 1993b. "Report on the U.N. World Conference on Human Rights on European Trafficking in Women." photocopied report. Utrecht: STV. 15 June: 2

———. 1994. photocopied flyer. Utrecht: STV.

Stoller, Robert, and Ira Levine. 1993. *Coming Attractions: The Making of an X-rated Video.* New Haven: Yale University Press.

Swedenburg, Ted. 1988. "Occupational Hazards." paper presented at the American Anthropological Association's annual meeting, 18 November 1988. Phoenix, Arizona.

Synn. 1991. "Street Smart Health Care." *Pony XPress* 2 (summer): 38

TAMPEP informational brochure. 1994. Amsterdam: Mr. A. de Graaf Stichting.

Tannahill, Reay. 1992. *Sex in History.* New York: Scarborough House.

Taste of Latex 8. 1992.

Taussig, Michael. 1987. "History as Commodity." *Food and Foodways,* vol.2; Harvard Academic Publishers: 160.

Tchudomirova, K., and P. Mardh. 1994. "A Study of Prostitutes in Plovdiv, Bulgaria." paper presented at the Second European Meeting on Migratory Prostitution. 29 March. Istanbul, Turkey.

Thoits, Peggy A. 1989. "The Sociology of Emotions." *Annual Sociological Review* 15:317-342.

Tornado. 1991. "Love for Sale." *Pony XPress* 2.

Trinh Minh-ha. 1987. "Difference: a special Third World Women's Issue." *Feminist Review* 25 (March).

———. 1987b. "Questions of Images and Politics." *The Independent,* May.

Tucker, Robert. 1978. *The Mark Engels Reader.* New York: Norton, P. 71.

UN Treaty Series. 1949. "United Nations Convention for the Suppression of the Traffic in Persons and the Exploitation of the Prostitution of Others." UN Yearbook 1949, vol. 96, P. 271-319

UNESCO and the Coalition Against Trafficking in Women. 1991. "Report on the International Meeting of Experts on Sexual Exploitation, Violence and Prostitution." Pennsylvania State College. April.

van Royen, Marjon. 1993. "Het is toch nooit de carriere die je moeder voor je droomt." *NRC Handelsblad* 6 March:1 & 2.

Vance, Carole S., ed. 1984. *Pleasure and Danger: Exploring Female Sexuality.* Boston: Routledge.

Verbeek, Hansje. 1987. "Priorities for a New Prostitution Policy." photocopied statement. December.

———. 1988. "AIDS and Prostitution." policy paper. Amsterdam: The Red Thread. April.

———. 1988b. "Editorial." *Blacklight* 1 (1). Amsterdam: The Red Thread.

Visser, Jan. 1988. "Safe Prostitution." photocopied statement. Amsterdam: de Graaf Foundation. November.

———. n.d. "Getemde Ontucht." 1994. Amsterdam: de Graaf Foundation.

———. 1995 *Vluggerties* 1:18..

Walkowitz, Judith. 1980. *Prostitution and Victorian Society.* Cambridge: Cambridge University Press.

Warland, Betsy. 1991. "Untying the Tongue." in *Intimate Wilderness,* edited by Judith Barrington. Portland: Eighth Mountain Press.

Watanabe, Teresa. 1988. "Smut dealers reeling from crusade on porn." *San Jose Mercury News* 24 January:1

Waters, Elizabeth. 1989. "Restructuring the 'Woman Question.'" *Feminist Review.* London.

Weeks, Jeffrey. 1981. *Sex, Politics and Society.* New York: Longman.

Weitzer, Ronald. 1991. "Prostitutes' Rights in the United States." *Sociological Quarterly* 32 (1): 25-34.

Wells, Jess. 1982. *A Herstory of Prostitution in Western Europe.* Berkeley: Shameless Hussy Press.

Wells Melanie. 1994. "Woman as Goddess: Camille Paglia Tours Strip Clubs." *Penthouse* October, p. 132.

WHISPER (n.d.). *Before You Turn Another Trick.* pamphlet.

———. n.d. "Oral history project of women who have survived prostitution." (audio cassette tape) #1, side 1.

White, Evelyn. 1989. "Reformed Prostitutes Take to the Streets to Help Their Sisters." *San Francisco Chronicle* 1 June:A-8.

Whorezine. 1992 16:8.

———. 1993 17:23.

———. 1993b 2:2.

Williams, Linda. 1989. *Hard Core: Power, Pleasure and the "Frenzy of the Visible."* Berkeley: University of California Press.

Winegar, Karen. 1994. "Ex-prostitute Pushes Education, Escape for Others." *Minneapolis Star-Tribune* 21 February:2-E.

Winokur, Scott. 1992. "Playground for Prostitutes." *San Francisco Examiner* 6 December:1.

Wolf, Naomi. 1993. *Fire With Fire.* New York: Random House.

Wolff, Rebecca. 1990. "Her Back Was Burnt with Irons: Chinese Prostitution in San Francisco, 1849-1924." unpublished master's thesis. Board of History, University of California, Santa Cruz.

Wong, May, and Christine Musitelli. 1995. "Outrage Follows Arrest." *Santa Cruz Sentinel* 4 February:1,6.

Woods, Karen Austen. 1993. "You Have Sex With a Condom." unpublished master's thesis, Department of Sociology, University of Auckland.

Index

"coming out" stories, of homosexuals, 226(n17)

Comitao Per I Diritte Civili Delle Prostitute [Italian self-advocacy group], 233(n1)

condoms
  in conference packets, 222(n13)
  failure of, 172, 233(n64)
  intimacy and use of, 172-174
  use by sex workers, 94, 114, 116, 121, 163, 167, 168, 169, 170, 171, 172, 175, 191, 198

Congressional Quarterly Researcher, 141

Connell, Robert, 29

CORP [Canadian self-advocacy group], 234(n1)

COYOTE [prostitutes' rights group], 70, 127, 143, 182, 186, 203, 205-209

cult of true womanhood, 44

D

Danner, Art, 80, 227(n49)

Davis, Angela, 224(n13)

Davis, Karen, 13, 17-18

Debbie Does Dishes [adult film], 33-34

Decentrale Controle Prostitutie (DCP), 157, 158, 199

de Certeau, Michel, 29

decriminalization, of prostitutes, 155, 156, 176, 214

de Graaf Foundation, 65, 102, 155-156

de Lauretis, Teresa, 26-27

disabled persons, prostitutes' services to, 194, 203-204

Doezema, Jo, 4, 8, 52, 75, 98-99, 102, 103, 182, 183, 222(n4), 228(n22)
  interview with, 117-122

domination workers, 192-193

"Don't Turn Pros into Cons", 3, 229(n23)

"Downtown Vigilance Committee" (San Francisco), 141, 143

drug addiction, 151, 152, 154, 168, 178, 184, 198, 202, 207, 232(n58)

drunkenness, 120, 124, 207

Duggan, Lisa, 31

Dutch Foundation Against Trafficking in Women (STV), 48, 55, 59, 60-66, 140, 222(n7), 225(n35), 229(n34)
  principles of, 53-54

Dutch National Council of Churches, 55, 56

Dutto, Joe, 230(n52)

Dworkin, Andrea, 19, 22, 29, 30

dyke, 26, 30, 217

E

East Europe, migrant prostitution in, 53

Educating Nina [adult film], 33

Elizabeth, 213

Elshtain, Jean Bethke, 14

emotions, 226(n16), 227(n39)

EMPOWER, 56, 175

Encounter of Ecuadorian Women Sexual Workers, 234(n1)

English Collective of Prostitutes, 233(n1)

Enloe, Cynthia, 43

Equal Rights Amendment, 24

eros, sex and, 13, 17

erotic dancing, 100, 101, 106, 170

Europe, anti-trafficking groups in, 54

exhibitionism, 192

F

family, sale of women by, 48

"fantasy stimulation" activity, 232(n57)

Fatal Attraction, 36

Female Sexual Slavery (Barry), 46, 47

"feminism", 222(n9)

Femme Productions [adult film company], 34

Finland, sex trade in, 6, 93

Finstad, Liv, 49-50, 51, 71, 77, 212

Flax, Jane, 211

Fraser, Nancy, 16-17

Freewoman, 11

French Collective of Prostitutes, 233(n1)

Freud, Sigmund, 124

Friends of Women Migrant Workers in Asia, 56

Future Sex, 23

G

gay sex, 31, 112, 124-125

gedoog beleid [tolerance policy], 136

genitals, photo exhibition of, 191-192

Germany, prostitution control in, 160-161, 176

Gillman, Sander, 45

Giobbe, Evelina, 98

"Golden Showers" (Califia), 68

Goldman, Emma, 227(n49)

Gran Fury, 191

Grazyna, interview with, 58-60

Greece, ancient, prostitution in, 194-195

Griffin, Susan, 17

Group O [Swedish self-advocacy group], 234(n1)

g-spot, 217, 218

H

Haft, Marilyn, 70

Hartley, Nina, interview with, 33-36, 102